D1418193

Becoming one

Emotionally, Spiritually, Sexually

JOE BEAM

HOWARD
PUBLISHING CO.

Our purpose at Howard Publishing is to:
• *Increase faith* in the hearts of growing Christians
• *Inspire holiness* in the lives of believers
• *Instill hope* in the hearts of struggling people everywhere
Because He's coming again!

Becoming ONE © 1999 by Joe Beam
All rights reserved. Printed in the United States of America

Published by Howard Publishing Co., Inc.,
3117 North 7th Street, West Monroe, Louisiana 71291-2227

02 03 04 05 06 07 08   10 9 8 7 6 5 4 3

Library of Congress Cataloging-in-Publication Data
Beam, Joe.
    Becoming one : emotionally, spiritually, sexually / Joe Beam.
    p. cm.
    ISBN 1-58229-078-4
    1. Marriage—Religious aspects—Christianity. 2. Intimacy (Psychology)—Religious aspects—Christianity. I. Title.

BV835.B36 1999
248.8'44—dc21
                                                    99-047709

Edited by Philis Boultinghouse
Interior design by Stephanie Denney

Author's Note: Because everyone's particular situation is unique, the ideas and suggestions contained in this book should not be considered a substitute for consultation with a psychiatrist or trained therapist.

Scripture quotations not otherwise marked are from the Holy Bible, New International Version. Copyright © 1973, 1978, 1984 International Bible Society. Used by permission of Zondervan Bible Publishers. Other Scriptures are quoted from The Holy Bible, Authorized King James Version (KJV), © 1961 by The National Publishing Co.

Dedicated to Terry Northcutt
Not only is he a true Christian gentleman,
but without him there would
be no Family Dynamics

And to the Staff of
Family Dynamics Institute
A dedicated team of hardworking
people who really believe that
by the power of God
we can change the world

Contents

Preface ix

Introduction: Intentional Intimacy 1

Chapter 1: The Craving for Intimacy 7
            God Created Us for ONEness

Chapter 2: The Triune Nature of Intimacy 27
            *Learning How to Love—Sexually, Emotionally,
            and Spiritually*

Chapter 3: Repairing Intimacy Diversions and Drains 53
            Understanding How Intimacy Is Generated

Chapter 4: Developing Emotional Intimacy, Part 1 77
            Learning Intimacy from the Inside Out

Chapter 5: Developing Emotional Intimacy, Part 2 103
            Learning How to Make Intimacy Grow

Chapter 6: Developing Sexual Intimacy, Part 1 131
            Opening the Door to Sexual Ecstacy

Chapter 7: Developing Sexual Intimacy, Part 2 153
            Becoming Consummate Lovers

Chapter 8: Developing Spiritual Intimacy—As a Couple . .177
            Removing Barriers to the Deepest Level of Intimacy

Chapter 9: Developing Intimacy with God—Personally . . 207
            Becoming His in Mind, Body, and Spirit

Appendix: Overcoming Negative Sexual History 231
            Getting Past the Bad to Enjoy the Good

Notes 261

Preface

"Why a book on intimacy?" you may ask.

Well, to tell you the truth, it took me awhile to fully understand the need for such a book as well. As founder and president of Family Dynamics Institute, a nonprofit organization designed to help families become all that God intended them to be, I thought the seminars our Marriage Division was currently offering were more than sufficient to help couples find fulfillment and happiness in their marriages. But that view has changed during the last few years.

One of Family Dynamics Institute's most successful courses is our *His Needs, Her Needs* seminar, based on the excellent book of the same name written by Dr. Willard Harley.[1] Thousands upon thousands of couples have gone through this eight-week, interactive course offered through local churches, and we've seen God work mightily in the marriages of those couples. We rejoice at every letter or phone call telling us how God is using the *His Needs, Her Needs* course to change marriages for the better. Often, the calls report not that the course *changed* a marriage but that God actually used it to *save* a marriage.

Our results are so amazing that one of our graduate couples, Jim and Karen Smith of Myrtle Beach, South Carolina, found themselves being interviewed with me on ABC's *Good Morning America* because of what the course did for them. When the reporter asked me why the course is so successful, I tried to explain what happens when you put twelve couples, a trained facilitator from their church, and God all in the same room. God takes control of everyone there who will yield to Him, and relationships change dramatically. (I don't think the reporter understood my point.) The course is a powerful, God-given tool that teaches husbands and wives how to understand their spouses' emotional needs and how each can make practical plans to fulfill those needs in the other.

You may think I'm bragging, but we at FDI continue to be absolutely amazed at what God does through the course. Sorry if I seem to carry on, but you would too if you'd experienced it.

As effective as the *His Needs, Her Needs* course is, however, it eventually became clear that more was needed. While the good reports on that course haven't slowed, more and more of our graduates—especially women—began asking, "What's next? Where's the next level? We're now understanding each other in ways we never thought possible, and we know now that we will be married for life. *Nothing* can ever tear us apart! But we still aren't where I want us to be. As much as we are fulfilling each other, I feel that there's something missing. Can you help us find it?"

At first the question puzzled us. From our present perspective, we now realize that we reacted like—I almost hate to say it—"typical" males. While women comprise 60 percent of our company, the males who serve as vice president of our Marriage Division and as president of FDI weren't "getting it." We had concentrated on what the graduating couples were *doing* for each other. And what they were doing was bringing excellent results. What else could anyone want? That's when we finally noticed it wasn't "anyone" who was asking. It was women. Almost always women.

I began researching the need for this book by the simple act of analyzing the happiness of my own wife, Alice, one of the sweetest people God ever placed on this planet. People who've never met her tell me they know she's a saint simply because she's still married to me! That sounds like a joke, but there's more truth to that than you might initially imagine.

Alice and I married the first time on June 7, 1969. That marriage lasted until 1984, the year we divorced and went our separate ways.[2] Three years later, on June 14, 1987, we remarried. Just to make sure she knew how much I love her and that I will never leave again, we reconfirmed our vows in November 1997. We jokingly tell people we're not sure if that means we've been married two times or three. All I know is that I don't want to lose her again. Ever. If anyone strives to be a good, loving, intimate husband, it is I.

As much as I want to be that kind of a husband, once I started examining this "intimacy thing," it didn't take long to realize that Alice was wanting more intimacy than we had.

Ouch.

"Okay," I admitted, "at least in my marriage the need exists."

Next, I went to Terry Northcutt, vice president of our Marriage Division. Together we analyzed what we'd already learned about relationships from the thousands and thousands of couples who had been through our courses in the last few years. To add to our accumulated findings, we asked each couple graduating from our courses to complete a detailed "before and after" questionnaire regarding their relationship, and I interviewed graduate couples I met as I traveled. The next thing we did was to gather information from the thousands of trained facilitators across the continent who lead our marriage seminars in their local churches. Finally, we sought the expertise of others who have done research on marriage and family relationships. I read research from reputable scholars like Dr. Nick Stinnett at the University of Alabama, Dr. Robert Sternberg at Yale, Dr. Mike Johnson at Penn State, and Dr. John Gottman at the University of Washington. I also sought the services of Linda Eller, a wonderful Christian researcher in Nashville, to help us gather the most up-to-date, valid information available on the subject of intimacy.

In addition to all this, Terry Northcutt and I bring to this book and seminar a combined ministry experience of more than fifty years. We both hold earned degrees in Bible, and we both strive for a deeply spiritual relationship with God. On our staff at FDI, we also have other ministers as well as several people who hold responsible, spiritual positions in their respective churches. Above all, our loyalty to God and deep respect for His word serve to keep the book, the workbook, and the accompanying course biblically accurate.

You hold in your hands the accumulated work of years of research based on up-to-date, validated information. But more importantly, it is based on information we've gleaned from the real experts—the thousands of couples who have shared with us what makes marriages work.

We make a suggestion that will help you gain more from this book. Buy a blue highlighter and a pink highlighter. When the husband reads something in the book that he thinks is very important, he highlights those words in blue. The wife does the same thing in pink. That way, each of you will see what the other is keying on. You'll also discover what you both see as essential, because your overlapping colors will produce a light purple.

Intentional Intimacy

For many, the idea of *becoming one* in marriage sounds wonderful. For others, it feels stifling and demanding. For still others, it's a pipe dream for the unrealistic romantic. What about you? What did you think when you read the title of this book?

Can two uniquely individual people really become one—sexually, emotionally, and spiritually? And even if it's somehow possible, is that really what we want?

Not only is it possible, it's what you were created for. It's what God had in mind for you all along.

But if you're like most people, you've not had great success with intimacy. Oh, when you were dating you may have thought you'd found your perfect soul mate, but not too long after the honeymoon, reality set in, and you have long since resigned yourself to the "fact" that intimacy was just a romantic dream.

The truth of the matter is, however, that even if you've given up on the dream, the yearning is still there—though it may be buried so deeply within you that you've not contemplated it for years. But it drives you just the same. Your God-given need for oneness is the driving force behind much of your behavior, thoughts, and longings. A lack of intimacy may very well be the source of that restless, unhappy feeling that so many of us have come to live with.

But it doesn't have to be that way. You hold in your hands the first step to finding the oneness with your husband or wife that you've always wanted—that God created you to have.

Here's the promise I make to both husbands and wives: If you will live out the principles taught in this book and do the exercises in the accompanying workbook, you and your spouse will develop a union better than any you've ever imagined. No matter what your marriage is like right now, no matter how you feel about your spouse today, the principles in this book can create new feelings of love and intimacy where none exist or enrich the loving relationship you may already have.

Yes, gentlemen, there will be plenty of action (translate that *physical*). And, yes, ladies, there will be depths of feeling, closeness, and warmth that will be ultimately satisfying. But each of you must be aware, this book waves no magic wand. There is work to do. Sometimes tough work. But the payoff is worth every bit of it.

This book can also be an excellent starting point for engaged couples. If you put the principles contained in this book into your marriage from the very start, you will avoid much heartache and your relationship will soar to levels unknown by many who've been married for years. But we do offer one word of caution. Chapters 6 and 7 are about sexual intimacy. And because of our Christian values, we hold to the view that sex should be enjoyed only in marriage. When you come to the chapters on sex—especially chapter 7—you would do well to defer working through that material until after your wedding.

We strongly recommend you read this book in conjunction with the accompanying workbook, *Becoming ONE: Exercises in Intimacy.* The chapters in that workbook correspond to the chapters in this book and present a threefold strategy for implementing what you learn: (1) the workbook carries you through biblical exercises so that God directs you in your growth; (2) it offers questions, charts, and graphs to help you find where you are in your relationship; and (3) it gives you guidance on how to decide where you want to be in your relationship, how to make a plan to get there, and how to make that plan work. We suggest that you each have your own copy to work in so that neither person's answers are affected by what the other has written and so you can share your answers in your own time frame.

If your church offers the *Becoming ONE*[1] interactive seminar, enroll in it for eight weeks of focused work on developing greater intimacy in your relationship. Plan to have fun, laugh a lot, maybe cry a little, and work intensely—perhaps like you never have before—on achieving all the happiness and joy God intends you to have in your relationship.

One last note before we start: Because we use several stories in this book, you may wonder if they are real stories of real people. Yes, they are real, but you need to know that we protect identities. Sometimes we do that by changing facts to disguise the location or situation. Other times we merge two or more stories of real people together into a composite story that represents situations we've encountered. Only when a person's last name is used do we tell a story just as it happened without disguising or protecting the involved parties. So if you read some story and think, "That's me!" rest assured that it isn't unless you see your entire name in the story, and that only happens when the person or couple gave us permission ahead of time.

As I said, whether you just read this book, work through the

3

accompanying workbook, *Becoming ONE: Exercises in Intimacy,* or do both as you grow through the eight-week course in a church setting, you will have to put out effort to make your marriage all you want it to be. But the benefits of all that work are fantastic.

We at Family Dynamics Institute have prayed that by the grace of God this book will lead you to greater levels of fulfilling love for each other. If you will join your prayers with ours and put into practice the principles set forth in this book, your relationship will grow to new heights and new depths.

*B*oth men and women crave intimacy, but both often go unfulfilled because each seeks it so differently. Men want action. Women want feeling. From day one they're set up to misunderstand each other. (page 12)

❧

*I*f you feel lonely or if you long for a relationship very different from the one you have now, it's almost a sure thing that you don't have true intimacy in your marriage. (page 16)

❧

*O*ur experience with thousands of couples makes us extremely confident of this: With God's help you can make your marriage all it should be and all you crave it to be—no matter what it's like now. (page 24)

❧

*S*truggles with sexual temptation or unacceptable emotional involvement with a person you're not married to don't necessarily mean you're evil at heart; they may mean you're unfulfilled. (page 22)

Chapter 1

The Craving for Intimacy
God Created Us for ONEness

He walked into my hotel room with a mumbled "hello."

Though my life's work is helping people and though I enjoy it very much, I employ a policy that never allows people to come to my hotel room. Never. But Sam had seen an ad in his local newspaper advertising that the president of Family Dynamics was speaking at a local church. Hoping that I might deliver him from the demon tormenting him, he found my lodging and implored a meeting until I yielded.

Now he stood silently before me, head hanging and shoulders drooping, until I directed him to the worn sofa situated in the middle of the room. I took the only other chair the proprietor had thought to furnish. Without looking up, Sam started into his story. It was the same story I've heard from countless others who, by their own actions, have caused the walls of their lives to crash in on themselves and everyone they love.

He'd been married twenty years, but for some time now, his relationship with his wife had barely existed. They'd drifted apart, taken up separate interests, and spent little time together—except during social functions, like church. They weren't sure they loved each other anymore. At least that was Sam's perspective.

Just two weeks before—on a whim—he had wheeled into a strip bar. Strip bars weren't a part of his lifestyle, and under normal circumstances they held no temptation for him. But on that particular night, he was feeling empty, alone. He was looking for something; he just wasn't sure what it was. Without any acknowledged thought process, he walked through the door into a world that had never existed for him before, unaware that he was leaving a world to which he might never return.

It was quite an eventful night.

By the time the sun groggily crawled over the horizon to reveal its own bloated, flushed face, Sam was recovering from his drinking binge while finishing breakfast at an all-night greasy spoon with a stripper half his age. They'd talked about life, dreams, and the futures they wished for but feared might never be. He told me how they'd instantly hit it off on some deep level, how she understood him like no one ever had, and how he had always longed for this kind of friendship with a woman.

Within a week he'd left his wife, rented an apartment, and moved in with this twenty-something whose trade in life was erotically enticing drunken men to give her their money.

Quite a rapid change for a churchgoing, pillar-in-the-community businessman and father.

Too much change. He couldn't live with it.

After just a few days with his newfound "soul mate," Sam had awakened to the realization that he didn't want to spend another night with this stripper. Guilt consumed him, and he surprised himself by discovering that he missed his wife—the woman he had convinced himself he had no affection for whatsoever. Bewildered and disoriented, he told the stripper to leave and spent the rest of the day wandering about in dazed confusion until he noticed the ad in the newspaper. That's when he tracked me down—the stranger he hoped could fix all this.

All my religious and moral values were offended by his actions, but I felt no anger toward him. What he had done was wrong—very wrong—but I was more interested in saving him than chastising him. Besides, I don't think I could have awakened any more guilt in him than he already felt.

As he finished telling me about the events of the last two weeks, he looked at me and asked the question I knew was coming. Not only did I anticipate the question, I knew the answer.

"Why?" he begged. "Why would I do a thing like that? It's so foreign to everything that I believe, everything that I am. Can you tell me why I'm doing what I'm doing?"

I paused just for a moment as an involuntary sigh escaped, then replied gently, "Sam, more of us have struggled with that question than you can ever know. I think I know exactly what is driving you— the same thing that drives so many people to misguided actions. It's the search for *intimacy*.

"You crave a warm, intimate, close relationship with another human being, and you were trying desperately to find something, someone, who promised to give it to you. Even though you didn't know what to call it, you knew that you wanted someone to share your very self with—your hopes, your dreams, your fears. That's what you thought you'd found in your stripper.

"But somehow, you've managed to discover what so many haven't yet figured out: *Sex and intimacy aren't the same thing*. That's why you told the stripper to leave. You longed for intimacy, but all you got was sex.

"If you ever had intimacy with your wife, you lost it long ago. But you don't want it lost. You want it so badly that your misguided search has cost you what little intimacy you had left. Sadly, your search is taking you farther from the treasure you seek."

I talked longer, fleshing out the thoughts above, until he interrupted my soliloquy by beginning to cry. Not the gentle, quiet weeping of tender moments. No, it was the bitter, angry expression of grief that accompanies a crushing discovery. With wonderment washing his eyes, he nearly shouted, "You're right! Oh, my God, you're right!"

Ultimately, I convinced Sam to call his minister. I sat listening as he laid out the skeleton of the story over the line, asking if the minister would go with him to tell his wife. They worked out a time to meet, talk in more detail, and pray before visiting with her. When Sam finished the conversation, I prayed with him and sent him on his way.

He left with a mixture of horror and hope.

I didn't know which of those emotions would find its fulfillment.

I knew that by the grace of God I'd started Sam on the right path, but I also knew that his own sinful actions had strewn that path with danger, pitfalls, and seemingly insurmountable obstructions. I watched through the curtains as he drove away, praying again for God's will to be done for Sam and his wife. I wanted to have hope for them. Maybe his wife would forgive him and, despite what he had done, work toward intimacy. Maybe he could focus on his relationship with her, find forgiveness, and find what he was seeking.

Maybe.

MY OWN STORY

The reason I was able to so easily identify what Sam really wanted is that I, too, had to discover my intense need for intimacy the hard way. I have been in situations and done things of which I'm terribly ashamed. Many times in my life I've had to face overwhelming guilt, trying to figure out *how* I got into some situation or *why* I did some sinful act.[1] I vainly tried to understand myself by analyzing environment, childhood events, potential genetic flaws, satanic traps, and even the possibility that at heart I am fatally morally flawed.

At one time or another I blamed each of those causes, but my understanding of my struggles wasn't to come through self-analysis. God decided to teach me a different way.

Because God sees me in a different light than I see myself—the light of grace—He continually gives me the ministry of helping people who struggle and fail as much as I do. He's done it for as long as I can remember. Not only does He graciously use me to help them, He often uses them to explain me to me.

It was during one of those times when I was helping another struggling Christian that I suddenly realized what God had been revealing to me through others for years. I finally understood that very often it is a person's drive for *intimacy* that misguides him or her into sin. As soon as that awareness blossomed, I immediately understood my own struggles and, better yet, the final solution to them.

I'd been seeking intimacy with God and a good marriage with Alice but had never seen the two goals as more than indirectly related. Instantly I knew that the only way to develop the godliness and wholeness I craved was to seek intimacy with God *and* with Alice as a unified goal. Unless I could accomplish that, I would struggle spiritually for the remainder of my life.[2]

As soon as I experienced that "aha!" I realized that because intimacy was missing in our marriage, Satan's forces had been able to lead me astray.[3] For the first time, I finally saw the truth that I would later share with Sam. *Intimacy* is the key. We seek it from the moment we are conscious that we are alive and continue until the moment we have our last conscious thought on this planet. Only when we live in an intimate relationship with another person *and* an intimate relationship with God do we have the very treasure we live our lives to find.

God made us that way.

OUR GOD-GIVEN CRAVING FOR INTIMACY

God Himself placed the desire for intimacy within each one of us. He made us with two powerful carvings that permeate or motivate nearly everything we do:

1. Every human craves intimacy with another human.

2. Every human craves intimacy with God.

Understanding those two undergirding drives within human nature gives great insight into many of our actions, both logical and illogical, holy and sinful. They explain a lot about *why* we do what we do. Sound simple? Maybe it should be, but it gets complicated because of the difference in men and women.

One thing we at Family Dynamics Institute have discovered is that while both men and women *need* the same kind of intimacy, their approaches to trying to fulfill that need aren't always the same. Though we refuse to stereotype, we have noted in our work with thousands of men and women that there are some general characteristics that tend to be repeated within genders.

For example, we have learned that men tend to focus more on the *actions* of intimacy while women tend to focus more on the *feelings* of intimacy. Not every man. Not every woman. But enough of each that many people find themselves unfulfilled in their search for intimacy, even though they are married to a person driven by the same craving.

Why?

Many men think that being intimate with their wives means having sex with them. If one man describes the night before with his wife as being intimate, most other men would think he was saying they made sexual love. Even when you remove sex from the equation, a man is still more likely to think that intimacy with his wife is *doing* something for her, like building her a gazebo in the backyard or bringing her breakfast in bed. For many, if not most, men, intimacy is something you do.

Women, on the other hand, are more likely to view intimacy as a *feeling* of closeness that may not be associated with any action at all. She wants conversation, sharing, warmth, and affection. She can feel those things just sitting on the sofa with him, daydreaming. He, on the other hand, is much more likely to want romantic encounters, uninhibited passion, or a saucy, seductive telephone call in the middle of his workday.

Let's illustrate further. A man like I'm describing would complete a rather energetic lovemaking session with his wife by falling into a contented sleep, having experienced intimacy as he defines it. If his wife is like women I'm describing, sleep may not come so easily for her. Suppose they had drifted apart emotionally, even in dimensions so small the husband may not have noticed. In a situation like that, she may lie there for hours after their lovemaking, wondering where their marriage is failing, before finally escaping into a restless sleep filled with wishes for some magical rekindling of their relationship. The *act* of intimacy had taken place, satisfying him, but the *feeling* of intimacy didn't exist for her. He thought they had both experienced intimacy; she felt that neither of them did.

Who is right? What is intimacy? Is it an action or a feeling?

In reality, both actions *and* feelings play a crucial role in real intimacy. In a sense, it's like faith in James 2. It exists in the heart (feeling), but the only way it proves its existence is by what it does (action). The actions aren't intimacy; they are merely vital signs that prove that intimacy is alive. You can no more replace intimacy with actions than you can replace faith with works. But intimacy isn't just feelings either. A claimed faith that never demonstrates itself isn't faith at all. In the same way, a proclaimed intimacy that doesn't express itself in actions isn't intimacy. True intimacy means more than having an active sex life, and it means more than warm, romantic feelings for a knight in shining armor. It means investing time and effort into satisfying the deepest longings of each other. It means making a safe place to share the secret parts of yourselves—your hopes, your dreams, your fears. It means sharing in a physical union that is open and free, ranging from touching to sexual fulfillment. It means having fun with each other. It means growing together spiritually and in your own personal relationship with God. Isn't that what you really want? I know I do.

The Craving for Intimacy with Another Human

From the very beginning, God has shown us that we humans desperately need intimacy with another human.

> So the man gave names to all the livestock, the birds of the air and all the beasts of the field.
>
> But for Adam no suitable helper was found. So the LORD God caused the man to fall into a deep sleep; and while he was sleeping, he took one of the man's ribs and closed up the place with flesh. Then the LORD God made a woman from the rib he had taken out of the man, and he brought her to the man.
>
> The man said, "This is now bone of my bones and flesh of my flesh; she shall be called 'woman,' for she was taken out of man." For this reason a man will leave his father and mother and be united to his wife, and they will become one flesh.[4]

To understand yourself and your mate, please take the time to think this passage through carefully. Likely you've read it or heard it many times, but see it afresh as we dig into its depths. It holds the key to the most powerful drives within us.

When God made Adam, He left him as a lone creature with no counterpart. Every other animal had a mate, but not Adam. God wouldn't complete the creation of humankind until man *craved* the completion. To make sure that Adam grasped his incompleteness, God directed him to name all the animals so that in that naming process, poor Adam would come to a great and crushing realization: Not only was he different from the others in terms of intelligence and spiritual dimension,[5] but of all God's creatures, he was the only one *totally* alone. The only one without a matching part.

Interestingly, the Hebrew word translated *alone* in Genesis 1:18 is written in English as *bad*. Perhaps that's coincidental, but it seems almost prophetic—as if God looked forward in history to a time when people would speak English and wanted to give them a message, as if he wanted them in their own language to comprehend that it's *bad* for a person to be alone. We know God feels this way because it was He who said, "It is not good for the man to be alone."[6]

But the greater dimension of the Hebrew word for *alone* means a "piece or part of something." And this also applies: Adam was only a part or piece of the whole. He was made to be a part of something that did not yet exist in totality. Only when God made the woman was the process finished.

Verse 18 of Genesis 2 uses the phrase "help meet" (KJV) or "helper suitable" (NIV). In the original Hebrew, that phrase means someone to correspond to or match the other. That's why Adam was so alone: His corresponding or matching part didn't exist yet. God made Eve to *complete* Adam. And of course, Adam, in turn, completed Eve. Humankind requires two parts to make the whole: a man and a woman. By the design of God, each needs the other.

As soon as Eve came into existence, Adam *knew* that she completed him. She was his ideal and perfect match, his corresponding being. The two of them together would make one. That's why the text says, "For this reason a man will leave his father and mother and be united to his wife, and they will become one flesh."[7]

One flesh.

United.

God created us with this need for intimacy with a mate. We've craved it from the beginning of the world. And He created this union to be the closest relationship on earth—even closer than our relationship with the father and mother who gave us life and sustenance. And since God made humankind with this strong need for intimacy with a mate, it exists for all people who have lived or ever will live on this planet—except for specific individuals whom God has intentionally gifted for singleness.[8]

If your life seems empty or unfulfilled, it may well be because you don't feel the intimacy with your spouse God designed you to have. If you experience feelings of loneliness or occasionally find yourself longing for a relationship very different from the one you now have, it's almost a sure thing that intimacy hasn't reached its intended level.

The Craving for Intimacy with God

Not only did God create us to crave intimacy with our spouses, He also created us to have just as strong a desire for intimacy with Him. And just as a human alone is only a part of the whole, people without God are only a part of what God intended them to be. Hear this well: *You will never achieve intimacy with your mate to the level God intended if each of you doesn't also strive for intimacy with Him.*

Don't underestimate the power of what you just read. It isn't just "religious" talk; it's the absolute truth. Let me say it again: If you want the deepest level of intimacy with each other, you must first each develop a deep level of personal intimacy with God. If you try to develop marital intimacy without intimacy with God, you will short-change yourself and your mate.

What makes me so sure of that? Again, it's the way God made us. Let me illustrate that from the Bible by sharing the outpourings of the inspired psalmist as he articulates his deep craving for intimacy with God on high.

> O God, you are my God, earnestly I seek you; my soul thirsts for you, my body longs for you.... Because your love is better than life, my lips will glorify you. I will praise you as long as I live, and in your name I will lift up my hands.... On my bed I remem-

ber you; I think of you through the watches of the night.... My soul clings to you.[9]

"Your love is better than life." Quite a statement, isn't it? He sounds like a man completely lost in his love for a woman. But it isn't that kind of intimacy he craves here. It's just as intense, but it's directed not toward another human but toward God Himself.

Whether you recognize it or not, you, too, have that kind of longing for the presence of God.[10] That need is just as inherent in us as our need for union with another person. But just as some people are too misfocused or unfocused to understand their need for intimacy with a mate, others are too misfocused or unfocused to understand their need for intimacy with God. The craving is there but buried under layers of misdirection and misunderstanding.

If a person says he or she doesn't need God, does this mean the need is not there? No; it just means that the need isn't acknowledged. And because it isn't acknowledged, the person is missing out on the most fulfilling relationship he or she could have—intimacy with God. Unfortunately, it means missing out on the second most fulfilling relationship as well. A lack of intimacy with God affects not only your relationship with God but also your relationship with your spouse.

That even applies when one spouse craves and seeks intimacy with God and the other doesn't. That couple's intimacy suffers as well. If either of the spouses varies greatly from the other in any of the three areas of intimacy (sexual, emotional, and spiritual), they drift farther apart rather than coming closer together. But if both come closer to God, their intimacy grows dramatically.

Notice in the following diagram that if one spouse grows closer to God (moving up the side of the triangle) while the other spouse remains at the lowest point on his or her side of the triangle, the distance between the spouses increases.

But if both spouses move closer to God (each moving up their respective sides of the triangle), the distance between the spouses decreases. In other words, by coming closer to God, they come closer to each other.

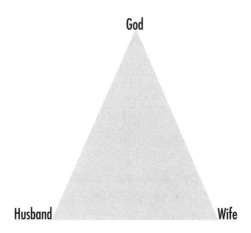

God

Husband   Wife

ONENESS

Alice and I learned this firsthand. We'd just finished a very special weekend that I called Wounded Believers. With more bravado than courage, I'd called a Christian couple I didn't know in Atlanta and asked them if I could take over their house for an entire weekend. Because God had blessed this couple financially, they owned a rather large dwelling that could accommodate a large group.

I brought about thirty.

Everyone there was a Christian who had been through some type of spiritual suffering—some because of their own actions and some because of what others had done to them. The idea was that we Wounded Believers would spend an intensive weekend in spiritual study and growth. We'd worship, pray, study, share, and, if needed, confess. No schedule guided us. We ignored clocks. We stopped and cooked when we wanted to eat. We ended our sessions late and drifted off to sleep in the wee hours. Our focus was completely on how each of us could restore or renew our relationships with God.

Exhausted physically and emotionally, Alice and I were the last ones to leave on Sunday afternoon. Alice has a servant's heart and wouldn't leave the donated house until it was absolutely perfect. That's one of the things that makes her so special. As we drove on the three-hour trip home, we talked little and thought a lot. During the drive home, Alice suddenly said, "You're different somehow."

I looked at Alice as she said it and thought, "Yeah, I am. And it's not just on the surface. Something happened to me deep inside, and I didn't even notice it as it happened. I just know that I'm different. Changed. Better."

During that weekend, my own relationship with God changed and, as a result, I changed too. I wasn't hyped or exhilarated. I was calm. Calmer than I'd been in years. And at peace. At peace with God. At peace with where I was in life. At peace with myself.

While the weekend affected Alice in very dramatic ways as well, it seemed to affect me more. It didn't take long to figure why. I needed it more. She was closer to God than I. I'd let too many things get too important and too demanding to keep myself on an even spiritual keel like she had.

What happened next was one of the most profound experiences of our marriage.

Alice said, "I've lied to you."

Surprisingly, her statement didn't startle me. No defenses came up. No adrenaline rushed into my bloodstream. None of my normal reactions that might have slammed me on hearing those words.

"Really? About what?"

It's not important for you to know what the lie was. In the context of many things it could have been, it wasn't even that big a deal. She had manipulated something because she was trying to protect me from feeling bad, and now she wanted to set it right. The lie wasn't the important thing. What was happening in our relationship was. We talked with complete openness and honesty. We each shared our hearts with each other without any defensiveness, dodging, or denigration. We talked more intimately than we had in years.

And it was all because of a deeply spiritual weekend where each of us had worked on his or her own relationship with God. By becoming closer to Him, we had changed for the better our relationship with each other.

We recommend that same process for you.

By now, you've seen that God's natural order for men and women is that they be *one*. So let's make the word *one* easy to remember. Forming it into an acrostic we see:

O – our
N – natural
E – element

Becoming ONE simply means fulfilling and living within *our natural element*. It isn't supposed to be unusual or extraordinary: Instead, it's the union that God intended from the very beginning. When two people marry each other, ONEness is the way it's supposed to be! So from now on, when we refer to becoming one, we'll do so with capital letters. Becoming ONE. Achieving ONEness.

Two parts that make a whole.

Two people becoming ONE.

That's what you wanted when you married, wasn't it? Wholeness. Completeness. ONEness.

WHAT HAPPENS WHEN INTIMACY IS MISSING?

The sad truth is that the vast majority of marriages—even Christian marriages—have failed to achieve ONEness. Too many husbands and wives live in marriages that range from empty and unfulfilling to miserable, often wondering how in the world they got into their marriages and wishing for a way out. We at FDI continually hear a statistic that our work with thousands of couples leads us to believe is accurate. It says that only one in four marriages is happy.

One in four.[11]

Scary, isn't it?

If true, this means that 75 percent of married couples exist in a marriage without the intimacy God intended. Unhappy and unfulfilled, they remain in their marriages for one reason or another—religious values, children, economic reasons, lack of alternatives, and the like. Some accept their sad state, believing that nothing can be done, and try to find other things in their lives to fulfill them. Others cannot accept such an empty union and grow angrier by the day, fighting and quarreling until the marriage explodes into fragments that even professional marriage therapists cannot put back together. Still others try to ignore the need, pretending that things are okay, until one day one of the partners finds that he or she has fallen in love with someone new.

Maybe your marriage is one of those unfulfilled ones. Is it possible? Might you be unfulfilled and unhappy in your marriage? If you have the accompanying workbook, *Becoming ONE: Exercises in Intimacy*, the first exercise in chapter 1 should help you get an idea of how satisfied you really are. We suggest you complete it and see. Why? Because if you aren't happy in your marriage, then you—like the rest of those in the 75 percent category—are a perfect target for satanic attack. No Christian should be naive enough to think that Satan's evil ones would bypass such a great opportunity to sow their seeds of discord, discontent, and deceit.[12] If you've settled into lethargy about your marriage, bad times *are* coming.

Don't think that everything will be okay and that you should just accept and endure a marriage without intimacy. Incomplete marriages—marriages that have not achieved ONEness—may seem acceptable on the surface, but the people who exist in them continually find themselves confronted with temptations or failings that wouldn't exist—or at least wouldn't have the same level of power— if ONEness existed in their marriages. Their susceptibilities to these pitfalls aren't because of some inward evil or lack of moral fiber, though they may end up committing moral evil. Their struggles with sexual temptations or unacceptable emotional involvements or excessive striving for success, fame, and recognition or a host of other character weaknesses come as an indirect result of their unfulfilled need for complete intimacy.

Remember Sam? He didn't walk into that strip bar because of sexual addiction or even overpowering sexual temptation. Sam didn't know it, but what drove him into that bar was his craving for intimacy—sexually, emotionally, and spiritually. Because he didn't understand the true inner need that propelled him, all he keyed on was his lack of sexual fulfillment. Too godly to openly seek out a paramour, he instead paid to watch provocative women. In his emotionally confused state, he was unaware that once he crossed that barrier, he opened himself up to whatever impulse seized him next.

His unconscious search for intimacy led him into an act of degrading sin.

Don't be so spiritually and emotionally naive as to think that a similar delusional process couldn't happen to you or your spouse.

GOD WILL GIVE YOU ONENESS

If you have the intimacy we've talked about thus far, praise the Lord! But if your marriage isn't all it should be, God is not happy with your marriage. As we saw in Genesis 2, He created us to find fulfillment in marriage, and that is what He wants for *you*.

If God doesn't accept your lack of ONEness in marriage, then neither should you!

If you don't have ONEness, don't have it on the level you feel it should exist, or just want more of it, what can you do?

We believe we can help. That's why we developed this study; the accompanying workbook, *Becoming ONE: Exercises in Intimacy;*[13] and the interactive course, *Becoming ONE.*[14] You don't have to live your whole lifetime—or even another year—without having what God intended for your marriage. God not only *wants* you to have intimacy in your marriage, He tells you *how* to have real, fulfilling intimacy—and we will show you His plan throughout this book.

Demand ONEness. Work for it. Do what it takes to achieve it.

Strive for the ONEness God wants you to have with the person to whom you are *now* married. No matter what you feel about that person at this moment—love, mild affection, hatred, or emptiness—you can and will have the intimacy God intends. All you have to do is follow His direction. We've seen it happen time and again.

The following story of one couple illustrates how pursuing intimacy with God and with your spouse can reap rich rewards. A couple of years ago, I briskly entered an auditorium filled to standing room only by thousands of people impatiently waiting for the speaker to arrive. That's why I moved briskly: I was the tardy speaker. A hurting couple had commandeered me in the parking lot and wouldn't release me until I heard their hurt and told them where to find the cure. Now, making my way down the overcrowded side aisle, mumbling apologies to the people I was stepping on and tripping over, I found myself suddenly brought up short by a giant of a man standing determinedly in my way.

"You Joe Beam?" he arched his eyebrow and bored his eyes into me as he asked, making me a little unsure of whether I wanted to identify myself.

"Ahhh, yeah, ummm, I'm Joe Beam."

"My name's Brad, and this is Thelma," he said as he magically produced a bashfully smiling, petite lady from behind him. "We were married for twelve years before we split up. When I left, I couldn't remember ever loving her and just wanted to be free of her, her family, and anything else that had to do with her. You felt the same way about me, didn't you, honey?"

She smiled more broadly in reply.

"Well, anyway, our preacher wouldn't give up on us. Kept telling us that God could fix this if we'd let Him, but that just sounded like preacher talk to me, you know? Finally, just to get him off my back, I agreed to go through your *His Needs, Her Needs* course at church. Thelma had already said she'd go."

At that point, he got misty-eyed and hugged her tight against him. "Man, did I ever see the power of God! He worked on me for those eight weeks, bringing me closer to Him. And when that happened, something changed in the way I thought about Thelma. I don't even know that I can explain it except to say that I don't think I would ever have come to love her if I hadn't first learned something about loving God.

"Thelma and I struggled through the tough parts of that course as we did all the things you told us to do on the tapes and in the handbook. We worked hard, not because we wanted to, but because we got to liking the folks in our group and didn't want to let 'em down, and because I was beginning to grow in God like never before. I don't know that I can tell you the exact moment it happened, but one day I realized that I loved this woman. And I found out that she never stopped loving me.

"I just want to make sure you tell these people that God can do anything with a marriage, no matter how bad it is. If He can turn me around and give me love and a great marriage with my wife, He can do it for anybody. If you just do what God tells you to do, you get what God promises. You tell 'em that for Brad and Thelma."

I did tell them, and now I'm telling you: God can do anything in your marriage—no matter what it's like right now. If you love each other now, He can show you how to love with deeper levels of intimacy. If you don't love each other, He can create love in your relationship in ways that defy comprehension. Just as He created our world from absolutely nothing, He can create deep, abiding, intimate love in your heart even if none lives there now.

He is Creator.

He can do it.

Trust Him.

But remember, if you want deeper, more fulfilling intimacy with your mate, you must first develop deeper, more fulfilling intimacy with God.

Personal Application

If you have the accompanying workbook, *Exercises in Intimacy,* we recommend that you complete the exercises there. If you don't, we give Personal Applications at the end of each chapter in this book to help you apply what you're reading to your life.

1. *Remember your dreams.* Try to remember the dreams and expectations you had about marriage when you were a child or young teen. Write as many of those dreams and expectations as you can.

2. *Review and reflect.* Review what you've written to find which of your childhood expectations about marriage involved your desire for intimacy. Reflect on what those expectations tell you about how you could be most fulfilled in marriage now.

3. *Share together.* As a couple, make a time when you will have no distractions and share with each other your reflections from activity 2 above.

4. *Talk openly.* Talk openly about what would fulfill each of you and how the two of you together could develop your relationship to that level.

To have every nuance of the intimacy God designed you for, you and your spouse must focus on all three of its dimensions: sexual, emotional, and spiritual. (page 31)

◦⌒◦

When sexual intercourse occurs without sexual union—without sexual *intimacy*—it cannot completely fulfill. Even if it's physically stimulating or erotic, a crucial element is missing. (page 33)

◦⌒◦

You'll likely not find the intimacy you crave until you know which dimensions of your relationship are lacking. When you've figured that out, you can start discovering new depths within each other. (page 41)

◦⌒◦

Don't expect your spouse to tell you the truth as long as you subtly communicate to him or her that you prefer a lie. If you want truth, we'll show you how to get truth. (page 50)

The Triune Nature of Intimacy

*Learning How to Love—
Sexually, Emotionally, and Spiritually*

As her husband took the pulpit to finish the service, she appeared beside me at the back door of the auditorium begging an immediate audience. I glanced at the packed house, mumbled something about all these people who in just minutes would be wanting to speak to me, telling me good-bye on this last night of a very successful revival, and asked her if she could wait a few minutes. Her eyes pleaded eloquently, speaking volumes, while her voice said only a quiet but urgent "please." Whatever it was that she needed, she needed it now. So taking one last measure of how much longer the service might last, I gently grasped her arm and guided her into the foyer.

That wasn't far enough for her.

She kept moving until we were down the hall and in a room where no one could disturb us. Or overhear us. With the clicking of the door latch, she swallowed a deep breath and started her story at the end rather than the beginning.

"I told him it's over. I did it this afternoon. God's been working on me all through this revival, and I just couldn't do it anymore. I thought you should know so you can pray for me."

Being in the marriage business, I knew that she'd just told me one of two things, but I wasn't sure which. Either she was leaving her husband, or she was leaving her lover. I had no knowledge of a lover or even a suspicion of one, but at FDI we've learned not to be surprised by anyone doing anything. So I asked, *"What* is over?"

She didn't cry or dissolve into emotion—not remorse or humiliation or panic. Looking me in the eye, she maintained the strength she must have exerted to do what she'd done earlier that day.

"I told the man I'm falling in love with that it just can't go on. What we're doing isn't right, and we have to stop now. He agreed because he didn't have much choice. I mean, he knows I'm a minister's wife. What's he gonna do, wreck his business by the scandal of pursuing me and breaking up my home? Everyone in town would castigate him for stealing a preacher's wife. So I just left him standing there and drove out of his life."

I wondered if she were as tough as she acted and immediately realized that she couldn't be. Some vulnerability had led her into the sin. Therefore, she wasn't nearly as invincible as she now presented herself. I knew that time was running out and that hundreds of voices would soon fill the hall outside our cubbyhole, but I had to ask.

"How? How did you get into this, Suzanne?"

She told a story of gradually losing the intimacy in her marriage with Wayne. He stayed busy ministering to so many people that he hardly had time for her or their children. They seldom talked anymore, made love only rarely, and drifted farther apart spiritually as Wayne concentrated on caring for the people in his flock. That's when she met Karl. He'd bought the service station down the street where she purchased gas and had her car repaired. He was funny, interesting, and most of all, attentive to her. Before long, she was getting more than gasoline there. She began finding excuses to drop by to have something checked on her car, and while the mechanics knowingly took their time getting to her car, she'd hang around Karl's office drinking coffee and talking about life. By the time she realized she was falling in love with him, she didn't feel guilty. He loved her, too, he said. One sin led to another until she found herself planning her new life with Karl and her escape from Wayne.

I could have diagramed it for her if we'd been in a room with a chalkboard. It isn't hard to do. At Family Dynamics we've heard so many similar stories from so many people that we've drawn it out in a model that we use in some of our seminars.[1] I could have shown her the process by which she'd first fallen in love with Wayne, what made that love diminish, and the process that led her to replace that lost love with Karl. But I didn't have time to teach her all that. I would be leaving her city the next morning and might never see her again, and I wanted to make sure she would have the strength not to return to Karl. So instead, I asked an important question.

"What do you feel for Wayne right now?"

She didn't hesitate: She'd thought this through already. "I love him. But I love him like a brother," she replied.

When I asked her to describe what she felt for Karl, she became much more descriptive: "He's the most wonderful person I've ever known. He understands me like no one ever has. He's smart and handsome and sensual and kind and caring and..." Her descriptions went on for some time. Obviously the love she felt for her husband and the love she felt for her paramour were quite different.

I agreed with her that she likely did love both men, each with a different kind of love. Then I began to teach her, "Because Christians tend not to sin without finding some rationalization, you eventually would have completely quit loving Wayne, finding every fault in him that you could until you finally convinced yourself you never loved him at all. I mention that because maybe you're already feeling that in some ways. It wouldn't surprise me or scare me if you said you didn't love him. We hear people say that regularly and have learned to ignore it. First, it's irrelevant. We can teach you how to love someone even if you don't feel love for that person right now.[2] Second, you'd only be saying you never loved him because you'd need to believe that in order to justify leaving him.

"I'm glad you say you still feel love for Wayne, even if it's just as a brother. That gives us a place to start. As best I can, I will try to explain what has happened and is happening to you, but I'll only do that if you promise to attend one of our three-day seminars with Wayne so we can help you get to where you need to be.

"Are you ready to learn?"

Of course she was. The same conviction that led her to stop the relationship that day also led her to do what was needed to do to save her marriage. And she did attend one of the seminars with her husband, Wayne. That was three years ago. Today they are happily married, and he ministers effectively for a growing church, though he places his family before his flock now. We were able to help them develop a deep intimacy with each other, but we had to start by helping both of them understand what intimacy really is.

A TRINARY VIEW OF INTIMACY

Would you like to know what I shared with Suzanne and Wayne? Wonderful. I really want to share it with you. But I ask your indulgence as I did theirs. We have to start with a subject that *seems* to have nothing to do with intimacy, love, or relationships but in reality lies at the very center of all those things. It has to do with the way God made us.

We are three-dimensional creatures.

That's right, three. We are body. We are mind. And we are spirit.[3] It's not difficult to see that the foundation of our discussion on ONEness comes from these three dimensions. For in this book, we are talking about a three-dimensional intimacy: sexual intimacy, emotional intimacy, and spiritual intimacy.

The Sexual Dimension of Intimacy

We know we are flesh. All we have to do to confirm that is glance in the mirror or hold our hands in front of us and look at them. Our bodies comprise an important part of what we are. The psalmist said it well as he sang of God's forming him in his mother's womb:

> You knit me together in my mother's womb. I praise you because I am fearfully and wonderfully made; your works are wonderful, I know that full well. My frame was not hidden from you when I was made in the secret place. When I was woven together in the depths of the earth, your eyes saw my unformed body. All the days ordained for me were written in your book before one of them came to be.[4]

Notice that when the psalmist sang of the formation of his body, he spoke of the formation of his very being. "You knit *me* together.... *I* am fearfully and wonderfully made.... When *I* was made in the secret place...when *I* was woven together." He didn't see himself as some spiritual being living in a body. He realized that he was a spiritual being who was *also* a body. Your body is part of who you are and what you are. When you die, you will vacate your body;[5] but you won't stay bodiless long. On the Resurrection Day, you will get a new body based on the seed that this one is.[6]

Remember that point: Your body is part of your very being, not just a "house" you live in while on earth.

When God created humankind, He created us with a drive for self-perpetuation that we call the sex drive. When we humans yearn to join ourselves in sexual union to another human of the opposite gender, on some primal, core level, the drive is to procreate. In that sense, we are like the rest of the animal kingdom. But God designed a dimension into *human* sexuality that He apparently didn't give the rest of the animals. We not only enjoy sexual union for procreation, we enjoy it for other essential reasons as well. Sexual union fulfills much more than the inherent need we feel to populate the earth;[7] it fulfills strong and varied emotional drives as well—including the drive for ultimate intimacy with another person.

Sexual intimacy is important because an *essential* way that two humans become ONE is through the joining of their bodies. Since our bodies are part of who we are, and not just something we live in, the joining of two bodies in sexual intercourse is the joining of two beings. When we join our bodies in sexual union, we become, in essence, one person. When God spoke of the union that happens when a man and woman leave their families of origin to start a new family, He said, "They will become one flesh."[8] He saw the union of Adam and Eve as so complete that He viewed them as one flesh (one person) to the point that He called them by one name.[9]

Not only do God-created body parts blend together perfectly in sexual intercourse to make one from two, but two people who lovingly and willingly join in this union become one in ways that transcend the physical. They become one through the *learning* and *knowing* accomplished through that sexual interaction. Thus, the King James Version says that Adam "knew" his wife and she conceived. "Knowing" in that passage means more than observation and reflection. It carries the secondary meaning of the Hebrew word used there, *yada* (yaw-dah').[10] *Yada* is used in this passage and elsewhere in the Old Testament to describe sexual union. It means either to know by observing and reflecting or to know by experiencing.[11] As used in this verse, it means that Adam *experienced* Eve in every sense of the word and that by that experience he *learned* his wife; he gained knowledge of her, and she gained a knowledge of him on a level that goes deeper than conscious cognizance. Their learning of each other contributed to the depth of their ONEness. Becoming ONE sexually blends more than two bodies into one body; it blends two people into one person, two strangers into a unique knowing of each other.

No wonder God considers sexual union so holy that it is reserved only for the marriage bed.[12]

True sexual union is far more than just sexual intercourse. Sexual intercourse may fulfill a part of us, our bodies, but sexual union fulfills more.

If complete sexual fulfillment is not a part of your marriage—if sexual intercourse occurs without sexual *union*, without sexual *intimacy*—don't fear. As we move through this book, we will show you how to have both. God intended that you have not only sexual intercourse but fulfillment through the uniting of the two of you in sexual intimacy. That dimension of a couple's relationship is too crucial to allow it to be anything less than it is meant to be.

The Emotional Dimension of Intimacy

From a biblical perspective, the mind is made up of two parts that comprise a third. We have *intellect* and *emotion*, and when they join together, they make up the *heart*.[13] In this book, we focus on the *emotional* aspect of the mind because intimacy takes root in our feelings rather than our logic.

Perhaps Melissa, a graduate from one of our marriage seminars, can help us understand this dimension of intimacy. When Melissa and her husband, Willie, came to our seminar, they were on the verge of divorce. What they learned in our course saved their marriage—no small feat—but that wasn't enough for Melissa. She called me one afternoon wanting *more*.

"I don't know how to describe it," she began, "but something's missing. Now don't get worried. We're okay. I love Willie, but the problem is that it's not like I *want* to love him. We've come so far in our marriage since we went through your *His Needs, Her Needs* course, but I feel like there must be another level, and whatever that is, we haven't reached it. The best way I can describe it is that I want to daydream about him in the middle of the day or feel so empty when he's on a business trip that I can't stand it. I want him to be my prince that I just can't live without."

She paused and then timidly asked, "Am I being too girlish? Is this just some latent adolescent dream? Because, Joe, it seems awfully powerful to me. I love the man, but I want to love him more. I want us to be so in love with each other that neither of us can get enough of the other. I want us to be able to share our secret dreams, our hopes, our fears. I want us to be so intermeshed that we can see into each other's souls. Tell me I'm not being silly. Tell me we can have this kind of relationship.

"And while you're at it, tell me how."

I chuckled because I knew her choice of words was meant to amuse me, but I also knew she was serious.

My mind raced through all I'd learned about love and intimacy. I remembered reading one researcher's conclusion that women who throughout their marriages see their husbands as Prince Charming live happier lives. It sounded like Melissa wanted to feel that for Willie, but Willie, bless his heart, doesn't fit *my* impression of Prince Charming.

Apparently, he didn't fit Melissa's either.

Then I mentally shuffled through what I'd read about codependency and wondered if what Melissa wanted was even healthy for her. Or Willie. It took only a moment or two to decide they had no risk of that delimma.

Finally I asked myself if she was being immature, acting like a teen rather than a thirty-five-year-old mother of four. Should she be pining over a husband away on business? Could she actually have a relationship so wonderful that she'd daydream about him while he was at work? Can those things happen in the real world with real people?

Yes, I concluded, they can. Then I had to ask myself if it only happened in women, if a married man with four children could feel the same way about his wife. Again, I concluded that yes, it could happen.

All that mental processing took about two minutes, during which Melissa apparently thought we'd lost connection because she interjected, "Are you still there?" She fell patiently silent when I apologetically mumbled, "I'm thinking."

"Okay, Melissa, I'm ready to respond to your questions. No, I don't think you're being girlish or silly. And, yes, I think this is doable. I think you and Willie can have what you describe. Can't promise it, but I do think it can be achieved."

What Melissa wanted was emotional intimacy.

As we continued to talk, Melissa shared something more about her relationship with Willie: "I hope I don't embarrass you by saying this, but our sex life isn't what it should be either. Oh, it's *physically* satisfying. It just isn't *emotionally* satisfying. Sometimes I find myself fantasizing about being with someone else—some romantic man without a face who sweeps me off my feet. Instantly I know he sees deep within me and understands all there is to know about me. When he touches me, I'm raised to levels of excitement like I've never known. But when I open my eyes, it's just Willie, and I feel so disappointed. Oh, I'm not trying to make Willie sound like he's a terrible lover. He really is a good lover—slow, careful, and considerate. But I want something more."

I'm not a sexual therapist, and I tread lightly when talking with people about the specifics of their sex lives—especially when talking just with the wife.[14] Therefore, I didn't directly pursue what Melissa was telling me. But I knew that I'd just heard something important: Melissa believes Willie to be a good lover, but in her mind being a good lover isn't enough.

Intimacy in its complete form is not just an act, like sex; it is also a union of *hearts*. It's true that every time a married couple has sexual intercourse, they experience one level of intimacy. But that doesn't necessarily mean they experience the level of intimacy that fulfills and creates the closeness that Melissa craved. To reach its full effect, intimacy must first be in the heart before it takes place between bodies. Otherwise the beautiful ONEness that God designed sexual union to bring doesn't take place as it should. The sexual encounter may carry some fulfillment—even some satisfaction—but it cannot, by itself, create the intimacy we humans really crave.

Why?

Because sex—as God intended—isn't just physical. Physical ONEness without emotional ONEness is incomplete—no matter how much our bodies participate. Melissa's body involved itself in sexual union with her husband. But her emotions went elsewhere.

Our emotions are the part of us that initially separated us from the other animals. It is the part of us that must be fulfilled if we are to rise above the animals and have true intimacy.

The other animals join sexually when it's time to procreate and have no concern for a long-term, intimate relationship. Even animals that mate for life don't feel what humans feel or think like humans think. When animals' mates are destroyed by predators, they hold no wakes, attend no funerals, nor enter grief counseling to learn how to get on with their lives. When it's time to mate again, they seek a suitable partner and continue filling the earth with as many offspring as possible. God simply didn't give them the emotions and feelings that He gave us; they cannot think and feel as we do.

If we ignore the emotional part of ourselves, mating just to produce offspring or attain gratification without developing a relationship with a lifetime partner, we lose a primary part of who we are. We must have intimacy—not only sexual intimacy, but emotional intimacy as well.

From my conversation with Melissa, I knew that until Willie understood her tremendous need for emotional intimacy, he could never provide for her the relationship she craved. He could be the greatest lover since Don Juan and still have a wife who chose to exclude him from her emotional fantasies.

The Spiritual Dimension of Intimacy

The spirit is as much a part of a human as is the body and mind. Even though it cannot be seen by sophisticated imaging systems or weighed on delicate scales or measured with precision lasers, it is nonetheless real. While scientists tend to ignore what they can't track, record, or predict, according to the God who made us, we *are* spiritual beings. He Himself formed our spirits within us.[15]

Our spirits are at the core of our innermost being. At death the spirit leaves the body, but it continues to exist in another realm[16] until it returns to be united with the resurrected body. It appears to be the part of us God described when He said, "Let us make man in our image, in our likeness."[17] Therefore, it is in our spirits that we worship God as His Spirit guides us. When we have union with God, His Spirit lives in us, testifying with our spirits that we are His children.[18]

So, what, if anything, does that have to do with intimacy between husband and wife? Put on your "thinking cap" for just a brief moment of theological study, and the answer will become apparent.

When some of the Christians in Corinth were satisfying their sexual drives by engaging the services of prostitutes, the Spirit of God led Paul to tell them to stop! But the reasoning he presented gives us an interesting insight into something that happens when two people come together sexually: When they join physically, they join spiritually.

> Do you not know that your bodies are members of Christ himself? Shall I then take the members of Christ and unite them with a prostitute? Never! Do you not know that he who unites himself with a prostitute is one with her in body? For it is said, "The two will become one flesh." But he who unites himself with the Lord is one with him in spirit.

Flee from sexual immorality. All other sins a man commits are outside his body, but he who sins sexually sins against his own body. Do you not know that your body is a temple of the Holy Spirit, who is in you, whom you have received from God? You are not your own; you were bought at a price. Therefore honor God with your body.[19]

Undeniably, Paul makes it clear that the sin is one of body, but he also points out that one reason Christians shouldn't have sex with a prostitute—beyond the fact that God said they shouldn't do it—is that in the sex act they become *one* with the prostitute. That certainly fits everything we're learning. Two people in sexual intercourse have a special kind of ONEness. But Paul goes even further. Notice his key arguments about a sexual encounter between a Christian, Christ, and a prostitute.

1. If you are a Christian, your body is a member of Christ (*member*—a word that means a limb or part of the body). A Christian's body is part of Jesus' body (v. 15).

2. Having sex with a prostitute makes the Christian one body with the prostitute (v. 16).

3. The implied argument is that the Christian's having sex with the prostitute somehow sets up a situation where Christ is one body with her. And Jesus *doesn't* intend to be part of that! (vv. 19–20)

Maybe you're thinking the same thing I thought when that argument first hit me many years ago: "Now, how in the world could Jesus become one body with a prostitute when a Christian has a sexual encounter with her?" The answer is that when the Spirit of Christ lives in a person, Christ becomes one with that person in spirit (v. 17). Therefore, the implied union between Jesus and the prostitute takes place in a spiritual sense, not in an actual physical sense. By the very act of having sex with the prostitute, the Christian is having more than just a physical union with her; he is also having some kind of spiritual union with her—a spiritual union that neither Jesus nor the Spirit wants any part of.

That principle leads us to believe that when married couples join together in the marriage bed, they join more than their bodies—they join their spirits. If that is true, there is an even more important issue to consider: To what *degree* is God involved in that spiritual union, and can our own spirituality affect His involvement?

Of course, God sanctions sex between husband and wife, even if one or both of them aren't Christians.[20] But if, indeed, sex carries a spiritual dimension, then wouldn't it have to be true that if one is committed to God and the other isn't, their sexual coupling is missing something? A spirit in union with God joining itself to a spirit *not* in union with God can't have the same level of intimacy experienced by the joining of two spirits who both know God.

Sex can be just sex. Or it can be a thousand times better when based on emotional intimacy. Or it can be even better than that. The joy and fulfillment of emotionally intimate sex increases exponentially when the couple also shares spiritual intimacy.

Several years ago, a wise and spiritually mature brother in a church I attended taught some of us younger men about this wonderful dimension of sexual union. He said, "Gentlemen, sometimes when my wife and I have a particularly fulfilling sexual experience, we get on our knees and join in prayer. Holding hands and lifting them to God, we thank Him for each other. We thank Him for the wonderful gift of sex for those who are married. We thank Him for the enjoyment we just had and will have again. We know that He's in that room with us, just as He is in every other part of our lives. We don't have to hide from Him like Adam and Eve did. We don't feel guilt and shame, just an inner peace that comes from knowing that we are right with Him and right with each other.

"If ever in your marriage you can't—or won't—pray with your wife immediately after making love to her, something's wrong. You have a flaw in your relationship, and it needs fixing.

"Fix it."

At that time in my life I thought him to be a tad eccentric. Now I know that the man had discovered what so many people—even those who love God with all their hearts—miss. The spiritual dimension of a marriage affects everything else in it, even the sexual part. As a matter of fact, we'll show you in a later chapter that if you really want to bypass all sexual hang-ups and inhibitions, you can absolutely do that if you first establish spiritual intimacy with God and with each other. Couples who pray together, study and meditate on the Word together, and serve God in their lives together add a depth to the relationship far beyond anything that any humanly based advice or education can bring. And when that spiritual intimacy—along with sexual and emotional intimacy—exists, a couple has finally achieved everything that God intends for them to have in their relationship with each other.

Physical ONEness.

Emotional ONEness.

Spiritual ONEness.

THE ONENESS MODEL

Borrowing from a model created by Robert Sternberg of Yale University depicting the different kinds of love,[21] we at FDI have created our own model. We call it the ONEness Model. Each side of the triangle below represents one dimension of intimacy.

Emotion

The three dimensions of intimacy shown above can actually be put together in different combinations to form seven different kinds of intimacy. We determine these different kinds of intimacy by considering whether a couple has intimacy in just one dimension or a combination of dimensions. (Actually there is an eighth kind of intimacy—nonintimacy—which exists when a couple has *no* intimacy in either body, emotions, or spirit.)

1. Spirit Only: Spiritual Intimacy

If two people shared only their love for God and their intimacy with Him, they would have only spiritual intimacy with each other. They would be brother and sister in the Lord,[22] but they wouldn't have the relationship that God intended for them as husband and wife. To have intimacy *only* in spirit is better suited to the immediate intimacy we feel upon meeting Christians we don't know; it certainly shouldn't be the only intimacy in marriage.

I vividly recall a couple I met years ago who lived together in the same house but in different bedrooms. Because the woman had been married before, their church believed that their current marriage was sinful and said they would be committing adultery if they joined sexually. The elders of the church demanded that they divorce, but for the sake of their children, the couple wanted to remain married. The church agreed to allow that only if they promised total celibacy. And that's exactly what they did.

Because of their deep faith in God, both maintained a deeply involved relationship with their church. They read their Bibles, prayed earnestly, and served God to the best of their abilities. Truly, they enjoyed only one kind of intimacy in their marriage—spiritual.

Unfortunately, they couldn't let themselves be emotionally intimate because they knew that would lead them into sexual intimacy. To prevent that and to ensure celibate lives, they distanced themselves from each other emotionally, interacting only with cold civility. Their emotional distance finally turned into bitterness and contempt. Eventually they wouldn't even drive to church in the same car. The only thing they shared was their love for God. Think God was happy with that? I don't. Surely God shakes His head in dismay when He sees his people missing the wonderful intimacy He designed for marriage by living together without emotional and sexual intimacy.

Spiritual intimacy is wonderful in marriage, but it *must* be mixed with other intimacies.

2. Body Only: Sexual Intimacy

We've already seen in 1 Corinthians 6 that two people who share their bodies become one flesh, even if no other element of intimacy exists.

But when emotional intimacy has faded—because of the pressures of life or just indifference to each other—and when one or both lack intimacy with God and spiritual intimacy with each other, a couple will grow farther and farther apart. That's easy enough to see. However, each still has a sex drive, and the most convenient place to fulfill that drive is with each other. Even though emotionally and spiritually separated, they may continue to be sexually active with each other. Sound improbable? Many couples have walked into our three-day facilitator training seminars—not to become facilitators but to see if there is any hope for saving their marriage—and sometime during the three days told us that they have an active sex life with each other but no other type of intimacy at all.

Ironically couples who are united in body alone may even feel great passion in their lovemaking, but the passion isn't for the mate. It is a passion for excitement and gratification. Most often these couples lack even physical excitement, and their perfunctory and routine sex life serves only as a means of release or relaxation.

Because the *intensity* of passion inevitably fades with age, after a while, even those who once had shared passionate lovemaking find that the only thing holding them together is convenience or commitment. Things like financial considerations, religious convictions, lack of alternative choices in lovers, or a desire to care for the children keep them in what they might describe as a loveless marriage. They may even say they love each other, but in fact, their love is empty and joyless.

Sex is a key element in marriage and a key element in every human being that God made. But a marriage that is held together only by sexual intimacy is desolate and barren. The passion almost always fades, and all that's left is emptiness.

3. Emotions Only: Emotional Intimacy

Some couples find the intimacy of shared emotions. They find friendship and understanding, feeling close to each other while opening their lives and telling their feelings to one another.

Perhaps the closest New Testament concept to what they experience is found in the koine Greek word *koinonia* (koy-nohn-ee'-ah). The New International Version translates it sometimes as *sharing*, other times as *partnership*, and yet other times as *fellowship*.[23] On our model we call it *emotional* intimacy. It occurs when two people find the wonderful friendship that comes from immersing themselves in each other. They live their lives as open books and feel total and complete acceptance.

Several years ago a friend of mine, J. Wayne Kilpatrick of Birmingham, Alabama, told me that his wife was his best friend. That was in the days before Alice and I divorced and remarried, and I remember thinking how wonderful it would be to have your spouse as your best friend. Obviously it takes work. More than that, it takes the willingness to share your actions, thoughts, and secrets with each other. Alice and I couldn't have that then because I couldn't tell her what I was doing, much less what I had done. My thoughts and secrets were mine alone because I was too terrified of the consequences of sharing them with her. Alice and I work on having this intimacy now. While I wish it had been true throughout our marriage, I can honestly say that I'm now more open with Alice than with any other person on this planet and that I feel more acceptance from her—no matter what I tell her about what I do or think or feel—than from anyone else.

She has become my best friend.

Emotional intimacy. We strongly recommend it. But even it alone isn't enough. True ONEness requires intimacy of emotions, body, *and* spirit.

4. Spirit + Body: Heartless Intimacy

In describing spiritual intimacy earlier, we told you of a couple who lived together in the same house but shared neither their hearts nor their bodies. The only commonality existing with them was their love for God and their union as brother and sister in Christ. As you read their story, maybe you shook your head in dismay and wondered how any two people could live together like that. Well, if that story made you ponder, think about this: Our perception is that most Christian couples (maybe as many as 75 percent) live together in *heartless* intimacy. They share their love for God, attend church together, and teach their children to do the same. They have some level of sexual activity—at least enough to prevent either from looking for sexual satisfaction elsewhere. But their intimacy involves only two-thirds of their beings. They share in spirit and they share in body—they just don't share in emotions.

That was the situation Melissa was in when she called asking if there was another level for her and Willie. They already shared a degree of sexual intimacy—though Melissa obviously wanted deeper intimacy even there—and they also shared spiritual intimacy. During their tenure in the *His Needs, Her Needs* class, Melissa and Willie both found Jesus and became Christians. That new dimension of their lives was exciting to watch as they became stronger in the Lord and in His service. With the fervor often found in new converts, they voraciously dug for every spiritual nugget they could garner from God and His Word.

But Melissa knew they were still missing something.

What Melissa and Willie hadn't yet learned was how to share intimacy at the *emotional* level. Remember what she said? "I want us to be able to share our secret dreams, our hopes, our fears. I want us to be so intermeshed that we can see into each other's souls." If Melissa could develop emotional intimacy with Willie, she wouldn't be dreaming about an imaginary Don Juan as they make love. Even their spiritual intimacy would increase as they learned to share what they're learning about God on more than just an intellectual level. If they could grow in emotional intimacy, Melissa would soon discover that she had found the elusive "missing" part of their relationship.

Our experience with thousands and thousands of couples has shown that the one element most often lacking in Christian marriages is *emotional* intimacy, and sadly, many have settled for this *heartless* state of intimacy—thinking they'll never find more. I'm glad Melissa refused to settle.

5. Spirit + Emotions: Celibate Intimacy

One of the greatest love stories in the Bible isn't about a man and his wife but about a man and his buddy. Don't worry; it has *nothing* to do with homosexuality. Instead, it has everything to do with two men who shared a deep and abiding love for the Lord God and who shared a deep and abiding emotional intimacy with each other.

Jonathan and David loved each other so much that after Jonathan's death David cried, "I grieve for you, Jonathan my brother; you were very dear to me. Your love for me was wonderful, more wonderful than that of women."[24] David and Jonathan shared two very special parts of their lives: their spirits and their hearts.

What did David mean when he said Jonathan's love was "more wonderful than that of women"? It certainly didn't mean they felt sexual passion for each other. No one could read the multiplied stories of David and think him anything other than a passionate heterosexual—too passionate at times! What David and Jonathan shared was an intimacy of both spirit and heart.

Each man loved God intensely, and they felt the same about the kingdom of Israel. They shared a kinship in their prowess on the battlefield—at the very mention of their names, their enemies were brought up short. They understood each other on a level that few ever experience. David and Jonathan were best friends.

But God wants more than friendship for you and your spouse.

When a husband and wife share faith and loyalty to God and become friends to the point of letting down the barriers to their souls, they share a blessed union; but it still falls short of what God intended if it isn't coupled with sexual intimacy. Even as couples get older and the sex drive doesn't have quite the same urgency, the enjoyment of two people for each other in the marital bed should last a lifetime.

Some of the saddest letters I receive come from people whose spouse can no longer function sexually but won't get help to overcome the problem. Allie wrote me a couple of years ago. Her husband is a well-known businessman. Sometime in the two or three years before Allie wrote me, he had become impotent. She didn't know whether the problem was physiological or psychological. He didn't either. And the reason neither of them knew was that he refused to seek any kind of help to solve the problem.

He would say to her, "Look, I'm the man. I'm the one with the sex drive. If I can live with this, you can too. So just leave me alone and let me get on with my business. Am I not good to you in every other way? Don't we spend hours walking on the beach just talking? Don't we give of ourselves in every way to God in heaven, serving Him here by serving people? What more do you want?

"I refuse to be humiliated by going to either a medical doctor or a shrink to see what's wrong with me. I'm okay with this, and you should be too."

But she isn't. Just because he convinced himself he feels no need for sexual union doesn't mean that she doesn't. In a later chapter on sexual intimacy, we'll see that Larry actually sins—directly violating Scripture—by ignoring Allie's sexual needs. His sexist view that if the man doesn't need fulfillment then the woman shouldn't either is as wrong as it can be. She lives in misery and wrote me, a friend of the family, to ask what she should do about the problem.

When I conduct our *Love, Sex & Marriage* seminars across the nation, this question finds its way into our question box nearly every time. Sometimes a woman writes it about her husband. Sometimes it's a man who has great sexual frustration because of a problem with his wife. Always the basis of the question is the same: "I can't seem to get through to my spouse that I need this. My spouse is content to have our intimacy be of the heart and spirit. But I *crave* sexual intimacy. What can I do?"

Mates who think that spiritual and emotional intimacy is enough are only fooling themselves. Not only do they put their spouses under undue susceptibility to temptation, they also miss a crucial dimension of the intimacy God intended. True ONEness comes from sharing in all three areas of a person—emotional, spiritual, *and* sexual.

Reserve celibate intimacy for your closest spiritual friend. Your spouse deserves all of you—spirit, emotions, and body.

6. Emotions + Body: Romantic Intimacy

When two people have both emotional intimacy and sexual intimacy, they have what most people define as *romance*.

Many people might see this as the ideal relationship—two people growing closer and closer to each other emotionally and enjoying sexual fulfillment in the process. Actually, it's more than most Christians I've dealt with ever experience.

Even those who have no knowledge of God can have this kind of intimacy, and there are a veritable plethora of books, courses, videos, audios, infomercials, and the like that claim to guarantee it. We think that as you work through the subsequent chapters of this book, you will learn to achieve this level of intimacy. But before you set your sights on this kind of intimacy as your ideal, let's look at one more.

7. Spirit + Emotions + Body: ONEness Intimacy

As we've stated, true ONEness intimacy exists when a couple shares all three parts of themselves with each other. It isn't enough to share one part of yourself with your spouse, not even two parts. God made you to blend in totality. You become one spirit, one body, and one heart. When you have true ONEness, you seek God together and grow closer to each other by growing closer to Him—like we demonstrated in our God-husband-wife triangle in chapter 1. You also seek to understand and accept each other in every part of your lives—what you've done, what you're doing, what you're going to do, and how you feel about anything and everything. And you find a way to keep passion burning in your relationship so that you find complete and total sexual fulfillment in each other.

This is God-intended, God-inspired ONEness.

THE COMPLETE ONEness MODEL
Types of Intimacy

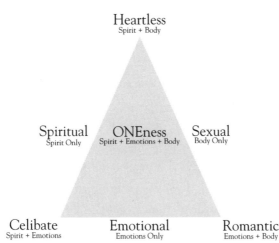

Heartless
Spirit + Body

Spiritual
Spirit Only

ONEness
Spirit + Emotions + Body

Sexual
Body Only

Celibate
Spirit + Emotions

Emotional
Emotions Only

Romantic
Emotions + Body

Personal Application

It's time to make the application of all you've learned in this chapter in your marriage. If you have the accompanying workbook, *Becoming ONE: Exercises in Intimacy*, turn to chapter 2 of that book now. If you don't have the workbook, you can still apply what we've learned. Here are some exercises you and your spouse can do together.

1. Write on separate pieces of paper where you think your marriage falls on the ONEness model. Choose the type of intimacy you think best describes your relationship. Remember, if you don't think you share body, emotions, or spirit, you aren't on the intimacy model at all. We call that a state of nonintimacy. But don't despair. God can help you find complete intimacy even if you have to start from scratch.

2. Now write down the kind of intimacy you want to have in your marriage.

3. Read each other's assessment. When you read what your mate has written, do not attack, belittle, or in any other way show censure or lack of acceptance for what your mate feels. You'll *never* develop emotional intimacy if each cannot say what he or she has done, is doing, or feels without receiving rebuke or retribution from the other. Any sign of a lack of understanding or acceptance will shut down all honesty and openness.

One of my students years ago came to my office to tell me he'd made a big mistake. His new wife had asked him what he honestly felt about their relationship, so he'd proceeded to tell her. He cocked his head at a serious angle and intoned, "I've just learned my first lesson about women. Don't answer them honestly; just tell them what they want to hear!" Apparently she'd cried when he gave his answer, and that had unnerved him. He had decided that from now on he would avoid all controversy by lying.

Whether his wife knew it or not, she was the one who taught him to make such a sad choice. Don't do the same with your spouse. Listen with acceptance even to those things you don't want to hear or don't like hearing.

You or your mate may be surprised at what you read. You may learn that you are both much better off than you thought. On the other hand, you may discover that things aren't as good as you perceived. For example, your mate may think you lack a dimension of intimacy you thought you had. Whatever you learn, don't be discouraged. The remainder of this book will help you develop intimacy in any areas you are currently lacking.

4. Write down what you can do to increase intimacy in areas you both desire. Then write what your spouse can do. Now verbally share what you've written. Listen to each other as you share your hearts. In this exercise, you are explaining what would make you feel more ONEness with each other and what it is that you want that you don't now have.

If you both have the same intimacy goal, begin now to talk about how you can get to the *kind* of intimacy and the *level* of intimacy you want to attain. The remainder of this book is designed to show you how to reach complete intimacy—emotionally, sexually, and spiritually. So no matter what you've learned, take heart and keep reading!

When intimacy isn't developing as it should, it's probably because energy is being directed at the wrong things. If you really want intimacy with your mate, you first have to examine your life. (page 59)

Sometimes we discover that what we thought we desire isn't what we desire at all. If that's happening to you—if you're mistakenly seeking the wrong thing—your confused actions will take you farther and farther from the fulfillment you crave. (page 64)

Even when you understand how to develop deeper levels of intimacy with your spouse, you may foolishly be causing your spouse to feel less intimacy for you. (page 68)

Just as soon as you remove diversions and repair drains, you're ready to learn how to develop intimacy with God and with each other. (page 74)

Repairing Intimacy Diversions and Drains

Understanding How Intimacy Is Generated

"Joe, you know that I'm a good man at heart. I love my wife, love my children, and love the Lord God Almighty. I've spent almost all my adult life trying to serve Him with all my ability. I've taught classes at church, worked as a parent volunteer with the teens, and even spoken at a few special events. I read my Bible and try to do what's right.

"Why just this morning, when I realized that the cashier at a convenience store had given me too much change, I got out of my car and went back in to give her the dime that wasn't mine. Now you tell me, how can a man be that honest in matters of money and at the same time be contemplating divorce? Tell me, how?"

I didn't get a chance to answer. He kept talking with hardly a hesitation.

"Somehow Marilyn and I have lost whatever we once had. She's such a good person and a wonderful mother. It's just that we aren't close anymore.

"All I want to do now is hang out at the health club. I hate going home. It's getting to where I don't want to be home at all. All I can think about is lifting, running laps, and building muscle. Marilyn says I'm obsessed.

"I know I'm wrong to stay away from home all the time. And Marilyn's right—maybe I am obsessed. I know God can help, if I'd let Him. But it's more than *me* He's got to rescue. It's *Marilyn and me*. Our *marriage*.

"I'm confused and I'm lonely and I'm scared. What in the world do I do now?"

He settled back onto the sofa and stared into space, giving me time to think and pray for wisdom.

Sometime later I tapped his knee to draw him from his self-pitying reflections and cleared my throat. "Okay, Josh, I know where we need to begin. We won't start by telling Marilyn that you want to leave her. Stay the night at my house—I'll call Marilyn and make that okay somehow—and in the morning we'll begin at the right starting place. I'm going to help you discover the *diversions* you've allowed to diminish your intimacy with Marilyn. We can't talk about how to become closer to your wife until you know why your feelings of intimacy have been diverted from Marilyn and refocused on other things like working out for hours at a time."

His eyes told the tale; he didn't have a clue what I meant by *diversions*. But I ignored his incredulous expression and went to call Marilyn. His skepticism didn't upset me: Many Christians have difficulty seeing in themselves what they can easily see in others. A good man like Josh doesn't just fall out of love with his wife: Something had interrupted his relationship with Marilyn; our first step was to find out what.

Over years of working with many, many couples, I learned that people can't develop intimacy with their spouses until they first repair any diversions that keep intimacy from occurring. In the first chapter of this book, we discussed the fact that we all crave *intimacy*—even if we don't call it by that name. Even if we don't crave it consciously, we crave it subconsciously, and much of our behaviors and attitudes are driven by that inborn desire. In chapter 2, I shared the three dimensions of intimacy and the seven types of intimacy that are created from different combinations of the basic three dimensions. What you learned there can help you understand where you are in your intimacy with your spouse and what your intimacy goals should be.

It might seem that the next logical step would be to tell you *how* to have the intimacy God intended—and that's exactly what we'll look at in chapters 4 through 9. But we cannot proceed without pausing here, now that you know what intimacy is, to help you discover if any *diversions* to intimacy exist in your relationship with your spouse.

THE INTIMACY TURBINE

Think for a moment about how we use a river to create electricity. We build dams to funnel the river through giant turbines, and as the force of the water spins those turbines, they produce electricity. (Forgive me for the overly simplistic explanation.) If some natural catastrophe or man-made intervention *diverts* the water, nothing spins the turbines and they produce no electricity.

The same kind of thing happens with intimacy. Intimacy is like electricity in that it is produced by indirect means. It is a by-product of other elements. Send enough water with enough pressure through turbines, and you get electricity. In a similar way, if you combine enough of the right *elements* with the right *intensity*, you get intimacy. Unfortunately the opposite is also true: Divert the river and electricity stops. Similarly if the elements that create intimacy for one's spouse are diverted to something or someone else, the process of developing intimacy with the spouse will come to a halt.

The "river" that runs through our hearts isn't composed of water, of course, but of three elements: communication, time, and action.

- *Communication*. For intimacy to grow, two people have to know each other on more than a superficial level. Communication that develops intimacy isn't just sharing ideas or thoughts but interacting on a deeper level. Communication is a verbal (and sometimes written) intercourse, a sharing of your life—what you've done, what you're doing, and how you feel.

- *Time*. We tend to develop the greatest levels of intimacy with those people with whom we spend time—quality time in generous quantities. It takes time to communicate on intimate levels. It takes time to fulfill the sexual and emotional needs of another person.

- *Action*. While sharing leads to the opening of one's heart so that intimacy can grow, it is the intentional effort to fulfill a person's sexual and emotional needs that gives intimacy solid roots in that heart. Only when a person *acts* can we know what he or she really is and whether he or she speaks truthfully.

As we return to our turbine illustration, think of the combination of these three elements as the river that "generates" intimacy, and think of the heart as the dam encasing a line of intimacy-producing turbines. A person has one turbine that generates intimacy for God, another generating intimacy for his or her spouse, and yet other turbines generating intimacy for friends or relatives. Each turbine generates a level of intimacy consistent with the supply of the "river" of communication, time, and action directed into it. Turbines receiving greater portions of the river produce more intimacy, and turbines receiving lesser amounts produce equally reduced levels of intimacy.

We contend that people should direct more of their river (communication, time, and action) toward the "turbines" of God and spouse. We have only so much energy to spend in *communication*, only so much *time* to invest in relationships, and only so much effort to expend in *action*. If we distribute those elements throughout several turbines, giving each equal amounts, we develop little intimacy for any of them. If we focus on God and our spouses, we can develop the level of intimacy we want with each of them. Then based on our priorities, we can distribute the remaining time, communication, and action. Our children are higher on our priority list than aunts and uncles, best friends are higher than casual acquaintances, and so on.

Maybe the following diagrams will help make this clear. On the first diagram, God and spouse receive greater portions of our intimacy-producing elements—communication, time, and action—than do the other people in our lives; thus, we develop greater intimacy with God and spouse than with others. On the second diagram, everyone receives the same amount of our intimacy-producing elements, and no one is prioritized.

The Correct Flow

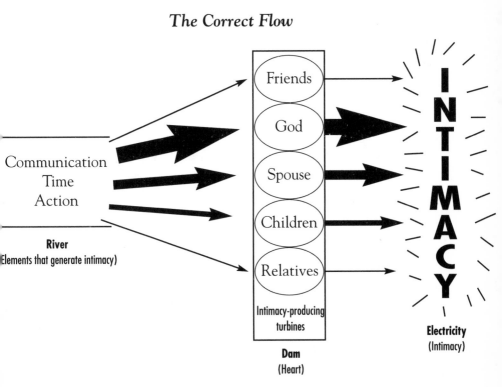

The Incorrect Flow

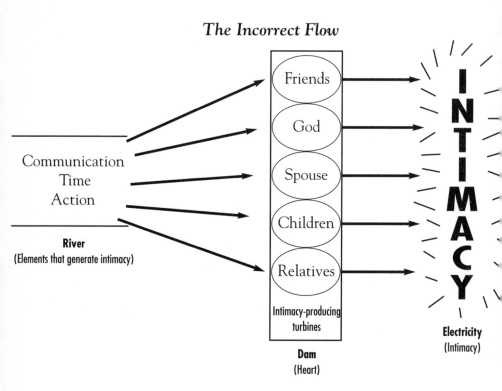

While these two diagrams represent two ways of approaching intimacy, neither of them illustrates what happened to Josh. It's probably obvious that Josh lost intimacy with Marilyn (and with God) because he no longer focused his energy on maintaining those relationships. What may not be so obvious is *why*. Before I could help him regain that lost intimacy, Josh first needed to know what had *diverted* his "river." Even if he worked harder at *communicating* with Marilyn, spending *time* with her, and intentionally *acting* to fulfill her needs, their intimacy would not have been rekindled if something else were *diverting* that power to its "turbine."

Because Josh admitted his nearly fanatical obsession with exercise, I knew that he had more than a simple case of "incorrect flow." An *intimacy diversion* had intercepted the communication, time, and action he should have been giving his wife. I surmised that he likely also had a diversion drawing away his focus on God as well. If I had sketched it out for him, it would have looked something like this:

The Diverted Flow

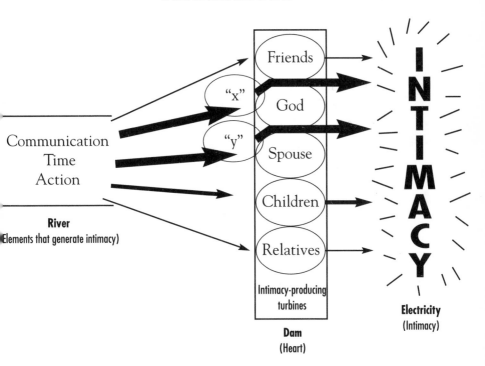

Even if Josh tried to increase his communication, time, and action flow toward Marilyn, he could never regain intimacy with Marilyn if at the same time his stronger effort was to focus his energy and concentrate his time in working out. His efforts toward Marilyn would be short-lived and superficial. Before he could rekindle his intimacy with Marilyn, he must first remove the *intimacy diversions*.

"Well, what's so profound about that?" you may be thinking. "Anybody can see that he has to rearrange his priorities before he can resume intimacy with Marilyn."

Maybe. But then again, maybe his obsession with exercise wasn't the real diversion but only a *symptom* of an altogether different diversion.

INTIMACY DIVERSIONS

To understand how intimacy diversions work, read this familiar story from the life of Jesus.

> Now a man came up to Jesus and asked, "Teacher, what good thing must I do to get eternal life?"
>
> "Why do you ask me about what is good?" Jesus replied. "There is only One who is good. If you want to enter life, obey the commandments."
>
> "Which ones?" the man inquired.
>
> Jesus replied, "'Do not murder, do not commit adultery, do not steal, do not give false testimony, honor your father and mother,' and 'love your neighbor as yourself.'"
>
> "All these I have kept," the young man said. "What do I still lack?"
>
> Jesus answered, "If you want to be perfect, go, sell your possessions and give to the poor, and you will have treasure in heaven. Then come, follow me."
>
> When the young man heard this, he went away sad, because he had great wealth.
>
> Then Jesus said to his disciples, "I tell you the truth, it is hard for a rich man to enter the kingdom of heaven. Again I tell you, it is easier for a camel to go through the eye of a needle than for a rich man to enter the kingdom of God."[1]

For many years I preached about this young man as if he were a legalist looking for a loophole. I thought he wanted to know just how little he could get by with and still go to heaven, and I thought that Jesus had pulled him up short by demanding total surrender. Only recently have I been able to see this passage in a different light—a light that may open your eyes to your diversions. This young man wasn't a legalist; he was a *lacker*.

Often when I preach around the world, I ask audiences if they feel as if something is missing in their relationships with God. Inevitably, a majority of the hands go up. These aren't people from the general populace in buses or malls or civic auditoriums. They are religious folks who love God—at least in some fashion—and want to go to heaven. They attend church regularly and sometimes serve as the very pillars of those churches, yet they still feel that something is lacking.

Lacking. That's the same word the young man used when he asked Jesus, "What do I still lack?" The koine Greek word used in this passage, *hustereo* (hoos-ter-eh'-o), means "come too late, through one's own fault to miss, fail to reach, be excluded...be in need of...be less than, inferior to."[2] It's in that last sense the word is focused here: The young man is asking, "In what respect am I still inferior?"[3] or "In what way am I still less than I need to be?"

Ever felt that way? Have you ever felt that by some fault of your own you were missing something, had failed to reach a promised level in your relationship with God, and felt excluded from what other Christians seemed to have with Him? If you've ever felt that, have you also wanted to have a private conversation with Jesus where you could let Him look into your heart and see all that's there and all that isn't? To find the intimacy that's missing, would you want Him to tell you the truth about you because you know you are much too good at lying to yourself to figure it out on your own? Me too. And all of us who've felt any of that can relate to the frustration this young man felt as he approached Jesus with his request to find why he "lacked" the relationship with God he wanted.

He began by asking Jesus what he should do to inherit eternal life. When Jesus ran through a litany of commandments, the young man apparently felt a strong degree of exasperation. He'd been *doing* all those things, and they hadn't worked. He knew that despite doing

61

them, he *still* lacked something. So he just blurted it out. "What am I missing?! What do I lack?"

Jesus told him.

"If you want to be perfect," He began. The word we translate "perfect" here is the word *teleios* (tel'-i-os), which means "having attained the end or purpose, complete, perfect...of age, full grown, mature, adult...fully developed."[4] It's in that last sense the word is used here: Jesus is saying, "If you want to be fully developed, here's the next step."

Fully developed. Sounds like the kind of intimacy we crave, doesn't it? Jesus was telling him, "If you want all there is to have—the whole of it without anything missing—then this is what you do. This is how you have a complete relationship with Me.

"Put Me before everything else in your life. Everything."

In terms of our illustration, we can say that Jesus told this young man that he must remove all *diversions* funneling his river away from God. To this young man, that message meant that he had to separate himself from the vast array of material wealth he'd accumulated. Jesus looked right into his heart and saw that the young man's money took precedence in his life. It stood as the diversion keeping him from developing intimacy with God. It was the "turbine" into which this young man fed the most attention. He could never put God first, loving Him above all else, if he loved his money more than he loved God. After all, who has time to commune with God through Bible study and prayer when business calls unrelentingly? Who can dedicate his time to God when he must work endless hours ensuring that his money makes him more money? Who can focus his life on serving God when the primary focus of his life is to do the things that must be done to maintain wealth? In the diversion model we drew earlier, we would replace "x" with the word *wealth* when describing this young man's diversion from God. It isn't a sin to have money; God Himself made Job, Abraham, Lot, Solomon, and others rich. But it is a sin to let wealth, or anything else, divert you from intimacy with God.

Three Categories of Diversions

We could come up with hundreds of diversions that might pull our focus away from our spouses—everything from the practical to the psychological—but we don't have the space or inclination to make such an exhaustive list. Instead we summarize all diversions into three categories:

1. A thing

2. A person

3. An emotional need (usually for something intangible)

From our own lives we know that these three categories exist. Some people find themselves distracted by a *thing* like money, others by a *person*, and still others by an unfulfilled *emotional need*.

It's not too difficult to imagine how the pursuit of some *thing* like money or power could divert our river of energy from what's really important in our lives. That's the kind of diversion that distracted the rich young ruler. The Bible also speaks of people whose desire for praise comes between them and God.[5] I've personally seen people allow a desire for fame or power completely divert their focus from God, resulting in the loss of all feelings of intimacy with Him.

It's also easy to understand how the desire for a certain *person* could become an intimacy diversion. That's why Jesus said that those who come to Him must not only put Him before any*thing*, they must put Him before any*one*. He said things like, "If anyone comes to me and does not hate his father and mother, his wife and children, his brothers and sisters—yes, even his own life—he cannot be my disciple."[6] And He said, "Anyone who loves his father or mother more than me is not worthy of me; anyone who loves his son or daughter more than me is not worthy of me; and anyone who does not take his cross and follow me is not worthy of me."[7]

That's why in our diagram we drew the turbines for spouse and children *beside* God's, not in front of. No one should interfere with or divert our energy from Him. No one. Not mother, father, son, or daughter. Especially not a lover.

As strong as the pull of a person or the craving for a thing can be, sometimes the strongest diversion of all is a desire for something less tangible—the fulfilling of an *emotional need*. In *His Needs, Her Needs*, Dr. Willard Harley Jr. explains emotional needs, especially those he calls "most important emotional needs." He says that when they are not fulfilled, we tend to feel loneliness, emptiness, or frustration. When they are fulfilled, we tend to feel contentment, happiness, or even ecstasy.

Every person has his or her own emotional needs, and we don't mean to imply in any way that having those needs is bad or that we should ignore fulfilling them. They are very much a part of the human experience. Our point is that when an emotional need is unmet, people are either consciously or unconsciously driven to find a way to fulfill it. Unfortunately, our efforts to fulfill them may lead us away from God or our spouses if our relationship with God or our spouses seems incapable of meeting the need.

Sometimes a desire that on the surface appears to be for a person or thing is really a desire for something more intangible. One night I heard a woman say that she was headed to a local nightclub and that the first man who said he loved her could have her. No, she wasn't looking for sex. Not even for a person, at least not in the way we're discussing here. She was looking to fill a powerful emotional need— the need to *feel* loved. Now there's nothing wrong with this need— just as there's nothing inherently wrong with desiring certain things and people—but because she was directing all her energy toward this emotional need, she had no energy to direct toward God or toward a relationship that could ultimately give her the real love she craved. Her emotional need to be loved actually stood as the diversion that kept her from real love.

Josh's Diversions

Knowing that unfulfilled emotional needs are sometimes the diversions that prevent intimacy with our spouses, I didn't make the automatic assumption that Josh's obsession with his health club was the initial diversion from his wife. Yes, it's possible that a godly man like Josh could become so obsessed with what began as a hobby that he violates his covenant with his wife and ignores the will of Almighty God. But it's also possible that his obsession resulted from a crafty satanic attack aimed at an emotional need whose lack of fulfillment so frustrated Josh that his desire for it loomed larger than his commitment and dedication to God and his wife.

With some time and effort, I finally uncovered the fact that Josh felt an overwhelming need for respect and admiration and that this unfulfilled emotional need became the driving force behind his emotionally moving away from his wife, Marilyn.

Josh had a strong desire to feel that Marilyn respected him. As his desire intensified, he started seeing almost everything she did or said as evidence of her contempt for his manliness. For example, one morning he told her he'd fix a leaky faucet before the weekend only to find she'd fixed it before he returned home that evening. While some men would have thanked her for saving them the trouble, Josh interpreted her action as an indication that she didn't think he could do it.

I eventually discovered through subsequent work with Josh and Marilyn that his perception that she didn't respect him had no basis in fact. But as long as he believed it to be true, it was true for him. And as long as she was unaware of his feelings, she continued to do and say things that appeared to indicate her lack of respect.

As Josh's self-esteem plummeted because of what he was convinced was a disrespectful wife, he became that much more focused on excelling at work. At least, he thought, he would be appreciated there. He started spending more hours at the office, volunteering for extra assignments, and he became the most proficient employee in his division. His desire for the praise of his boss and the envy of his coworkers crowded out any time for Marilyn. But their praises weren't enough. Not having his wife's respect continued to make him feel inadequate, no matter how much he excelled at work. He finally began to think that he needed to bulk up his muscles, work away his encroaching love handles, and prove his manhood by achieving near physical perfection. His emotional need to feel respected as a man, coupled with his belief that his wife didn't respect him, became the diversion that siphoned his communication, time, and actions away from Marilyn and toward the quest to prove himself manly.

Not only was his "intimacy river" diverted away from his wife, it was also diverted away from God. His lifelong focus on God and His church gradually subsided to the point that church became a burden and God got only a grudging "how do you do" on Sundays.

His obsession with work and exercise wasn't the actual diversion, just its symptom. Ending his membership at the health club or quitting his job wouldn't refocus Josh's energy on Marilyn. The true diversion—his craving for admiration and respect—would continue to prevent their relationship from growing.

What about Your Diversions?

If you've been emotionally moving away from your spouse, or if your spouse has emotionally been moving away from you, the cause may well be an intimacy diversion.

How would you know if that was happening?

It would be nice if we could just ask Jesus—like the rich young man—wouldn't it? "Lord, is there something keeping me from finding intimacy with my spouse?" Obviously we can't ask Jesus face to face, but perhaps we can accomplish a version of his experience. Close your eyes and visualize the following scene. Imagine that Jesus just walked into the room where you are right now and sat down across from you, waiting expectantly. You know He's come to tell you of any diversions to intimacy with your spouse and is waiting for you to speak; so you clear your throat, nervously stumble through a few niceties, and then get to the subject. "Ah, Jesus, what do I need to do to have true intimacy with my spouse? What is it that I still lack?"

Now wait for His answer. Don't read any farther until in your imagination you hear His answer.

Did you do it? Did you visualize that conversation with Him? Of course, you were just imagining, but what did He answer in your imagination? Why do we ask? Because whatever your mind conjured up could be quite revealing.

Okay, enough imagination. Now ask Him for real—in prayer. Ask Him what, if anything, you still "lack." Ask believing He will answer. Maybe He'll confirm the answer you got in your visualization exercise—maybe He'll let you know that the person or thing or emotional need flitting around the edge of your mind is a real diversion to intimacy with your husband or wife. Or maybe He'll let you know by something that will be said by your spouse or one of your children or your minister. Maybe you'll see it on the next page of this book or in the next passage of Scripture you read.

Whatever it is, ask Him to make it clear to you.

When in your heart you feel you know what it is—if there is anything at all—ask Him to remove the diversion, heal it, or do whatever He needs to do to get you past it. Let *Him* decide how to deal with the diversion; don't try to figure it out yourself. Ask Him to rearrange the priorities in your life so that the person or thing no longer stands as a diversion. Ask Him to fulfill your emotional need in a godly way. Ask Him to use your spouse in a powerful way to fulfill your emotional need. But listen to His decision. It's much too easy to rationalize and believe that things are changed when they aren't. If you say, "Okay, God, here's what I'm gonna do about that...," you may end up not dealing with the diversion at all, even though you convince yourself you have.

Some diversions cannot be repaired by *reprioritization;* they must be *removed* altogether. That's apparently why Jesus told the young man that he had to give all his wealth away. To keep it and pretend to love God wouldn't do. Sometimes that's how it is in our marriages too. Sometimes it's impossible to funnel *any* of our energy into a diversion and still have the intimacy God wants us to have with our spouses.

Make sure you don't fool yourself into thinking reprioritization is all you need if the real solution lies only in removal.

INTIMACY DRAINS

Sometimes a lack of intimacy in a marriage is caused by an intimacy *drain* rather than a diversion. Diversions keep a person's communication, time, and action from being *directed* to the right "turbine" in his or her heart. Drains work differently. They keep the intimacy generated by the "turbine" from being *felt* by the person it's intended for. This occurs when a person does the right things but those right actions are negated by wrong actions. In Family Dynamics Institute's interactive marriage seminar *His Needs, Her Needs,* we lead couples through an examination of what Dr. Willard Harley calls "love busters."[8] He defines love busters as any repeated habits of one mate that cause the other to lose affection and positive feelings toward him or her. We don't mean to reproduce that material here because Dr. Harley covers it so well in his book *Love Busters.* But we must at least point out that sometimes we do things that we think should be producing intimate feelings in our mates, but those actions don't have that effect at all.

For example, if a husband spends great quantities of time communicating with his wife in an open and meaningful way but also shames her in public by ridiculing her or explodes in tantrums toward her, he negates all his positive efforts by his negative behavior. The negative behavior in a sense "drains" the effect of intimacy-producing elements. At best, the other spouse feels nothing in return. At worst, the spouse feels anger, rejection, or some other negative emotion.

Intimacy drains are any actions done repeatedly that cause the other spouse to lose affection and positive feelings. For one person that might be feeling manipulated. For another it may be something as seemingly innocuous as chewing ice. For others it's something that a spouse *doesn't* do! For example, some would experience a major intimacy drain toward a spouse who regularly forgot special days. An intimacy drain is *any* behavior that you do or *fail* to do that keeps your spouse from feeling intimacy for you.

We diagram that concept this way:

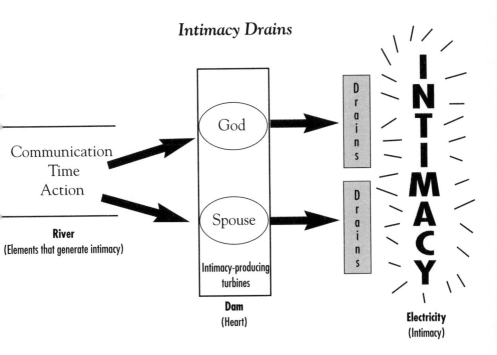

Intimacy Drains

Communication
Time
Action

River
(Elements that generate intimacy)

God

Spouse

Intimacy-producing turbines

Dam
(Heart)

Drains

Drains

INTIMACY

Electricity
(Intimacy)

The intimacy drain is a barrier that soaks up any and all positive behavior, rendering it powerless to create intimacy in the spouse it is aimed at.

When Intimacy Diversions and Drains Are Rooted in Sin

Sometimes intimacy in marriage is impossible because of ongoing or unconfessed sin. If Jesus came to visit you, would He uncover sin in your life—possibly sin that sprang from an intimacy diversion? That's what happened to Josh when he became so obsessed with exercise that he neglected his family. His desire for admiration and respect redirected his "river" so that he became involved with his hobby in a sinful way.

So ask yourself this question: Is there any sin in my life that keeps me from having deeper levels of intimacy with my spouse? Not too fast now. Don't just skim over this. Think openly and honestly with yourself. For example, are you developing a relationship with someone that you have no right to? Are you lying to your mate about anything? Are you harboring anger or bitterness toward your spouse? Is there any kind of sin in your life that is keeping you from developing the intimacy God intends for your marriage?

If so, you need to get rid of it.

Now.

It doesn't have to be something as major as adultery or spousal abuse; it can be any inconsideration or unkindness toward him or her. Peter wrote that husbands should be considerate of their wives and treat them with respect "so that nothing will hinder your prayers."[9] If you treat your spouse badly, it affects the way God hears you.

Do you have any sins between you and your spouse that keep your intimacy from growing? If you know there's sin in your life, here's how you start fresh in your relationship with your spouse.

1. Candidly confess your sin to God, even though He already knows it. Be specific and detailed in your prayer about it. Lay it out before Him. Ask *Him* to remove this sin and all the desires or weaknesses within you that give it power. Don't ask

Him to "help" *you* get rid of it; make sure you specifically ask Him to do it and to do it powerfully. Also ask Him to fill with His love the emptiness left in you by the removal of the sin and your desire for the sin.

2. Ask God to heal or fulfill the desire that led to the sin. For example, I urged Josh to ask God to fill him with a sense of value and worth so that he wouldn't react so sensitively to perceived slights by his wife. You may need to ask God to make you less sensitive or to soothe the pain of a memory or to replant love in your heart for your spouse. It's crucial that you deal with the underlying problems that provide Satan's forces with avenues of attack. The desires that led to your sin can lead to more sin unless they are healed or repaired. Ask God to do it and surrender to do or feel or believe whatever He tells you.

3. Tell your mate, if you can do so without fear of reprisal. Later in this book we'll show you how to share things that might initially hurt your spouse, but we aren't ready for that yet. At this point, only share with your mate if you can comfortably do so. If you can't tell your mate the sin you confessed to God, find a balanced, mature Christian and tell him or her. (We strongly suggest you tell a person of the same gender as you.) There is great power in confession to bring sin to a halt and to unleash the healing power of God.[10]

Go ahead. Stop right now and talk with God and talk with your mate, if appropriate, or a trusted Christian, if not. I'll be right here waiting for you when you come back.

DO YOU REALLY WANT TO KNOW?

What would happen if you approached your mate with the same question we led you to approach Jesus with earlier? "Honey, what can

I do to have a closer, more intimate relationship with you? Do you know of anything that I am placing in front of you that is *diverting* intimacy from you? Does any of my behavior or lack of behavior drain intimacy from our relationship?" The queried spouse might respond in one of three ways.

1. The first possible answer could be, "Nothing. There's nothing diverting your intimacy away from me. There's no behavior that is draining the intimacy from our relationship." (Of course, if the spouse who asked the question feels there is something lacking, that answer wouldn't help.)

2. The second possible response might be, "The only thing you lack is that you aren't doing *enough*. You aren't spending enough time with me, talking enough to me, or doing enough of..." If your mate responds by saying, "You're not doing enough," you should honestly examine yourself to see what intimacy diversions are keeping you from focusing your time, communication, and action on your spouse. (Unfortunately this answer doesn't tell you what that diversion might be.)

3. The third possible answer could be, "I know what is getting your attention and diverting your attention from me." Or, "I can tell you exactly what behavior [or lack of behavior] is draining intimacy from our relationship. It's..."

If you asked that question of your mate, which of those three answers would your want to hear? If something is diverting your focus from your spouse, would you honestly want your spouse to tell you what it is, if he or she knows? If some behavior is draining the intimacy from your marriage, do you want to know? Are you willing to change?

Our experience is that *most folks don't want to know.* We've seen over and again that quite often the "offended" spouse does know what the diversion is—or at least has strong suspicions—and does try to bring that diversion to the attention of the "offending" spouse. Unfortunately the usual response when a diversion is pointed out is outright denial that it exists or efforts to explain it away as meaningless. Often guilt, sin, ignorance, or a combination of the three keeps the mate from admitting the diversion.

As long as a person refuses to admit that the diversion exists, that person never can develop the intimacy he or she consciously or subconsciously craves with his or her spouse. Ignored diversions become stronger, drawing more attention and resources. Unrepaired drains continue to suck the intimacy right out of a relationship. Only admitted diversions can be abandoned or replaced into different priorities, and only acknowledged drains can be repaired.

If you want the closest, most intimate relationship with your spouse that any human can have—the kind God intends you to have—you *must* discover and remove diversions and repair intimacy drains that prevent you from having that intimacy.

Personal Application

If you decide that you really *do* want to uncover the intimacy diversions and drains that you are responsible for, we are ready to help you eliminate them. The best way to do that is to complete the exercises in chapter 3 of *Becoming ONE: Exercises in Intimacy*. If you don't have that accompanying workbook, here's what you need to do:

1. *List any diversions* that you know are taking your focus from your mate or any drains that are negating other positive actions. These diversions may be anything from your children, to your parents, to your career, to a craving for affection. The drains could be annoying habits or some sin that absorbs you. Admit these to yourself and confess them to God.

2. *Tell your spouse*. It may be that you fear sharing the information. If you carry great fear of that right now, wait until we show you

in later chapters how to share those things you are afraid to share but need to share. If you know you should share it now, please do so. You'll be amazed at how effective your spouse can be in helping you remove a diversion or repair a drain once you've admitted to him or her that it exists. As we teach people in our *His Needs, Her Needs* course, spouses can and should fulfill the emotional needs of their mates.

3. *Ask your spouse what diversions or drains he or she sees in you.* Look your mate in the eye and ask with all sincerity and courage, "Tell me, honey, what barriers or diversions exist to our relationship? Tell me what you see in me or what you know exists as a diversion in my life that keeps me from developing the deepest levels of intimacy with you. Whatever it is, we'll find a way to remove the problem and develop the intimacy we need with each other."

Remember, your spouse won't answer honestly if he or she fears any retribution or reprisal from you. Therefore, don't do this exercise unless you are willing to hear the answers, willing to admit the truthfulness of what you hear, and ready to do something about it. If you lash out, rebuke, or argue, forget about getting to the level of intimacy you need.

Just as soon as you remove those diversions and repair these drains, you're ready to learn how to develop intimacy with God and with each other.

*W*hen a couple drifts apart, often the real problem *isn't* their differences, but the perceptions each has of those differences. If either holds a misguided view of self, their differences seem even worse and cause more problems. (page 83)

⌒

*I*f you don't love yourself as God intended, how do you expect to love your spouse or your children as you should? The very foundation of love starts with loving yourself in a godly way. (page 89)

⌒

*L*earning to love self means learning to accept your imperfections, including the reality of your weaknesses, faults, and failed dreams. As long as you don't accept the truth about yourself, your efforts for valuable change will end in frustration. But when you accept yourself as you are—admit all the truths about you and see your lovableness anyway—you will find yourself changing naturally—for the better. (page 97)

Chapter
4

Developing Emotional Intimacy, Part 1

Learning Intimacy from the Inside Out

"We have nothing in common."

He said it flatly, no emotion, without so much as a glance at his wife who sat in a chair to his right not more than a foot away. I shifted my gaze from him to her just in time to catch her slight wince as she tightened her lips and narrowed her eyes. She obviously didn't like what he'd just said, but she made no reply. He seemed to have no emotion within him, and what feelings she had were very carefully controlled.

"I'm not quite sure how we wound up together," he continued. "We were young, foolish, feeling a compulsion to marry because everyone else our age was. The first few years are more of a blur than anything, but the last few have been a man-made hell. I want out, but I don't want to hurt our children. I also know that our church won't accept a divorce. In our little town I'm considered a community leader. Divorce and excommunication from my church won't play well there. But we're to the point where I don't know what else to do.

"There's no one else. I mean I don't have someone waiting, and I assume Theresa doesn't either. It's just that we don't have any life together except the kids and church and a rare—very rare—session of lovemaking." He then slipped into a semisarcastic tone and said, "Somebody told us you work miracles, so we're here for ours."

I studied my steepled fingers for a moment and then replied, "Maybe miracles only come for those who want them. Do you really want God to work a miracle that would fill you with intense love for Theresa?"

He didn't reply verbally; he just fixed a baleful stare on me and sat in arrogant silence.

"What about you, Theresa? Do you need a miracle to be in love with Blake?"

I admired her continued emotional control as her tone of voice belied the hurt in her eyes. "No. I don't need it." Tilting her head toward Blake, she said, "*If* you can believe it, I love him now." Her arched brow added the unspoken question, "*Can* you believe I could love a jerk like this?" but Blake didn't notice. He still didn't look at her, not even to be polite as she spoke.

"Yeah? Why? Why do you love Blake?"

Just before she spoke, I caught the quickest glimpse of what it must have been like for them thirteen years ago when they fell in love and wanted to be married. She smiled at the memory, but lost it immediately as Blake shifted nervously beside her. To keep from seeing him as he now was, she dropped her head and stared into the past, speaking of a Blake apparently quite different from the man staring out the window of my office. "What can I say? He's funny and smart and knows how to do everything. He can talk to anyone, anywhere; he can enthrall a room full of people with his stories. He's sweet and gentle and so thoughtful. When I'm with him, I feel as if no one else is in the room...or even on the planet. He loves God and he loves his children and he loves me." With that she jerked her head up and returned to the present. "At least that is how he used to be and how I think he still is under all that...that...whatever it is he's got himself armored with."

Armored. I thought it a good choice of words. The man had himself protected in some way, and the force of it was palpable. I wasn't sure if he wore it against everyone or only against Theresa. I'd never met him before today and had no previous experience with which to compare his current withdrawal. One thing was sure: He'd never love her again until his emotional force field weakened enough to allow penetration.

"Tell me, Blake, when did you quit loving Theresa?"

He sighed to let us all know what a waste of time this was and shifted back in his seat. Then he stared at the ceiling, making me wonder if from this point on he would treat me like he was treating Theresa—like a disembodied voice floating in the room instead of a person to be interacted with. "I'm not sure," he began, "but it was a long time ago. I kept learning and growing; she didn't. She could have, but she didn't want to. All she wanted to do was have babies and be a house mom. I traveled on business, and she always had some reason she couldn't go. I read extensively; she says reading hurts her eyes. I watch the news; she prefers soap operas. Somewhere along the line, we discovered we had nothing to talk about, no common interests, not even a common awareness of the world.

"I learned to find my intellectual and emotional stimulation elsewhere. Just because she wanted to vegetate didn't mean I had to. Now we're worlds apart, and I don't think we agree on more than a couple of major issues in our lives. We don't agree on how to discipline our children. We don't agree on which church to attend. We don't even agree as to whose parents we visit on Thanksgiving.

"She says, 'Talk to me. You don't talk to me.' So I try; but within minutes, we're in a terrible argument. We can't agree because we don't understand each other; we have totally different frames of reference. We've grown in completely different ways over thirteen years and don't work from the same foundation anymore. How can I talk to her when I know she's going to fight or pout or slam the door on her way out. I can't talk to a woman who doesn't care to understand what I'm saying or, when she does understand me, doesn't like what she's hearing.

"You know, being married to her is like living with a housekeeper who is sweet to everyone else but can't stand anything I think or say.

"I didn't want it to be that way, but that's how it's become. If you're gonna work a miracle, fix *her*."

As much as I disliked this man with his holier-than-thou self-righteousness, I knew that at least on one level he was right. If any miracle were to be worked, it had to start with Theresa. If Blake were telling the truth, he had tried early on to develop intimacy with her, but she had chosen a course of action that not only retarded intimacy's development but eventually killed it. Unless she learned to interact with him in a different way, they were doomed. It was true that he now treated her badly, but it appeared that his behavior originated in frustration with the way she distanced herself from him.

Beyond that, the most immediate problem at hand was whether we could break through the wall of resentment he'd built up and get them started on the path they should have followed thirteen years ago. It wasn't too late to start—it never is—but we'd never get them on the path to healing if Blake kept acting as he was now.

"Okay, Blake, we can do it. I don't have the power—never have and never will—but God can give you the 'miracle' you want. He can change Theresa. He can change you, too, even if you don't think you need to change. In just a minute we're going to pray with full faith that He'll do just that. You didn't answer me earlier, so I'll ask you again: Do you really want God to work a miracle that would fill you with intense love for Theresa? Before I ask God for the miracle, I need to know if you really want it—if you'll accept it. He doesn't do much for people who don't desire His actions, and He seldom gives the second blessing to people who don't appreciate the first. Now, if God changes your relationship so that you have consummate love and true ONEness intimacy, will you accept His gift? Is that what you really want?"

I figured I'd receive one of three answers. Either he'd stab me with that stupid, silent stare again, or he'd say yes, or he'd say no. Even if he said yes, that could mean one of two things. The first would be a true yes: He wanted it. The second would be a smiley-faced-lie yes: He would say it because that's what a good little boy should say.

"Yes." His shoulders sagged as he said it. "Yes. If God would work the miracle, I'd accept it. I wish I could be in love with my wife."

Ah, a true yes. We were in business.

There are four basic steps to developing *emotional* intimacy. In this chapter I want to share with you that first step—the step that Theresa had to begin with. In the next chapter, we'll cover steps two through four.

Here are the four steps to emotional intimacy:

1. Accept yourself as you are.

2. Share the facts of your life.

3. Share the feelings of your life.

4. Accept the other person as he or she is.

All four steps are essential, but the last three steps cannot develop as they should until you master the first one: *Accept yourself as you are*.

THE SOURCE OF BLAKE AND THERESA'S PROBLEM

Over time, Theresa revealed why she shied away from interacting with Blake as he would try to talk with her about a book he was reading or engage her in a philosophical conversation about something happening in the news. She felt inadequate. *Intimidated* might even be a better word.

Blake had a lightning-fast mind and a genius level IQ, while Theresa scored in the average realm. He read rapidly, understood even the most complex ideas quickly, and could discuss nearly anything with almost anyone. In social settings, she often fell silent because she hadn't kept up on the international event or hadn't read the book under discussion. As she would sit quietly in those situations, feeling left out and drifting into her own isolated world, she also drifted away from her husband. Of course he noted her detachment, but he misunderstood her reason for it. Each felt rejected by the other. He resented her withdrawal, and she resented what she eventually came to view as his intellectual arrogance.

She found few of the things which intrigued him interesting. On the rare occasion when she tried to have a conversation with Blake, he would soon make her feel stupid and uneducated, either by adopting what she perceived to be a condescending tone or by making some snide remark like, "You would know this if you just read something once in a while." As I worked with them, I became convinced that early on in their relationship he hadn't realized how much he hurt her with his remarks. But that made little difference. His words hurt, and they damaged her already poor self-perception even further.

Without doubt, Blake needed to learn how to communicate effectively with Theresa. While at first he didn't understand his part in their dilemma—because he honestly had tried to communicate, spend time with, and do things for his wife—his intensity and occasional air of superiority negated every good thing he tried to do and then some. Whether he realized it or not—whether he meant to or not—he at times was a real jerk to his wife. As they grew farther apart, he became a bigger jerk, developing an attitude toward her that prevented any love or intimacy from growing in their marriage.

By the time they reached me, neither of them believed they could live together in harmony and happiness. I knew they could. They could know it, too, if they just thought about it in the right way: They needed to remember the happiness they'd felt in their courtship; something had worked right between them, or they never would have fallen in love and gotten married. There is no law that says that people must have the same IQ, educational path, or abilities in order to love each other. Any two people can develop a wonderful level of intimacy, no matter what their differences. Blake and Theresa's problem didn't lie in their differences as much as it did in their *poor perceptions of those differences*. We had to change that.

And as badly as Blake now behaved, the first step to establishing emotional intimacy between them was to change Theresa. We had to change her misguided view of herself before we could change Blake's view of her and rid them of the animosity that existed between them.

Theresa could never communicate intimately with Blake until she first accepted herself. I knew we'd deal with Blake in the last step—accepting the other person as he or she is—but for now we had to start the process by helping Theresa learn to do step one. She had to learn to accept herself as she was.

Now, don't misunderstand; *accepting* yourself as you are doesn't mean that you must be *satisfied* with yourself as you are. It just means that you can't get to where you want to go if you can't admit where you are. We'll discuss this concept more later.

PRETENDERS AND DENIERS

People who play games with themselves or with the world around them can't honestly grow. They're either too busy *pretending* to be what they're not or *denying* that they are the valuable people God says they are.

Pretenders: Those Who Pretend to Be What They Aren't

We've all dealt with the first type of person, the "I must make you believe I'm someone of stature" kind. Once, while in the midst of a three-way business negotiation, our meeting was interrupted by a ringing cell phone. The woman to my right answered her phone and greeted the caller by name. I was working as a consultant to her company and knew the employee she was conversing with. She began instructing him on how to close a big deal they were apparently working on. She threw out names known to us all and numbers of staggering proportions. Because of my business relationship with her company, I knew it was barely surviving. They were hoping the deal we were currently negotiating would salvage it. There was no way the things she was saying on the phone could be true.

As we left, I cornered her. "What was *that* all about?"

"Oh," she casually replied, "sometimes you just have to make them believe you're something you're not. It's the way to fame and fortune—you know, 'fake it till you make it.'"

I'd heard of people who did business like that, but I'd never been a party to such dealings and didn't intend to start. I ended my relationship with her company on the spot. If a person pretends or postures or playacts with someone else, you never know *when* he or she is telling *you* the truth. They get so caught up in their fantasies that sometimes they themselves don't even know the truth.

Such pretension is devious in a business relationship; it's destructive in a marriage.

It even affects the pretender in negative ways.

People who pretend to be something they're not cheat themselves out of potential growth. How could anyone admit the need for personal growth if his or her philosophy is to "fake it till I make it"? That approach might make money, but it won't create happiness or wellbeing. It certainly sabotages the development of intimacy with another person. The other person could never know what was real and what was pretended. Maybe the pretender couldn't either.

Recently I witnessed a situation where a wife said flatly to her husband, "How do I know which is the real you? You wear so many faces and play so many games in your efforts to get ahead that I've come to doubt that I know you at all." Interestingly she made her comment in direct response to his promise that he would be whatever she needed him to be. Rather than hearing a pledge of self-sacrifice, she heard hypocrisy. His constant pretensions made his promise hollow.

Quite simply, people who pretend to be something they are not do so because they refuse to accept the truth about what they currently are. Living a lie perpetuates the lie. They'll pretend for the rest of their lives unless they learn to operate in the light of honesty and truth.

Honesty—toward self and toward others—is the only way to develop a life that is real and genuine.

Deniers: Those Who Deny Their Worth

The other kind of person who has difficulty accepting him- or herself is the person who is convinced that he or she is somehow inferior. Deniers simply cannot believe that they have any value within themselves. Unable to comprehend that they could have worth, they deny the very possibility.

Theresa fell into this category.

She dropped out of college to work so that Blake could finish his degree, and she never found enough time or motivation to return. If Blake appreciated the sacrifice she made to advance his career, he never thought to mention it. He swept into a world of high-powered people and spiraling stimulation, learning and growing rapidly as a result. She decided to be a homemaker and mother, and her time was dominated by tots in their terrible twos rather than enlightening books and scintillating conversation. There was nothing inherently wrong with this combination, and their marriage could have thrived. But something got in the way. What destroyed their intimacy was their own *faulty perceptions*. Although the role of homemaker and mother is one of the finest professions God ever created,[1] Theresa saw her role as less important than those who pursued a career. She'd never enjoyed the academic challenges of college and eventually interpreted that dislike to mean that she never could have finished anyway. That made her feel inferior—not only to Blake but to all her friends who had graduated from college or entered a profession. Those feelings of somehow being less than others kept her from enjoying the noble course of life she had chosen. In an effort to be more like Blake and those she admired, she tried to learn things on her own. When household chores were done and the kids were in bed, she tried to read. But she was so exhausted from her busy day that she regularly fell asleep as soon as she began. That convinced her that she somehow didn't have the intellect to read and understand, and she became even more frustrated with herself. As a result, when Blake cajoled her to read or discuss a book he was reading, she inferred that he was ridiculing her lack of intelligence.

Their path was set. She could have been enjoying her children and building a wonderful life with her husband. Instead she became hostile. She hid rancor in front of others but skewered Blake every chance she had in private, wanting to somehow make him feel as badly about himself as she did about herself. He answered with his own hostility. He likely knew on a subconscious level that her lack of self-worth drove her hostility, and so that's where he attacked her. He made insinuations and accusations designed to make her feel ignorant and unintelligent. Stupid on his part? It was more than that. It was sinful. But his sin wasn't rooted in an evil heart any more than her sinful actions were rooted in actual inferiority. Blake and Theresa were good people who had drifted into sinful behavior patterns. And their behavior was destroying their love and any chance they had of developing true intimacy.

Both Blake and Theresa were responsible for their unhappiness. If Theresa had developed a biblically accurate view of herself, she wouldn't have felt compelled to demean Blake in an effort to establish her own worth. And if Blake had been as wise as he was quick-witted, he would have seen that Theresa felt inferior, and he would have reassured her of her value instead of exacerbating the problem by his contemptuous behavior.

Once I asked him, "Does it bother you that your wife doesn't have a college degree?"

Blake seemed surprised at the question. "Of course not," he replied.

I pursued the matter: "Do you think you're smarter than she is?"

Shaking his head in confusion, he said, "I don't know what you're getting at. I know more things than she does because I'm exposed to more, but I don't feel superior to her, if that's what you're asking. She's as good at what she does as I am at what I do. I don't think my wife is stupid; I just get frustrated because she acts as if she doesn't want to learn or grow. I just want her to talk with me and think with me and not shut me out."

While it was true that Blake had failed to minister to the needs of his wife and was even cruel to her on occasion, I could clearly see that it was Theresa's lack of belief in her own self-worth that lay at the core of their problems. It was the starting block from which all their problems sprang—her poor treatment of Blake and his ever poorer treatment of her.

People who can't accept themselves as they are because of feelings of inferiority or helplessness don't only make themselves miserable; they make everyone around them miserable. If they aren't attacking, they're whining. If they aren't whining, they're making subtle put-downs of themselves in conversation. They act this way because they don't like themselves, and they want someone, anyone, to make them feel important. If anger, self-pity, or self-degradation gets them attention (and, therefore, a kind of importance), they will use those tools in increasing portions.

Inevitably they inflict their pain on the people closest to them—husband, wife, son, daughter, mother, father, or best friend—because they don't know how to handle the pain in any other way.

WHAT DOES GOD SAY ABOUT SELF-ACCEPTANCE?

As you might imagine, people in either category—pretenders or deniers—do not accept themselves as God wants them to. Does God actually speak to the problem of self-acceptance in the Bible? He most certainly does.

What Does God Say to the Pretender?

The pretender is easy to find in Scripture. God condemned people who love themselves in an improper way[2] or exalt themselves over others.[3] He lambasted those who "love the place of honor at banquets and the most important seats in the synagogues."[4] Rather than exalting ourselves, the Bible says, "Do not think of yourself more highly than you ought, but rather think of yourself with sober judgment, in accordance with the measure of faith God has given you."[5]

God wants us to live in truth and not lie to ourselves or to anyone else about who we are or what we've done. He says that our word should be as bold and bonding as an oath,[6] which means we must *always* speak the truth. "The LORD detests lying lips, but he delights in men who are truthful."[7] Jesus called people "hypocrites" when they pretended to be something they weren't. The word He used throughout the Gospels is *hupokrites* (hoop-o-kree-tace'), which means playing a part or being an actor. People who can't accept themselves as they are must pretend to be something they aren't, and God said He doesn't like that. His counsel is simple: Be real. Speak, act, and live in accordance with truth about everything—especially about yourselves.[8]

What Does God Say to the Denier?

God just as clearly teaches that the person who denies his or her value and worth is wrong too. As we read in the previous section, we are not to think of ourselves "more highly than we ought"; rather, we are to view ourselves with "sober judgment." So what is the "sober" way to view ourselves? Let's look at two simple principles to find the answer.

1. See Yourself from God's Perspective

First, instead of seeing yourself from your own perspective— whether falsely high or falsely low—see yourself from God's perspective. God sees you as so worthy and loves you so much that "He gave his one and only Son."[9] Your value doesn't rest in just what you do or in what you accomplish but in the fact that God loves you.[10] If any king on earth sought you out to give you wonderful gifts, dedicate his army to your protection, and offer you the opportunity to be adopted into his family, you'd feel unbelievably special. In reality, the King of all kings has done all this for you. You *are* unbelievably special.

His love instills you with worth. To deny your worth is to deny God's love for you.

2. Love Yourself

Finally, let's look at a command of Jesus that you've probably heard many times before. Jesus said, "Love your neighbor as yourself."[11] It doesn't take a Bible scholar, a language scholar, or a Christian psychiatrist to figure out that you can't do the first half of that command without doing the last half. We *can't* love others if we *don't* love ourselves! People who dislike themselves dislike everyone else (or at least most everyone else) as well. That's why guilt-caged people attack others[12] and why people unable to attain friendship undermine the friendships of others. They become perverse people, gossips: "A perverse man stirs up dissension, and a gossip separates close friends."[13]

Theresa couldn't help attacking and maligning her husband because she had a perverted view of her own self-worth. She couldn't love him as she should because she didn't love herself as she should.

So you see, when Theresa doubted herself to the point of believing she had no worth or value, it became impossible for her to give worth and value to Blake. Sure she loved him in some ways—she said so—but she couldn't give him consummate love because she held little or no love for herself. When he retaliated to her hostility—not understanding that it wasn't him she attacked but her own frustrations—he exacerbated the problem. His reaction didn't make her rethink and change; it convinced her that he, too, thought she was inferior, and it reinforced the very negative behavior they both hated.

God knew what He was saying, and the truth is basic: Only those who love themselves can love others! Maybe it would impress you more if you get a glimpse of how many passages of the Bible repeat that essential phrase "love your neighbor as yourself."

- Leviticus 19:18
- Matthew 19:19
- Matthew 22:39
- Mark 12:31
- Mark 12:33
- Luke 10:27
- Romans 13:9
- Galatians 5:14
- James 2:8

Do you think He's trying to make sure we don't miss this crucial truth? Love yourself if you want to learn to love others. If you don't love yourself as He wants you to, the need for that self-love will become the diversion that interferes with intimacy with others. Your desire for love will loom so large it will overpower any effort you make to give love.

THE PATH TO SELF-ACCEPTANCE
AND GODLY SELF-LOVE

But how do we put this self-acceptance into practice? We do it by accepting the truth about ourselves.

When Jesus interacted with real people who passed through His life—be they Pharisee or prostitute—He never hesitated to tell them the truth about themselves. He addressed Pharisees in Matthew 23 by calling them names like "hypocrites," "whitewashed tombs full of dead men's bones," and "blind fools." He pulled no punches, but told them the absolute truth. Why? So they would know to "first clean the inside of the cup and dish, and then the outside also will be clean."[14] They could never change until they accepted the truth about themselves.

But it wasn't only bad things or negative characteristics that Jesus wanted people to know about themselves. He once told a woman who lived as the "town sinner" in her community that she *loved deeply.* As she cried at His feet, unable to say a word to Him in her remorse and shame, He pointed out to her that she had love and faith in her heart. He then told her that He forgave her, even though she'd done horrible, sinful things.[15] She needed to accept the beauty Jesus saw in her so that she could learn how to love herself the right way and, in turn, learn to love God.

The Pharisees of Matthew 23 were pretenders. The woman in Luke 7 was a denier. Each believed lies that led them into sinful behaviors. Both needed to know this truth: *See yourself as you really are so that you can learn to love; otherwise, you'll never know how to love yourself and you'll certainly never learn how to love another.*

Pretenders know deep within themselves that they are pretending, and their awareness of that prevents them from properly loving themselves. They can't love the person they are because they're afraid to admit that person exists.

Deniers believe they are unlovable, and that faulty self-perception prevents their properly loving themselves. They can't love the person they are because they focus on wanting to be someone else.

The path to self-acceptance and godly self-love begins with (1) accepting your sinfulness, (2) accepting your physical imperfections, and (3) accepting your gifts and talents.

1. Accept Your Sinfulness

Both pretenders and deniers must begin by accepting the fact that we are all sinners and can only be saved by the grace of God. We are plagued with character flaws, we are tormented with temptations tailor-made for our specific personalities, we are haunted by our sinful pasts, and we can be sure that we will sin in the future. And sometimes, what haunts us is not our own sin, but sins committed against us by someone else—sexual abuse, rape, emotional abuse. But there's more truth to consider than the truth about our own sinfulness or our sordid pasts: There is the truth of God's love and the truth that Christ's blood makes us perfect in God's sight. Maybe the following breakdown will help.

1. You are an imperfect sinner with flaws, just like everyone else on the planet. We all sin and fall short of the glory of God,[16] and none of us is perfect.[17] When you think that others are better than you and that nobody could love anyone as bad as you, accept the truth: Others have just as many flaws, weaknesses, and sins as you—maybe more—no matter how godly and perfect they may appear to be.

2. God loves you no matter what you've done, what you want to do, or what has been done to you. He loves you so much that He sent Jesus for you, even though He knows everything you've ever done to hurt Him and the things you'd do tomorrow if you had the chance. "But God demonstrates his own love for us in this: While we were still sinners, Christ died for

us."[18] There is no sin, no matter how evil or degrading, that goes beyond His willingness to love and forgive.[19]

3. If you come to God through Jesus, He doesn't look at what you have done but sees you through the blood of His Son.[20] As far as He's concerned, you're perfect because of Christ's sacrifice— absolutely perfect.[21] Not because He denies the truth about you, but because He can and will *change* the truth about you.

These three spiritual truths become the bedrock for biblical self-love. Remember them and believe them. If you have trouble believing them, read *Forgiven Forever*[22] as your study guide to convince you.

2. Accept Your Imperfections

Not every person is gorgeous, brilliant, athletic, or magnetic. We each have unique characteristics given to us by God, and those varying characteristics make up a population that gives the earth all it needs. Accepting ourselves as we are also means accepting all our physical, mental, and other imperfections.

For example, I'm not particularly tall (5′10″), I have hair that grayed prematurely, and I am possessed of a large nose. All my life I've been called ugly. That label tormented me in high school and has followed me ever since. Just the night before I wrote these words, a man approached me after I spoke at a revival in a state far from where I live. He said, "I've listened to you on tape for years and thought from your voice you'd be a tall, good-looking man. Boy was I surprised! You aren't much to look at, are you?" With that he ambled away, chuckling to himself and muttering loudly enough for me to hear, "I thought he'd look a lot better than that."

Obviously I wasn't what he expected me to be. I can only assume he thought himself to be funny. I didn't. I've listened to people make fun of my looks since I was a child, and I see no humor in ridiculing another human for his or her physical appearance. None. But I didn't throw a verbal jab in response or even think about his senseless slur again until I sat to write these words.

Why?

Because God taught me to accept myself as I am—the way He made me.

When Jesus came to be one of us, He made it clear that physical beauty wasn't related to worth. Isaiah predicted of Jesus, "He had no beauty or majesty to attract us to him, nothing in his appearance that we should desire him."[23] Jesus came as an ordinary, regular guy, without handsomeness or personal magnetism. If He walked past you on the street, you wouldn't look twice. He came as a common man, who most certainly didn't look like those pictures people draw of Him. Isn't it funny how the artists make him a light-skinned, blue-eyed, long-haired, nearly blond, delicately featured European, when in truth, anthropology tells us that the common Jewish men of the first century were short, swarthy, dark haired, and large nosed? Most artists don't draw Him that way because then He wouldn't stand out; He wouldn't be handsome. We put such a premium on beauty that we change history to make Jesus beautiful, but He wants no part of that. He came looking like us regular folks.

Personally, I appreciate that.

If God chose to take on a human form that wasn't pretty, why should I worry that I'm not pretty? The only beauty we should care about is the beauty "of your inner self, the unfading beauty of a gentle and quiet spirit, which is of great worth in God's sight."[24] No person on this planet who accepts the truth of God will reject themselves because they aren't beautiful or handsome. They won't think themselves unlovable because they don't have all their fingers or toes or arms or legs. They understand that this body is at best a temporary dwelling and that the new body to come will have no imperfections at all.[25]

Two nights before I wrote this page, I was building a salad at a restaurant and noticed two young girls grazing down the other side of the salad bar. One was about the age of my Kimberly, and because I was feeling a bout of homesickness, I watched her for a moment. That's how I noticed the hands of the other girl, her sister, who looked to be five or six. She had only three fingers on each hand and struggled valiantly with the spoons as she tried to dip tomatoes and grapes and croutons onto her salad. As she turned to walk back to her table, the plate slipped from her underequipped hands and shattered across the floor. Before the sound of the splintering china faded, she began to cry a sad moaning sort of cry.

In a nanosecond, all sorts of thoughts and emotions ran through me. In my mind I was feeling what I imagined she was feeling: "I can't do it! I can't even carry a plate back to the table. I can't live a normal life. All the taunts and slurs other kids toss at me are true; I'm a freak, and I'll always be a freak." It was all I could do not to scoop her up and comfort her, telling her not to cry, that she wasn't a freak and that it makes no difference whether we have four fingers or only three. What matters is who she is on the inside, and...

But I knew I couldn't hold her or comfort her, because I understood that a strange man inserting himself brusquely into her life would scare her, not reassure her. So I stood and watched helplessly. Within a moment, her dad was there. He didn't panic over her dropped plate—he deals with her struggles every day and obviously knows how to keep everything in perspective. As a waitress shooed them away from the mess, saying, "It's all right, daddy; you just go on," he picked up his daughter, kissed her, and took her right back to the salad bar, staying a little closer to her this time.

I didn't know him, but I instantly liked him. He was teaching her that it didn't matter, that she *could* function in life, that her disability wasn't a major matter. He was teaching her how to love herself in spite of her difference. Just like God does. Even the ones of us with big noses and gray hair. Someday she'll have a body like all the rest of us in heaven, and I bet nobody...nobody...makes fun of a thing.

3. Accept Your God-Given Talents and Gifts

Not only does God want us to accept our bodies as they are, but through Paul He taught us we should be just as accepting of our talents and abilities. He told the Christians in the city of Corinth that God gives gifts to people as He chooses, gifting some with one thing and others another. Using the illustration that we are like different parts of a body—some a hand, others a foot, even others an eye—he wrote, "God has arranged the parts in the body, every one of them, just as he wanted them to be."[26] It's God who decides who should be a preacher, who should be a teacher, or who should be an administrator.[27] He decides who should be rich enough to give to the needs of others, who should be a servant, and who should be a leader.[28]

When you accept the fact that God gave you the gifts He wants you to have, you'll realize that you are no less important and no more important than anyone else. "We have different gifts, according to the grace given us.... Let [us] use [those gifts] in proportion to [our] faith."[29] God made Blake to be a man with above-average intelligence and expected him to use that gift. He made Theresa to be a woman with great love for her children and a mastery of homemaking. She had no reason to envy Blake or other women who were successful in business or academia; she had no reason to feel inadequate or inferior to them. She would probably be surprised to learn how many of them felt inferior to her as they came into her world and saw how effectively she operated there. Who wouldn't want to be a wonderful parent who could spend most of her time molding and crafting her children in godly ways?

Every person's gifts, particularly the special spiritual gifts given at conversion, contribute to society and to the church. Every person, without fail, is special.

Alice and I taught that to our children, even our retarded daughter, Angel. When we introduce her to people, we say it just this way: "This is our special daughter, Angel." We say that for two reasons.

First, we've sadly learned that some people lack even the most basic social skills and will ask right in front of Angel if something is wrong with her. They notice that her eyes aren't quite as crisp as others', or they see the occasional confusion that crosses her face. Then, seemingly without a thought to Angel's presence, they callously blurt out something like, "Is your daughter normal?" We spare Angel that insensitive humiliation by telling people as Angel meets them that she's different. But we do it in a way to let her know that we think her difference is a wonderful difference, a "special" difference.

Our second reason for saying that Angel is special is because we really do believe it. What's more, she believes it. She knows she's special, and that maintains her feelings of self-worth.

Theresa should have done the same thing for herself. After all, how important is it to her children, her husband, even to our society, that she serves as a good mother and an efficient homemaker? Very. That role in life is just as important as being a world leader, a nuclear physicist, or a medical doctor. We are all needed, and we are all important.

If you want to develop intellectual and emotional intimacy with your spouse, you must first learn to accept yourself as you are—your sinfulness, your physical limitations, and your God-given talents and gifts.

Satisfied Discontent

My early mentor, Paul Tarence, regularly quoted William James: "When I accept myself as I am, I change. When I accept others as they are, they change." He taught me over and again that it was okay to want to grow, to evolve as a person, and to set spiritual and other life goals, but he also taught me that *acceptance* precedes *change*. He explained the teaching through three basic concepts:

1. You must first accept yourself as you are before you can become what you want to be.

2. When you accept yourself as you are, you begin to grow spiritually, emotionally, and in other ways.

3. A Christian's desire to grow or change must always root itself in "satisfied discontent" rather than "dissatisfied discontent."

There's a big difference between "satisfied discontent" and "dissatisfied discontent." Dissatisfied discontent leaves us feeling helpless, hopeless, and unable to change. Satisfied discontent fills us with a desire to grow and the belief that we can. Satisfied discontent allows us to be satisfied with our current circumstances[30] yet able to set goals for our futures.[31]

When we see ourselves honestly, as we presently are, we can set valid goals for what we want to become. Then our goals won't be driven by desperation but by a genuine desire to grow and mature. We won't operate by greed for better circumstances or misguided attempts to earn love. We'll know we're loved by God and by ourselves.

For example, what if Theresa had said to herself, "Okay, I *don't* like college, and I *don't* like academia. I hate taking tests and find myself sometimes feeling 'dumb' when I'm around those brains. But I do love my husband and children, and I do a good job of being a wife, mother, and homemaker. That's a noble calling, just like being a college professor is a noble calling. What I do is just as important to society—and maybe even more important to my kids—as anything else anyone else on earth is doing. I see myself as a worthwhile human being who has value, and that means I can love me just as I am."

If Theresa had seen herself that way, she wouldn't have felt inferior to Blake or to any of her friends. When Blake wanted to discuss some matter he was reading or that was on the news, she could have said without hesitation, "Blake, I'm not familiar with that. Could you take a few minutes to explain it to me?" As he explained, she would have felt very confident to stop him as needed, "I'm not sure I got that. What does that mean?" If she had felt her own worth and had the confidence that naturally comes from knowing our worth, she wouldn't have been intimidated by what she didn't know. She and Blake could have had the intellectual interaction he craved, and both of them would have enjoyed it.

With her increasing confidence, she could have then explored other ways to learn, ways that she liked instead of facing the frustration of falling asleep as she tried to read. For example, she might have had the motivation to rent or buy books on tape and find ten minutes here or twenty minutes there to "read" as she ironed or watched her toddler play in the backyard.

Who knows, as Theresa accepted herself, she may even have wanted to attend college again and have Blake tend the children while she studied at night. She would have had that right, if she so desired.

Personal Application

1. Answer these questions if you don't have the accompanying workbook, *Becoming ONE: Exercises in Intimacy.*

- What, if anything, has happened in your life that makes you feel negatively about yourself?

- What could God do (that you *really* believe He can do) to help you get past any negative feelings you have about yourself?

- What would *you* need to do to allow Him to do that for you?

- . If you aren't happy with your body, look deep within and discover why. If you find an underlying emotional need ("I want to be loved," or "I want to feel important," etc.), how could you fulfill that emotional need without changing your appearance at all? (Think hard: There is a way.)

- How would you need to grow spiritually to come to full acceptance of the talents, gifts, etc. that God has given you?

2. *Share your answers with your spouse.* If any answer is too private or personal to share right now, give each other the privilege of "skipping" without prying or cajoling. Your goal is to help each other come to a better self-perception.

*E*motional intimacy begins when you share the events of your life with your spouse. We call this sharing facts. The more private and potentially threatening the fact, the more intimacy you feel for your partner when he or she hears it and accepts you anyway. (page 105)

*S*ometimes you *must* tell your mate the things you've done wrong, and sometimes you are much better off not to. The secret of a strong and intimate marriage is knowing what to share and what to leave buried. (page 108)

*T*he events of your life tell your mate *what* happened, but they don't tell enough about *who* you are. The only way the two of you can see into each other's hearts is when you share not just facts, but feelings. That's when your spouse learns all there is to know about you, even the parts you don't completely understand yourself. When you accept each other on that level, you'll begin to discover true emotional intimacy. (page 111)

*W*ant your spouse to talk to you, really talk? Learn to communicate your acceptance of his or her facts and feelings. (page 118)

Developing Emotional Intimacy, Part 2

Learning How to Make Intimacy Grow

"Okay, what's the formula? You know, the model? I've heard you speak too many times and have read the books you've written. From your research, reading, or experience, I *know* you can give me directions on how to get my dates to open up to me so I can tell more quickly if I'm wasting my time or not."

Tracey grinned as she fired that last sentence at me, and I grinned slyly in return. Even though she was joking about sorting through the men she dated more quickly, she honestly wanted to know if there was a methodology to encouraging open communication. Her question impressed me. Tracey showed maturity and insight by wanting to learn the methodology before she married. We work with people who've been married fifty years who haven't yet tried to learn.

You may recall that Blake and Theresa in the previous chapter hadn't yet learned to communicate effectively, and the effect on their relationship was extremely destructive. Maybe you haven't learned to share openly in your marriage either. Whether a person is single and "looking" or married and committed, the process is the same. Emotional intimacy comes through the four basic steps we introduced in the last chapter:

1. Accept yourself as you are.
2. Share the facts of your life.
3. Share the feelings of your life.
4. Accept the other person as he or she is.

In chapter 4 we discussed the first step: Accept yourself as you are. In this chapter, we will discuss the remaining three steps.

STEP TWO: SHARE FACTS OF YOUR LIFE

When two people first start sharing themselves with each other, they usually begin with the simple *facts*—where they went to school, where they work, or where they were born. They don't start off sharing personal, private feelings. For example, when you met the person who finally became your mate, you likely didn't start your first conversation with, "How many children would you like to have?" One young lady told me that a blind date asked her that before they'd gotten two blocks from her home. She told him to turn around and take her back home! When I asked why, she arched her brows at me and said, "He's a nut! I was afraid of the way his brain worked and wondered where he was taking me. Normal people don't approach getting to know each other that way!"

It's more likely that as you began to develop your initial intimacy with the person who became your mate, you didn't discuss probing issues but instead shared facts about yourselves. It's also very likely that the facts you first shared were facts you deemed nonthreatening—how many brothers and sisters you have, where you grew up, what you do for a living, what you do for fun. These facts all become part of the network of information that lets the other person know who you are. As you share such facts, you actually begin to develop a little intimacy with the one you share with because you allow him or her a look inside you. At the same time, this level of sharing doesn't reveal any truly personal information. This level of communication works well with strangers and casual friends, but we want a deeper level of communication with those we hold dearest.

There's another level of facts that we *do* see as potentially threatening. We think that if people knew *those* facts about us, they might reject us. So we keep them locked in our memories and share them only when we feel absolutely sure that the person who hears them will neither reject us nor use the information to harm us.

When we are able to share these intimate facts with someone and are met with acceptance, rather than rejection, that person takes on a certain significance in our lives, and we develop feelings of intimacy toward him or her. Therapists and other helping professionals are trained to anticipate these feelings of intimacy and prohibit them from entering the relationship between counselor and counselee. Preachers, counselors, priests, and lawyers frequently hear things about people's lives that those people may never have told another living human being. The sharer depends on the ethics of the professional to prevent repulsion and harm. They want someone else to know—to validate that the occurrence doesn't negate their value or worth as a human—but they can't trust anyone in their private lives to give them that affirmation.

So, what does that have to do with developing emotional intimacy in a marriage? It's really quite simple. When husbands and wives learn to share the facts of their lives with each other, intimacy grows. First they must learn to share the innocuous facts that are unlikely to evoke a negative reaction; then they can move on to the potentially threatening facts.

Start with the Innocuous

For many couples, intimacy would increase if they simply started sharing facts that are completely nonthreatening. For example, if a couple set aside twenty to thirty minutes every day to talk about their days—who they saw, what they ate for lunch, and the like—they could actually increase intimacy. The very acts of spending time together and communicating (two of the keys to intimacy) feed the intimacy turbine. It won't create as much intimacy as a marriage relationship deserves, but at least it would get the turbine spinning, and some intimacy would be created.

Sadly, many couples hardly talk at all. He wants to forget work when he gets home. She's had a horrible day and would rather forget that it ever happened. They each talk to the kids—if they talk at all—and communicate with each other only in short, essential statements. For these couples, the turbine has gone dry. It isn't producing any intimacy because *nothing* is feeding it. Wouldn't you agree that just a few minutes a day is a good first step to getting the intimacy going again? If it's "turning" at all, it's producing something! And that makes it easier to take it to the next level.

If you want to start increasing intimacy in your marriage, start talking more than you do now. Share the facts of your lives—nonthreatening facts. If you don't want to discuss your day because you don't want to relive it or because you feel that's too superficial, explore your childhoods. Each person could share a few minutes of some childhood event. Talk about your grammar school, your best friend in high school, your most fun family outing. As you share these facts of life with each other, you're developing intimacy with each other. You're sharing your lives, and that's as it should be. Before long, you won't be talking just twenty to thirty minutes but may find yourself on the back porch talking for hours into the night. When that happens, you're really spinning those turbines and intimacy is increasing!

One friend of mine answered my question about how he knew he was marrying the right person this way: "Hey, the other day we drove five hours to visit my parents. We started a conversation as we got into the car and finished it as we pulled into my parents' driveway. You ask me if this is the woman I really want to marry? Sure she is! She's my best friend."

As you share your past and your present, move on to sharing your future. Share your dreams, what you want to be, where you want to go, what you want to do. You have lots of things to talk about, but you'll only discover them *when you start talking*.

So go ahead, start talking. Spend quality time together—and in as much quantity as possible.

Move to the Threatening

Once you get used to sharing nonthreatening facts about your lives, gradually move to the facts you fear might cause your spouse to react negatively or reject you.

"Wait a minute. Just stop right there," you may be thinking. "If you think I'm gonna share the things with my spouse that I've been hiding for years, you've lost all contact with the way things are in the real world! I can't do that."

Sharing Past Sin

Deciding whether to share an old secret with your spouse is not always easy. A couple of years ago, a woman called me and told me she'd sinned against her husband years before. He didn't know and would likely never know if she didn't tell him. But the guilt and pain was preventing her from developing intimacy with him. She couldn't allow him deep into her heart because the knowledge of what she'd done continually haunted her, and the fear that maybe, just maybe, he would eventually stumble upon the truth never went away. She asked me what she should do: Should she tell him or try to put it behind her and go on with her life?

My answer surprised her. I first guided her to Ephesians 4:29 and pointed out to her that what we share with others should be "only what is helpful for building others up according to their needs, that it may benefit those who listen." I told her that I occasionally counsel people that a sin from years ago is better left buried than shared because of the pain it would bring to the hearer. "But," I interjected as I visited with this lady, "when any sin, no matter how far in the past, is affecting your current relationship with a person, the person has a right to know. Not only a right, but a need. If your continued feelings of guilt from the sin that God long ago forgave are preventing you from having the intimacy with your husband he deserves, you must remove that barrier by telling him. It's the only way to get on with developing true intimacy in your marriage."

If you're at peace with your spouse right now, that may sound like a ridiculous idea, but it's only when a couple shares all the facts of their lives—past, present, and future—that they reach the levels of emotional intimacy they deserve. Only if the three following conditions are satisfied is it okay *not* to tell: (1) you are confident that what happened does not stand as a barrier to intimacy in your marriage, (2) it would harm, rather than benefit your spouse to know, and (3) you tell no lie to your spouse. Even if the first two criteria are met and your spouse asks, "Did you...?" *always* tell the truth!

If the first two conditions are not true for you, and you still can't—or more correctly, won't—tell, it's likely because you're afraid that your spouse will emotionally abandon you, either walking out of your life or remaining only to punish you for what you've done. While that's an understandable and valid fear, what's your alternative? Live a lie? Spend the rest of your lives together having only a portion of what you should have, what God wants you to have? You can choose that if you wish, but it's a foolish choice. You sacrifice intimacy for safety—a safety that may only be a facade.

The woman with the secret past whom I just told you about didn't want to tell her husband. She was sure he'd divorce her and her life would be over. She told me that her parents would disown her, her kids would hate her, and her church would shun her. She had every reason in the world not to tell and only one reason to tell him: She wanted—truly and deeply wanted—the intimacy they didn't have but could have. Her guilt kept her emotionally distant from him. That meant she had no choice; she had to risk it all and tell him.

He did leave her for a few days. He felt shock and denial and anger and all the other things that accompany grief. Grief? Sure. He grieved the loss of the innocence he thought existed in their relationship; he felt everything to this point in their lives had been only a lie. But he loved his wife, and he saw what she was trying to do and why she humiliated herself in his eyes by telling him. And being an intelligent man, he began to understand her motive for telling him, he saw her remorse over her sin of many years before, and he came home.

They're still together, they're still in love with each other, and they're growing a relationship to be envied. Sure they have some bad days and flashbacks that hurt, but they now can have what they never had before. Intimacy.

To my way of thinking, it was worth all they had to face to get there.

Sharing Past Abuse

Some of the secrets we hide have nothing to do with our own sin, but with something horrible that was done to us by someone else. These secrets, too, can stand as impenetrable barriers to intimacy. Did you know that one reason the FBI doesn't know the actual number of rapes in America is because so many wives who are raped are afraid to report it? Why? They fear their husbands will reject them, think them somehow soiled, so they live with the secret. Of course, the secret affects their sexual response to their husbands. How could any woman surrender sexually to one man while still imprisoned by the emotional effects of a brutal sexual assault from another? How could she feel intimacy with a man she fears would reject her if he knew the truth of the horrible trauma of her life?

It's terrible when one spouse has to hide a certain fact of his or her life from the other. It lies as a hidden barrier and inhibits intimacy.

We at Family Dynamics frequently talk with people who can't tell their mates that they were abused as children. We work with people who are afraid to tell their spouses that they are addicted to drugs, are drinking too much on the sly, or are stealing money from their companies. Not only are they unable to turn to their spouses for the help they need to either stop or overcome their problem, they are unable to grow closer to their mates.

Some are so fearful of the possible recriminations of telling the truth that they actually allow their marriages to deteriorate to the point of divorce without ever telling their spouses the dark secret that is at the real root of their disunion.

Don't let that happen to you. If your past is hurting your present, share the parts of your life that you've never shared. Clean the slate, wash the conscience, share the secret. If a sin or abuse exists in your past, prayerfully ask God if it is a barrier to intimacy and if your mate or your marriage would benefit from your revealing the truth. If you can't get a clear course of action through prayer, seek out a professional Christian counselor and have him or her guide you to the decision. But never forget, confession heals.[1]

STEP THREE: SHARE YOUR FEELINGS

Perhaps you've noticed that if people are reticent to share facts, they feel even more reticence in sharing feelings. After all, a fact is what people do or what happened to them, and others can believe any number of interpretations as to why a person did something or why something happened. We reveal some, but not all, of our lives by sharing facts; only when we tell how we *felt* about the occurrence do we let another totally into our hearts.

For example, when I told you in chapter 4 that a man made fun of my appearance, calling me ugly, you got only a glimpse into what *happened,* not a glimpse into my *heart.* If I were to tell you that I hated him and wished some evil upon him as he walked away, you would have a different view of me than the one you got just by hearing the facts of the event. If I were to tell you that I didn't feel hatred at all but instead that I felt superior to him because he seemed to be poor and I have money, you'd get yet a different view. But in reality, I felt neither of those things. I was too busy to have any reaction other than a mild irritation. I quickly thought, "That guy needs someone to teach him how to treat people," but my attention was immediately turned to the next person waiting to speak to me. You see? One set of facts; several possible interpretations. That's the way life is, isn't it? It's not just what happens but how people *feel* about what happens that tells you the most about them.

What's the point? It's a wonderful thing to get couples sharing the facts of their lives—past, present, and future—but it's even more important that they learn to share feelings. Why? Because if we want the deepest level of intimacy, we want the person with whom we're developing it to know all there is to know about us, even the parts we don't completely understand ourselves.

As with facts, the place to start with feelings is with those that are innocuous and nonthreatening.

Share Innocuous Emotions

Because the feelings we hold about an event tell more about us than the facts of the event, we don't feel completely understood unless we know the other person understands our feelings. If you want to learn how to understand your mate, encourage him or her to share feelings when he or she shares apparently nonthreatening facts with you. For example, if a husband were telling his wife about a commendation he got at work, she could increase the intimacy factor of that interaction by seeking to understand how he *felt* about it. As he showed her the award and told her what it was for, if she were to say, "Honey, how'd you feel when you got it?" she would immediately increase the flow of his intimacy "river" toward her turbine.

If he believed that she really wanted to know what he felt deep inside and would share the emotion with him, he might respond, "You know, I was beginning to think I'd never get one of these. Sometimes I feel like I'm not quite as good at the job as Charley, and I've watched him get this thing every month for a year. Getting this commendation made me feel like I'm as good as he is, and to tell you the truth, that feels pretty good."

As he tells her this and as she hugs him in warm understanding, what started as a simple (yet beneficial) sharing of facts escalates into a wonderful sharing of feelings. His feelings of intimacy for his wife would grow because he'd know that she understands him as he really is and accepts him.

You might be thinking that she needn't go to all that trouble, that she should just assume he's happy he got the commendation and rejoice with him in his victory. But that isn't really true. There's something special that happens when we let people tell us how they feel. There are at least two reasons to hear our mates' emotions rather than assume we know how they feel: First, we could be wrong in our assessment of their emotions. After all, we don't really know what people feel unless they tell us. And second, people don't often get the chance to pour out their true emotions, knowing that the other person really wants to hear them—and most people crave such opportunities.

If a person were to say, "My spouse just doesn't understand me," what do you think he or she is likely referring to?

Emotions.

If the statement were in longer form, it might be something like, "She just assumes she knows what I feel, but she doesn't really know. How could she? She never listens to my feelings!" or "My husband hasn't a clue as to what I'm really like. He has this image of me, and everything gets interpreted through that image. If, once, he would listen—really listen—to my heart, he might begin to understand me."

Almost always these feelings would change dramatically if one's spouse would listen—and hear—what the other feels about anything. About everything. It is the closest connection one human can make with another. Understanding another's heart.

At first, just encourage your spouse to share feelings you think will be nonthreatening. Don't start with, "How do you feel about my mother?" but with "How do you like our neighbor?" Get used to asking, listening, sharing, and accepting innocuous feelings before you move to the ones that may cause friction.

Move to the Threatening

Sometimes we don't understand why we feel as we do, and we need someone to help us figure ourselves out. And sometimes we just need someone to reaffirm that we aren't evil or crazy or ignorant. Quite often we find ourselves with these needs when our emotional reaction to an event isn't what we expected. The feelings we have aren't what we think we should have, and that scares us.

When we find a person we trust enough to share those feelings with, we open the "river" to his or her turbine in a special way. We allow a great concentration of our energies and emotions to feed the turbines of the person who listens and understands our emotions, who accepts and loves us in spite of our emotional reactions. As a result, we feel the greatest levels of intimacy for this person.

Several years ago a woman came to me as her minister to tell me about a "date rape" that occurred while she was in college. A young man forced himself on her in her own apartment. She'd dated him before and felt comfortable enough with him that she'd seen no danger in allowing him in. They kissed awhile, and then he decided to take things to a far different level. As he forced himself on her, she fruitlessly tried to stop him. She obviously still felt the hurt as she told me the story—even though the rape had occurred years before. When she finished describing what happened, it was evident that she wanted to say something more. It appeared that either she'd left out some fact that she very much wanted to tell or that she wanted to express some emotion that she hadn't yet shown. Her hesitancy made it clear that whichever it was, she was afraid that if she said it, I would reject her in some way.

I tried to communicate support with my body language and quietly said, "What is it that you want to tell me about that night that you're afraid to?"

She hesitated for several moments, dropped her head, and stumbled into what she wanted to say. "I, uh, I fought him and, uh, I begged him to leave, but when he kept on I..." She sighed deeply, "I had an orgasm. I'd been feeling fear and anger and desperation, and then all of a sudden I was flooded with this tremendous feeling of excitement and pleasure. It lasted only for a moment and then all I felt was revulsion for him and for myself. That was long before I was married, and I was a virgin." She looked at me with guilt-filled eyes as she spat this last sentence. "Apparently I was a slut at heart—don't you think?"

She didn't understand why she'd felt as she did when that awful thing happened to her. Her body betrayed her, and her mind, for the briefest moment, cooperated. For years she'd carried the fear that what happened meant that she was somehow internally evil. She had never before trusted another person enough to tell what had happened. She certainly couldn't trust anyone enough to tell how she had *reacted emotionally.*

Her trusting me gave me a chance to explain to her that her reaction occasionally occurs in women being raped and that such a reaction certainly isn't because they like what's happening to them or because they are corrupt at heart. Actually it involves the same phenomenon that's at work when the doctor taps your knee with that little rubber hammer. You have an involuntary response because the right nerve endings were touched in the right way. Your will, your intent, your soul have no involvement at all. It just happens because the right stimulation reached the right apparatus. That same principle is sometimes at work while a woman is being raped. The orgasm doesn't come from some evil, lurking desire. Because of the horror of the rape, her mind isn't focused on her body, so her body just operates on its own. An orgasm may happen as an involuntary response to stimulation to certain nerves.[2]

I was able to assure the young lady that her only "sin" was possessing a body that worked as God designed it to work, though He intended such a reaction to occur in much different circumstances. She did no wrong. I was able to reassure her, "You aren't a slut, and you aren't evil. You were the victim of a cruel man."

From the moment that terrible thing happened to her she'd wanted to tell someone. Now that she had told me and now that I'd accepted her, helped her understand herself, and shown absolutely no rejection of her at all, I knew that as a result I'd gain intimacy in her heart. As her minister, I knew that I would now have to limit my interaction with her so that neither of us suffered undue satanic attention because of it.

That didn't bother me; it was part of the job.

What bothered me was that she'd been married five years and had never been able to tell her husband. She was so afraid he'd think her evil and reject her that she *couldn't* tell him. If she could have and if he could have shown her acceptance when she did, they would have grown closer by the sharing of the fact and the feeling that she was so afraid to share. He wouldn't have to have known about the involuntary response either. If only he could have held her and said something like, "I know your heart. You're not a slut," everything would have been okay, and their intimacy would have deepened tremendously.

Understanding this principle, I've tried to share my feelings openly with my wife. Earlier I wrote that after we remarried she wanted to know all that I'd done in our years apart, and she wanted assurance that I held back nothing from her. So I didn't just tell her the facts. When she wanted to know, I also told her the feelings. I didn't disguise or hide them. One reason our first marriage ended was because we hadn't developed intimacy in all its dimensions. And even though it took years in our second marriage to begin to learn how to develop it, I instinctively knew as we started the second marriage that we would never find the relationship each of us wanted if I hid my feelings from her.

It's tough when you're not only asked what you did but how you liked it, what you felt as it happened, and how you feel about it now. But I answered as honestly as I knew how. And though it hurt and wounded and cut to the heart, it slowly but surely forged a bond of intimacy between my wife and me. As you've seen from earlier chapters, we still needed more; we needed to learn to share spiritual intimacy before we finally found what we'd been looking for. But our emotional intimacy came as we shared what we felt—I with her, she with me—and as each of us accepted what the other felt, even when we didn't like what we heard.

Step Four: Accept the Other Person

In chapter 3 we learned that the "river" that feeds our intimacy turbines is composed of three elements: communication, time, and action. We also learned that the communication has to be more than the superficial, "how do you do" kind of talk; it must be the sharing of our lives. But the sad truth is that the level of communication needed for intimacy (and the time together that it requires) just doesn't happen in most marriages. Sometimes it's the wife who doesn't talk very much to her husband, but much more often it's the husband who won't communicate on any deep level with his wife.

In our marriage seminars, we hear countless wives ask, "Is there something you can do to get my husband to talk to me? He doesn't talk to me much except to say, 'Pass the salt' or 'You gonna eat the rest of that?' Why won't he talk to me?"

Even as we hear those comments, we also read that the number one reason men visit prostitutes isn't for sex; it's to talk—to have someone listen to their lives and their dreams.

During the years I lived in sin and away from Alice, I discovered that if you want company, all you have to do is sit in a bar and listen. Person after person will pour out his or her heart to you, if you'll just listen.

Naturally we at Family Dynamics had to wonder why so many wives say their husbands don't talk with them when at the same time we know that their husbands are likely talking to someone—a bartender, a friend, maybe even a lover. We've discovered in the last couple of years that a large number of men are paying three to five dollars a minute to talk to a person on a 900 line, not for sexual reasons—at least not primarily—but just to have someone who will interact with them nonjudgmentally. And even more men are writing increasingly intimate letters to newfound companions in "chat rooms" on the Internet.

Why? Why aren't people talking with their wives or their husbands? If we can't get them to share nonthreatening facts and feelings, we'll certainly never get them to share threatening ones. What is the problem? Why don't couples communicate on intimate levels?

We've found the answer to be twofold. Some don't talk to their mates because they cannot accept themselves as they are, as we discussed in the previous chapter. Others don't because they feel their spouses reject them when they do try to share what they've done, are doing, or plan to do. Since their spouses can't accept facts, they don't even consider that their mates would accept how they *feel*. They quit talking openly and honestly because they fear the recriminations of the conversations. They don't want to be made to feel unintelligent. Or they don't like accusations or anger or derisive laughs. They'd rather say nothing at all than feel the rejection of the person they're married to.

Accept the Other Person's Past

If you ridicule, reject, attack, or in any way punish your spouse for what he or she has done in the past, he or she won't be truly open about the present and future.

I remember well the preacher's wife who stayed with him after his affair. Three years after it happened, I asked her why she hadn't left him. She growled, "I'm staying with him so that every day for the rest of his life he'll remember what he did. I'm not here to love him; I'm here to punish him." And she meant it. Intently. Just being in her bitter presence was tough for me; you can imagine what it was like for him. Because he felt the call of God to preach, he endured her hatred, continual put-downs, and slanders in order to keep his marriage intact. He knew he had sinned, and he accepted his punishment. Of course, he never again told her the truth about anything he felt or anything he did that she might not like.

How do you think they fared?

Today he drives an over-the-road truck along with his new wife who is his co-driver. But you expected something like that, didn't you? You knew that he wouldn't live in that kind of relationship forever, even if she would.

Perhaps as you read that you thought, "But I can understand his first wife's anger." So can I. But her choice to continue in the marriage should have also included the choice to forgive. If you've been hurt but want to stay in your marriage, you, too, must choose to forgive. In FDI's *A New Beginning* seminar, we teach that forgiveness is a choice and that it includes three steps. The first two are essential, and the third is optional.

1. *Assign the person value again.* Rather than viewing that person as evil, you choose to see him or her as a flawed human, just like the rest of the people on the planet.

2. *Decide not to take vengeance.* You may have to call the person to justice, but refuse to do anything through the motive of appeasing your hurt. For example, reporting a child abuser is justice—essential justice—but it doesn't have to be vengeance. Forgiveness means that you choose not to inflict pain or consequence on the other person to compensate for the pain he or she caused you.

Note that both steps involve choices, not emotions. One may not be able to readily control emotions, but he or she can always make choices. A person can't remove the hurt by a simple act of will, but he or she can start on the path of healing by making the right choices.

The first two steps satisfy the biblical command for forgiveness; the third goes "the second mile."

3. *Restore or create relationship with the person who hurt you.* If you were raped by a criminal now serving time for the crime, you may wish to forgo this step. But if the person you need to forgive is your parent, sibling, child, or friend, you likely will gain from making this happen. If the person is your mate, you must complete this step if you want to stay married.

How can you restore your relationship after being hurt deeply?

Well, it certainly can't be done without completing steps one and two. Once you complete those, you basically start over, building the relationship the right way.[3]

Remember, since forgiveness is a choice, you can do it no matter how badly you've been hurt.

If you so choose.

Forgiving doesn't mean that you have to like what's happened. You are free to express your own feelings of hurt and anguish, but don't hit, slap, slander, talk about, denigrate, ruin the reputation of, turn the children against, or in any other way try to do damage to the one who has hurt you. God said, "Do not take revenge, my friends.... Do not be overcome by evil, but overcome evil with good."[4] No one can go back and "undo" the past. Acceptance of what has happened in the past is the best way to change the future. You cannot change the fact that it happened. Why not accept that it did—face reality—and go from there?

At Family Dynamics, we see multiplied numbers of couples each year learn to forgive and let go of their hurt over what's happened in the past, and we see them develop an intimacy that they never thought they could have. You can have this intimacy too.

Accept What the Other Person Feels

Even more crucial than accepting facts about the past is the ability to accept feelings. Most of us can't change our feelings at a moment's notice. We typically don't quit crying just because someone tells us to, nor do we lose all hunger just because a person tells us we shouldn't be hungry. We feel what we feel.

If you want your spouse to develop the deepest levels of intimacy with you, you must make it possible for your spouse to tell you what he or she feels by accepting those feelings as real whether you like them or not. Remember, by *accepting* what your spouse feels, you have the greatest likelihood of *changing* what he or she feels.

One couple I worked with was in the middle of a divorce. He'd fallen in love with another woman and was making every preparation to spend the rest of his life with her. As his wife asked me how she could save the marriage, I replied by asking her if she really wanted to save it when he was so head-over-heels in love with another woman. She said, "Yes. At heart I know he's a good man, and I know that he can get past this. I'm hurt. I'm devastated. But I don't want my marriage to end. Is there anything I can do?"

Without taking the space to tell you all that we discussed, I need to point out that I helped her understand the value of acceptance. "If you can love him with total acceptance—accepting him even though you don't accept his sin—he may change. Remember, stand strong against his sin; never accept that. But demonstrate to him that you understand what he feels for his lover and that you *accept the fact that he feels it.*"

That's just what she did.

Because so many people in his life had turned against him for what he was doing—his children, his church, his boss—he had no one to talk to but his lover…and now his wife. She became his only contact with the world he was abandoning. He found himself talking with her more and more as she gradually became his best friend, the only one besides his lover who understood and accepted him. She would listen to how he felt and say, sincerely and kindly, "I understand how you feel and think it must be wonderful to feel that kind of love for someone. I cannot accept your sin; you know you're wrong. But I accept how you feel about her and only wish that you could feel that way about me."

Think she did the wrong thing?

I don't.

I saw her turn this man inside out through her Christian compassion, while standing ever firm against his adultery. Her acceptance of what he felt meant that she accepted him, completely and unconditionally. That's what it took to shake him free from his sin. He left his lover and begged his wife for forgiveness and renewal.

Today they're happily married and both serving God.

Intimately.

Accept What the Other Person Is

Remember Theresa and Blake from the last chapter? Theresa couldn't share herself as she wanted with Blake because she believed that Blake didn't accept her as she was. She believed this not only because of her own low self-image but also because Blake had learned to hurt her by implying that she wasn't as smart as he. He tried to make her read and keep up on current events by humiliating her, foolishly thinking somehow that would motivate her. Of course, all it did was increase her conviction that she was stupid and incapable of learning. If he'd only thought to reaffirm her as she was, rather than trying desperately to make her into something she wasn't, he would have witnessed her growth.

Theresa didn't need a college degree or a genius level IQ to be a worthwhile person or a wonderful wife. All she needed was to know that she was valuable just as she was. When people feel that kind of acceptance and affirmation, they don't fear growth; rather, they *want* to grow and *believe* that they can. It's the confident who strive for the next level, not the fearful or timid.

Husbands and wives who put down, ridicule, or insult their mates will find that the most common reaction of offended mates is to retreat, not advance. Criticism and contempt are the quickest ways to drive a spouse away from intimacy. They don't want to please their unpleasant, insistent partner, nor do they set any growth goal to achieve. They stew in their own bitterness as their mates continually push.

Remember the adage, "When I accept others as they are, they change."

Of course, accepting your spouse as he or she is requires good sense. For example, if your spouse is an abuser, you should not accept the abuse. You must put barriers into place to make sure the abuse can't happen again. Accepting your spouse does not mean accepting his or her ongoing affair. It also doesn't mean there won't be consequences. It makes perfect sense to tell your wife the marriage can't continue if she intends to keep working with the man she had an affair with. And if your husband struggles with an ongoing temptation of any kind—sexual, chemical, or emotional—acceptance doesn't mean that you allow him to be in an uncontrolled, tempting environment.

But using good sense is quite different from refusing to accept a person or refusing to accept something that happened. Refuse to accept anything destroying either of you or your relationship, accept everything about your spouse that isn't actively sinful, and forgive all sin that's been abandoned.

If you want your mate to grow, affirm all that is good and holy in him or her right now. Don't try to make your spouse be what he or she isn't. Don't ever make your spouse think that your love and acceptance are conditional on his or her meeting some standard set by you— no matter how "right" that standard is. Be like your Father God by loving others as they are so that as they love you in return, you can gently guide and encourage them to be what they can be.

Above all, accept each other. Forgive when you need to forgive. Put boundaries to behaviors where they need to be. But always, always, make sure that your spouse knows that you accept him or her no matter what he or she has done or what he or she feels. When your mate believes that your love is unconditional, he or she will begin to tell you more and more and more. And emotional intimacy will grow like never before. You may be thinking, "It's too late. Too much hurt. Too many rejections. It would have been nice to do that, but we've gone too far." If you feel that way, that's certainly understandable.

It's just as certainly wrong.

Because we humans have the ability to choose, we never have to be enslaved by our pasts. Unless we choose to. We can just as easily choose to unfetter ourselves from our pasts and concentrate on creating better futures. The first step is to make that choice. The second is to act on it.

Because we've seen so many couples overcome hideous pasts to create heavenly futures, we believe that you can do it too. We suggest this formula:

1. Repent and express sorrow.
2. Ask for and pledge a positive future.
3. Work through the four steps to emotional intimacy presented in this chapter and the previous one.

Repentance means you really are sorry for what has transpired. But feeling it isn't enough. Express your sorrow as sincerely as you've ever expressed anything in your life. Don't use self-justifying words like "mistake" or "we both." Don't even use a mild-mannered word like "apologize." Say, "I'm sorry for what I've done," and then confess freely and openly how you botched it.

As you ask for another chance to create intimacy, pledge to do all you can to make that happen. Don't promise what you won't do. But if you can genuinely pledge to work as long and hard as necessary to make everything as it should be, you may just find yourself presented with the opportunity.

If the opportunity is granted, then read through the four steps of emotional intimacy once again. Understand them. Practice them. Watch intimacy grow.

WEDDING TRIANGLES

In the spring of 1998 I flew to Seoul, Korea, to speak at a spiritual retreat. My brother, Greg, an elder in our church, accompanied me on the trip, and he and I spent hours searching for just the right gifts for our wives, daughters, and parents. I also kept an eye out for a unique gift to bring the staff members of Family Dynamics. Finally, I found just the thing. Wedding ducks.

When a couple marries in Korea, they receive a colorful set of wooden ducks, one representing the male and the other the female. The newly married couple uses these cute little ducks as an aid to communication. For example, if a husband were to come home to find his wife's duck turned away from his, he would know that she was upset about something. Or, if he noticed that her duck was nuzzling his, he'd know she was feeling amorous. Of course, he in turn may use his duck to open communications with her about his feelings.

The staff of FDI loved the ducks, and we decided they are a neat tool with which couples can communicate. So I'm going to teach you how to make you own set of wedding ducks. Well, not exactly. Instead of a set of wedding ducks, you'll be making a set of marriage triangles.

While we readily admit that the ducks are more colorful and decorative, your triangles will have an extra dimension: In addition to being tools for communication between you and your spouse, they also help you know where you are in your relationship with God.

Are you ready? Start by getting two blank pieces of paper—the heavier the stock the better—and making a model like the one illustrated below for each of you. (If you would like a set of "his and her" color-coded models already drawn and cut, call 1-800-650-9995.) Using a ruler, draw as large a triangle as you can fit onto each piece of paper. Make sure the three sides of the triangle are all the same length because you will also draw four equally sized triangles inside this large one—one in each corner and one in the middle.

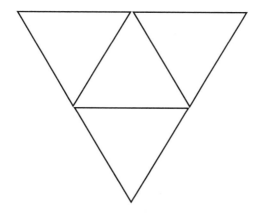

As you can see on the model, there are five triangles represented. The first large triangle you drew is the outline of the other four. Using scissors, cut out the large triangle so that your model is free from the sheet on which you drew it. Be sure not to cut any of the smaller triangles. Each of them must stay completely connected to the other.

The middle triangle represents your relationship with God. It also serves to remind you that an intimate relationship with God is the best foundation for achieving the most intimate relationship with each other. The other three triangles represent the three dimensions of intimacy—*spirit*, *body*, and *emotions*. Write those three words on your triangles as shown below.

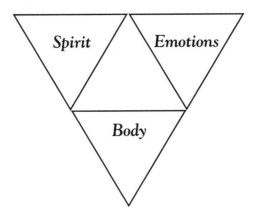

On the back of the triangle attached to the leg that says "Spirit," write "Spiritual Intimacy." On the back of the leg that says "Emotions," write "Emotional Intimacy." On the back of the leg that says "Body," write "Sexual Intimacy." If you aren't using color-coded triangles so that each of you can tell at a glance which is his or hers, jot your initials somewhere on your triangle.

If you've done this correctly, you'll notice that if you were to fold the three triangles upward, they would form a sort of pyramid, each side touching the other. We're not shaping this object this way because we believe in any occult or New Age power in pyramids. Perish that thought! We simply think it makes a nice 3-D object to help you assess your marriage.

Place your triangles on your dresser in your bedroom. When you feel that you have acceptable emotional intimacy with your spouse, fold up that side of your triangle. As you fold up other sides in the coming weeks, you can attach the sides to each other with scotch tape. Remember, at any time you feel your emotional intimacy is not what it should be, fold that side back down so that your mate will see that as he or she sees your triangle on the dresser.

See? Just like Korean wedding ducks, this model becomes a means of communicating. It helps each of you to begin the conversation about what you are feeling and what it is that you desire. Want greater levels of spiritual intimacy? Fold down that leg and your partner can see that. It becomes a visual clue as to how each of you feels about your relationship.

Always strive to become one heart by sharing what you think and feel.

Always.

And you'll develop a wonderful, fulfilling intimacy in your marriage.

Personal Application

1. *Pray for self-acceptance.* If you can't share facts or feelings with your mate because you feel inadequate or inferior, spend time in prayer asking God to show you how He feels about you. Jot down the talents and abilities He's given you. If you write down "none," you aren't yet looking at yourself as He looks at you. God made you special, and it's time for you to see how special He made you.

2. *Communicate facts about your past.* As you learn to accept yourself, make a list of the kinds of things you and your spouse may talk about. Jot down things from your past, your present, and the

things you'd like to do in your future. Make a game of communicating facts by making one night a "tell me about your grammar school" night and another "tell me what you'd like to do before you die" night. If you just plan a little, you can find many ways to share the facts of your lives. Write down which night of the week you'll reserve for this game. Then list enough topics for the next ten weeks. For example, "Week 1—Tell me about your funny relatives."

3. *Communicate feelings associated with facts.* Gradually start asking and answering how you feel about the facts revealed in your games. Start with events that you feel comfortable sharing your feelings about. Don't push for threatening feelings until your spouse is ready to share them.

*G*od made sex to be fun and enjoyable and fulfilling and exciting. It's supposed to be that way all our lives. You don't have to be twenty or thirty or even forty to have a great sex life. (page 135)

*W*e still encounter men who think their wives have little to no sex drive. We respond that if he believes that, it may be that one of three things is happening. The first would be beyond his immediate control: His wife may have physical problems or emotional hang-ups from her past. Professionals can help her remedy that. The other two possibilities would be directly related to him, not her. Either he doesn't understand how a woman's mind and body prepare for sex or he isn't a good enough lover to bring her to excitement. We can help *him* remedy that. (page 138)

*M*any sexual hang-ups we see in both Christian men and Christian women originate in theological misunderstanding. Taught that certain sexual practices are wrong, they either avoid them while longing for them or do them while feeling guilty. We open the Bible and set them free. (page 144)

Chapter
6

Developing Sexual Intimacy, Part 1
Opening the Door to Sexual Ecstasy

They were beaming when they picked me up at the airport and didn't lose any wattage throughout the entire seminar. He smiled at her, she at him, and they both smiled at anything or anyone that moved. Not those designed-to-dazzle smiles flashed by charismatic actors but genuine, wholesome, "can't help but smile back at them" smiles that emanated from pure hearts and fulfilled lives. Somewhere along the line, I may have met a happier couple, but I can't remember doing so. I've seen the loopy smiles of newlyweds who think marriage is "happily ever after," the situational smiles of longer-marrieds who enjoy specific pleasurable events, and the resigned smiles of the elderly who long since learned that good times aren't forever. But for pure, perpetual joy, Ernie and Sal stand out from the vast sea of people I've encountered. Just thinking about them makes me grin.

Both retired, they each serve in various volunteer capacities in their church and community. They married when they were young, raised children who now have families of their own, and currently mentor several of the younger couples in their church. It was in that role that they booked me to come and conduct our *Love, Sex & Marriage* seminar. Ernie and Sal had already trained to lead our eight-week marriage courses and wanted me to come to boost interest in their classes. Since our marriage division trains hundreds of facilitator couples all over America and Canada each year, I didn't know them personally until they met me at the airport. It took all of fifteen to twenty seconds to fall in love with them.

Throughout the Friday evening and Saturday seminar, they nodded their heads as I talked, and one or the other would occasionally insert an affirmation of what I'd just said or an addendum that made the point richer. I thoroughly enjoyed their involvement in every part of the seminar, but the place where they gave the greatest insight was their participation in our discussion of sex in marriage. Not only did they bless the other couples in the seminar, they gave me a picture of a wonderful sex life that was less clinical and more fulfilling than the view I'd held when I arrived. Oh, I like sex and teach about it openly everywhere I go. But Ernie and Sal gave it a living dimension of fulfillment, innocence, and happiness that I had never seen before.

Whatever they had, I wanted. For me and for every other husband and wife.

As we studied passages from the Bible—particularly those from Solomon's Song of Songs—the audience, as usual, sometimes fell very quiet and looked a little embarrassed. Not Ernie or Sal. They enthusiastically sang out their answers, without the slightest hesitation, using anatomical words that probably had never been uttered in their church building! As we moved to the session where I answered written questions anonymously submitted, they robustly entered into the discussion as energetically and as happily as if we'd been discussing an exciting game in the World Series instead of oral sex, sex "toys," and sexual hang-ups. Anyone in the room could see that they found sex refreshing and exhilarating and certainly not something to be ashamed of. Because of their age, no one thought they were being salacious or provocative. Because of their pure, innocent hearts, no one could think anything of them other than that they were truly in love with each other in every way and that they saw a wonderful sex life together as a natural part of that love.

At one point in our explanation of a passage in the song of Solomon, Sal chimed, "It sounds like Solomon may have been nearly as good a lover as Ernie!"

Ernie grinned, leaned toward her, batted his eyelids and crooned, "With a woman as alluring and as good at lovemaking as you, a man would *have* to be a good lover."

I laughed along with the rest of the audience and thought to myself that every couple—especially Christian couples—should have the kind of ONEness intimacy that Ernie and Sal shared. Every couple who does will have the same kind of sexual intimacy, where each could honestly say wonderful things about the sexual skills of the other. It's the way God intended us to be. Fulfilled spiritually, emotionally, and sexually. Settling for anything less is settling for an incomplete relationship.

If I could figure how to do it, I'd take them both on the road with me and have Ernie teach husbands and Sal teach wives what it means to love your mate in every way.[1] I'd love for my wife and daughters to be in Sal's class.

SEX IS GOOD

Several years ago when our daughter Joanna entered puberty, Alice pointed out that it was time for us to tell her the facts of life. We've always been open with all of our children about sexual matters, but now it was time for the "birds and bees" discussion that would fill in the gaps of Joanna's knowledge and ensure that she understood the sexual relationship from a spiritual standpoint.[2] We didn't want

Joanna getting her primary information about sex and sexuality from any other source—not her friends and not her teachers at school. Our intent was to emphasize that sexual intimacy is only one part of a relationship and that it would be sinful and unfulfilling to remove it from the spiritual and emotional intimacies that should accompany it in marriage. Teenage locker-room talk or clinical charts in a classroom wouldn't teach her that.

As we sat down with Joanna, I started with the words I hope she remembers throughout her lifetime. "Honey, the first thing you should know is that sex is good. It's the most wonderful way God gave a husband and wife to say 'I love you' to each other."

Sometimes audiences seem surprised when I tell them that's the first fact we taught Joanna. "You told a teenager that!" they gulp at me as I share this story in our *Love, Sex & Marriage* seminar. "Don't you know you set her up for temptation by telling her that sex is good and wonderful and stuff like that?"

No. In fact, just the opposite is true. By telling her the truth about God's intent for sex in marriage, we didn't set her up for temptation or sin or anything but a wonderful marriage. We're weary of dealing with young women who were taught for years, "Sex is bad. Sex is bad. Sex is bad..." and then later, "Oh, you're getting married tomorrow, then sex is good!" You can't undo a life of teaching in a couple of days, weeks, or months. We see too many young women, especially from Christian homes, who've been given such conflicting information about sex from their parents and church that they enter marriage with conflicting emotions about the sexual union they're about to have with their husbands. They want to enjoy lovemaking but feel somehow that they're doing something wrong, something shameful. We've had to help so many young couples with this struggle that we purposed not to have that happen with our daughters. Besides, we know that the forces of Satan work best in the dark, not in the light.[3] It's the misguidance and misinformation that teens get from each other or provocative TV shows and movies that sets up temptation. The truth—the light—gives the power to overcome those temptations.

Alice and I taught Joanna, "Sometimes you'll feel strong sexual urges when you're with a boy, especially in those times when no one is around and you want to hug and kiss and hold each other. When you feel those emotions, don't panic. Thank God He placed them in you and that someday you'll have a wonderful fulfillment of them in marriage. God made you this way, and it's good. But when you feel them, be aware that the emotions at work within you are strong and powerful. Don't be afraid, but know that the onset of those feelings means it's time to end your date and come home. The sensations and emotions you feel are God's way of giving you a preview of coming attractions that you are going to love and enjoy greatly. Don't ruin what's waiting for you by acting prematurely and turning what is supposed to be so good and holy into something sinful and shameful.

"God made lovemaking in marriage good. You must exercise the discipline to keep it good by waiting until marriage to enjoy it. After you marry, you'll pray many prayers of thanksgiving that you saved this unique ONEness for your husband."

And so we taught Joanna the truth. Sex is good. And we want you to be cognizant of that same wonderful truth as well. So we'll say it again. *Sex is good!*

Sex is supposed to be fun and enjoyable and fulfilling and exciting. It's fulfilling for the young as they marry, fulfilling for them as they age together, and fulfilling for them as they enter the autumn of their lives. God designed the sexual union to be good *all* our lives, for as long as we breathe and have sufficient health to join ourselves sexually to our spouses. You don't have to be twenty or thirty or even forty to have a great sex life. Ernie and Sal approach their seventies just as sexually fulfilled with each other as when they started their marriage nearly fifty years ago.

Have we convinced you yet? Sex is good!

If you think differently, you need to ask God to recast your thinking. If you have sexual hang-ups, fears, or frustrations, you need to ask God to "transform your mind" to His truth about sexual fulfillment. If sex hasn't been good for you in the past, it's probably because it was consummated in the wrong context. That doesn't mean that it can't or won't be good for you in your future. God can make it good from this point on, no matter what you've experienced before—even if you were abused as a child, even if you were promiscuous before marriage, even if you've been unfaithful earlier in your marriage, or even if your spouse was unfaithful.

If you have inhibitions or hang-ups or inordinate guilt or anger because of prior sexual history—either what was done to you or what you have done—please stop reading this chapter right now and go immediately to the appendix. In that special section you'll learn how God can and will give you a "transformed" mind about sex and how wonderful it can be for you.

If you believe God can give you a more wonderful sex life and ONEness—no matter how good or bad yours now is—read on.

SEXUAL FULFILLMENT

Sex in marriage is wonderful! But like all blessings, there can be an accompanying curse: When husbands and wives don't find sexual fulfillment in marriage, they will find themselves increasingly susceptible to sexual sin. To avoid that temptation, they have the duty before God to sexually fulfill their mates. That means that wives are to fulfill the sexual needs of their husbands and that husbands are to fulfill the sexual needs of their wives.

What the Bible Says about Sexual Fulfillment

Each man should have his own wife, and each woman her own husband. The husband should fulfill his marital duty to his wife, and likewise the wife to her husband. The wife's body does not belong to her alone but also to her husband. In the same way, the husband's body does not belong to him alone but also to his wife. Do not deprive each other except by mutual consent and for a time, so that you may devote yourselves to prayer. Then come together again so that Satan will not tempt you because of your lack of self-control.[4]

That passage clearly teaches several things about God's view of sex.

1. A crucial dimension of the marital "contract" or "covenant" is sexual fulfillment. When we marry, we should *expect* sexual fulfillment to take place in the marriage. That means that any spouse who knowingly and willingly fails to sexually fulfill the other violates the marriage covenant designed by God Himself.

2. God considers sexually fulfilling our mates to be a "marital duty." Other ways of translating that koine Greek phrase are "to pay what you owe" or "to pay what is due." God considers us literally indebted to sexually fulfill our mates.

3. The sexual needs of both mates—husband and wife—are given equal value and consideration. The wife doesn't exist as a sexual slave or sexual toy for her husband any more than he exists in those roles for his wife. Each has needs and each has a "heavenly contract" allowing him or her to expect and demand that those sexual needs be met.

4. Any deprivation of sexual fulfillment must meet three requirements: (1) it must be agreed upon by both wife and husband, (2) the period of deprivation must be temporary— "for a time," and (3) during the deprivation both partners should devote themselves to prayer.

5. God commands that husbands and wives resume their obligation to sexually fulfill each other quickly, before temptation overpowers either one.

Strong Sexual Needs Exist in Both Husband and Wife

Notice that in 1 Corinthians God gives the same instruction to both husbands and wives. This fact makes it clear that women have just as strong a need for sexual fulfillment as do men. This is a crucial point, because even now, at the beginning of the twenty-first century, many people still believe that women don't have the same sexual drive that men do. That's ridiculous. God made it clear thousands of years ago that He created the same need within both sexes and that He intends those needs to be fulfilled in marriage. Married men must fulfill their wives sexually; God commands it. And married women must fulfill their husbands sexually; God commands that too.

When we make the point in our seminars that women have just as much need for sexual fulfillment as do men, we often see arched eyebrows of disbelief in the audience. The difficulty many have in believing this biblical, psychological, and physiological truth is that they confuse the different *approaches* each gender takes to sex as a difference in their *need* for sex.

Several years ago when I was a very young and inexperienced minister, a husband came to me within six months of the day I performed his wedding ceremony with these startling words: "My wife's a pervert!"

Since both were members of the church for which I ministered, I gasped, "She's what? Are you sure? She seems so...so...sweet and kind and...*normal.*"

"Nope. She's a pervert all right. Something's wrong with her. She wants sex more than *I* do! Now you know that's not normal. She can't get enough. Every morning. Every night. Man, I gotta get her some help. Where do I go to find the person who can fix this?"

I remember three immediate thoughts hitting me as he whimpered his revelation:

1. I didn't need to be hearing this because I had to interact with his wife regularly.

2. Most men would be on their knees thanking God for a wife with that kind of problem.

3. Yep, she's a pervert.

Having no education in the matter, I thought just like my young friend. (I was just out of school and barely older than they.) I thought that men had strong sex drives, that women only got interested in sex occasionally, and that they only got interested after a series of specific events that no male knew or understood but that some unwittingly stumbled into on occasion. It would be years before I learned that women have sexual needs too. It's just that men and women approach sex differently.

Men and Women Approach Sex Differently

When I ask audiences in the *Love, Sex & Marriage* seminars how long it takes a man to be ready for sex, several women around the room instantly snap their fingers. While they exaggerate just a little, it is generally true that men can be prepared for sexual activity very quickly. Put the right stimuli before them, and their bodies rapidly make themselves ready for sex.

When I then ask the audiences how long it takes a woman to be ready for sex, we hear a chorus of witticisms that are almost always the same in every city.

"Four hours!"

"Three days!"

"I don't know; we've only been married twenty years!"

After the laughter subsides (mostly male), we gain agreement from everyone in the room when we say, "For men, sex is a reaction. For women, sex is a decision."

Until women decide they want to be involved in sexual activity, their bodies typically don't prepare for sex. Men may discover that their bodies are ready for sex even if their emotions or intellects say no. For women that's much less likely to happen. Sex starts in their intellects and emotions before making its way to specific parts of their bodies. It's usually only in the mental shutdown during some trauma like rape that a woman's body functions in total disregard of her emotions.

When a woman decides she wants sexual fulfillment, her body reacts at a much slower rate than her husband's. Unless he's hindered physically by age, disease, or psychological or emotional impotence, his rapid reaction to sexually provocative stimuli is to redirect blood to his penis. Very quickly he's physically prepared for intercourse.

Except in unusually sexually charged situations, her body prepares itself more slowly. Her body redirects blood to create swelling, and it also manufactures secretions to facilitate penetration by the penis. Her swelling is to create more friction and stimulation in her vaginal area, especially the clitoris. Not only does that enhance her pleasure, it enhances his by creating more tactile sensation for him.

Generally, these events only take place because she wants them to. Sex can take place without them—a man could force himself on her—but any swelling that occurs in that type of situation is likely from tissue being harmed because of penetration without lubrication. As we noted earlier, under duress, she may even have an orgasm because her mind has detached itself from what's happening. But the "pleasure" of the orgasm is fleeting, and the pain of the abuse longer lasting.

This slower preparation for sexual intercourse is what makes some men think their wives have weaker sex drives. But it means nothing of the kind. While it may take her longer to become ready, she may actually crave more sexual activity during their encounter than he can provide—especially if he is focused on his own pleasure. She also may need these sexual encounters more often than he. The reason a husband may not know this is that his wife may hesitate to tell him. Why? There could be many reasons, not the least of which could be that his too rapid lovemaking technique may be frustrating for her.

So don't confuse the different approaches to sex as an indication that men and women have different degrees of sexual needs based on gender. The amount of sex a person needs is more likely based on factors like temperament, what's going on in his or her life, and age than it is on gender.

Through the thousands of couples we've worked with through Family Dynamics, we've come to understand that in many, many marriages, it's the wife who needs sexual fulfillment more than the husband. And in most marriages, the balance of need sometimes shifts from one mate to the other, as life situations and circumstances change.

Men, don't let yourself be deluded into thinking your wife doesn't need sex as much as you just because she approaches it differently. As a matter of fact, you may discover that she wants and needs it more than you do once you learn to become a better lover. In the next chapter, we'll discuss verses from the Bible that tell you how.

From a completely pragmatic viewpoint, husbands will find that the best and most effective path to greater sexual fulfillment is to forget about themselves and concentrate on sexually fulfilling their wives! A sexually satisfied woman makes a much better lover than one who feels constantly put upon to meet the demands of a selfish husband. It just makes sense, doesn't it? If women tend to approach sex first from a mental and emotional framework, they will enter sex with a much better mind-set and more enthusiasm when their husbands concentrate more on fulfilling their wives' emotional needs than their own physical needs.

Sex and sexual fulfillment are two very different things. Animals can have sex. Only humans can sexually fulfill each other.

Sexual Fulfillment Is More Than Physical

The largest sex organ is the brain. We bring to our sexual unions our own unique set of emotions, experiences, expectations, fantasies, preferences, and inhibitions. Because of our unique constitution, we're the only animals God made who have to learn how to be good sexual lovers. In all the other animals, sex is instinctive. Certain visual or olfactory signals are given, received, and acted upon without need for any union beyond the physical act of procreation. Not so with us. Very little of our sexual union actually leads to procreation, and our sexual needs exist far beyond the core need to produce offspring.[5]

Sexual fulfillment for us isn't based in the planting of human seed. We can't consummate that physical act and go on our way with no thought of what just happened or what it means. For us humans, sex isn't about just making babies. Far beyond our child-producing years, we carry needs for sexual fulfillment. For us, sex is about becoming ONE with another person.

If that seems too elementary to discuss, we wish you could read the multitude of questions we've gathered in our *Love, Sex & Marriage* seminars. Some will make you laugh. Others will make you cry. Most will make you marvel at how little so many know about sexually fulfilling their mates. To illustrate, I'll share just a few of the questions here. Don't worry; we've weeded out any that are too explicit for this book.

> My husband thinks sex is forcing himself into me as quickly as he can and going to sleep as quickly as he's done. Is this what God intended?

> Can you teach my wife how important sexual fulfillment is to me? Can you help her understand I'm not some sicko because I want sex more than twice a month?

> My husband is impotent and won't see a doctor or talk to anyone about it. He says that if he's okay with it, I should be too; since sex is what a man needs, not a woman. He calls me names and makes me feel like a slut because I ask him to get help so we can have sex again. Who's right, him or me?

> My wife wants me to do all kinds of things to her in our love-making that bring her pleasure, but she doesn't want to do any of

those things for me. She just wants me to "do my part" when she's finally ready. Is that all I'm supposed to get?

My husband has made me feel so degraded and cheap for so many years that when we have sex, I want to get it over with just as quickly as we can. Are you saying I'm wrong to feel that way?

Each of these folks either doesn't understand—or are married to a person who doesn't understand—sexual fulfillment. *Physically*, two bodies melt together into a perfectly designed coupling. *Spiritually*, the joining of two bodies somehow brings about a union of the two spirits, as we learned from our discussion of 1 Corinthians 6 in chapter 2. And when humans allow themselves complete, uninhibited *emotional* sharing during their sexual union, the resulting ecstasy goes far beyond physical sensations.

Maybe we can say it this way: *Sex* is the physical dimension of intimacy. True *lovemaking* is the one act in which all three aspects of intimacy come together—emotional, spiritual, and sexual ONEness.

That's why the questions from our *Love, Sex & Marriage* seminar are so disturbing.

The husband of the first wife we quoted needs to learn that while forcing a quick coupling is sex, it isn't true lovemaking. It misses emotional intimacy altogether, and at the same time it bars his wife from feeling even physical intimacy.

The wife who thought her husband was a "sicko" because sexual fulfillment was important may need to be educated on God's plan for sex, or it may be that he hasn't learned how to make the experience satisfying for his wife.

The man who told his wife that men, not women, need sex shows ignorance not only of her body but also of his wife's desire for complete intimacy.

Being the recipient of attention and stimulation while not returning it, like the wife who wanted her husband to simply "do his part," indicates selfishness. A person focused on self will never find complete intimacy with his or her spouse.

And finally, by making his wife feel dirty and cheap, this last husband prevents his wife from opening herself to uninhibited emotional sharing.

What these people and many others need to learn is that sex is not only a physical matter. Sex is also emotional and spiritual. If you want to make your sex life all that it should be and all that it can be, consider the physical, emotional, and spiritual dimensions of everything you do together sexually.

As couples learn to share more intimately with each other, some invariably ask the question, "Are there 'dirty' or forbidden sexual acts that Christians must avoid?" Let's go to the Bible and find out.

SEXUAL PROHIBITIONS

When I was but a young minister, serving at my first church back in the early seventies, a new convert approached me with a question I was unprepared to answer. She was too new a Christian to know that there were some things good church folks just didn't ask (good for her!), so she decided to corner her minister just after Sunday services (bad for me!). She pulled me into the church nursery, bumping into young mothers as they scurried out the door with their charges to catch their husbands in the outgoing tide.

"I have a question, and you told me when I became a Christian that I should ask anything I needed to know, right? Well, my husband isn't a Christian, as you well know, and he wants me to do something I don't know that I can do now that I'm a Christian. So he told me to ask you about it. What does God say about a husband and wife having oral sex?"

My wife later told me that she happened to notice me through the window of the nursery and saw me turn starkly white and then blush bright crimson. She should have been in the room with me. She would have heard me stammer, stutter, and squirm. Mentally, I quickly ran through all my college Bible classes wondering where we would have discussed such a pressing issue. "Let's see, it wasn't in the prophets. No. Hmmm. Pentateuch? No. Maybe Proverbs? Hmmm, not there." I finally admitted to myself that the reason I didn't remember was that it had never come up in any of my Bible classes. My perception of the professors I'd studied under—with the exception of one—was that they would have dropped dead from embarrassment at the mention of such a topic, just after expelling the student who was audacious enough to ask. Realizing I hadn't a clue, I asked the newborn sister if I could get back to her later. I then spent the next few weeks in an amazing Bible study—especially for a young minister who'd never been taught to use the Bible to find answers to real-life questions.

I discovered that a great deal of what the Bible teaches about sex comes in the form of prohibitions. Don't let that make you think God is against sex. He made it! But He made it to be enjoyed in His design—not in any human aberration of that design. I finally realized that starting with the prohibitions was a good beginning.

The study was quite freeing. First, I learned that what many Christians said was prohibited sexually was not prohibited at all! When God is silent, we have no right to insert our own rules.

Second, freedom from those man-made prohibitions opened my mind to understand passages that indicate how a godly person's sex life should be. That happens with almost everyone. When couples in our *Love, Sex & Marriage* seminars discover their freedom, their sex lives begin to improve. They learn how to be good lovers by first casting off needless shackles of man-made inhibition.

Basically I found ten categories of sexual sin listed in the Old and New Testaments. I share them with you here.

1. Incest

God strongly condemned sexual relations with a "close relative" in the Old Testament. We call it *incest*. Relatives listed in the Bible with whom a person shouldn't have sex include:

- Mother[6]
- Father's wife—which probably means stepmother[7]
- Sister, half-sister, or stepsister[8]
- Grandchild[9]
- Aunt[10]
- Daughter-in-law[11]
- Sister-in-law[12]
- Daughter or granddaughter of woman one had sex with[13]

2. Homosexuality

In the Old Testament God strongly condemns sexual relations with a person of the same gender.[14] He condemns it just as strongly in the New Testament.[15] While it isn't politically correct to make this statement in the United States at the beginning of the twenty-first century, those who believe the Bible to be true find themselves compelled by their beliefs to speak boldly as the Bible speaks: Homosexuality is a sin.

3. Rape

If a man raped a married or engaged woman in the Old Testament, he was to be executed and the woman was held to be innocent and worthy of no punishment. If the woman could have summoned help but didn't, she was also to be executed.[16] If a man raped a single, unengaged woman, he was not put to death. The penalty was to marry her with no possibility of divorce, ever.[17]

4. Premarital Consensual Sex

In the Old Testament, if a man slept with an unmarried, unen-gaged woman who consensually engaged in sex with him, his penalty was to marry her (if her father wished) with no possibility of divorce.[18]

The New Testament made it clear that God expected sex to take place only in the boundaries of marriage.[19] Anyone guilty of sexual sin—called "fornication" in some Bible versions and "sexual immoral-ity" in others—will suffer spiritual death unless he or she finds God's forgiveness.[20]

5. Adultery

The Old Testament law definitely favored the male. In the Old Testament, adultery only occurred if a married woman was involved. A man who slept with a single woman didn't commit adultery since men could have more than one wife. While the word *adultery* often is used when referring to sexual activity, it refers to the violation of the covenant between husband and wife. Therefore, a man could sleep with other women and not commit adultery because it didn't violate the covenant with his wife. Rich and powerful men like King David or King Solomon had not only a multitude of wives but concubines, as well, to sate their need for status and sexual gratification.

Because in that male-oriented society, women couldn't have more than one husband, any sexual encounter with another man—married or single—was adultery. She violated the covenant with her husband.

God vehemently condemns adultery and listed the punishment as death.[21]

In the New Testament anyone—husband or wife—married to one person but sleeping with another commits adultery. "Marriage should be honored by all, and the marriage bed kept pure, for God will judge the adulterer and all the sexually immoral."[22]

6. Lust

In the Old Testament, God phrased it this way: "You shall not covet your neighbor's wife."[23] In the New Testament, Jesus said it like this: "You have heard that it was said, 'Do not commit adultery.' But I tell you that anyone who looks at a woman lustfully has already committed adultery with her in his heart."[24]

7. Prostitution

God detests prostitution.[25] In the New Testament He said through Paul, "Do you not know that your bodies are members of Christ himself? Shall I then take the members of Christ and unite them with a prostitute? Never!"[26]

8. Bestiality

Under the Old Testament law, any person, male or female, who participated in sexual activity with any animal was to be put to death along with the animal.[27]

9. Sex during the Menstrual Period

A basic principle of Scripture is "the life of a creature is in the blood."[28] Therefore, blood is always treated as holy—even in the New Testament.[29]

Understanding that principle helps us understand God's law in the Old Testament about sexual relations during the wife's menstrual period. He said that it shouldn't happen and listed the penalty as being "cut off" from the people.[30] Many today believe that particular part of the "blood law" was given primarily for health reasons—the people of the Old Testament did not have access to our modern hygiene or medicines—and thus that particular law has no application to Christians. Others feel that it demonstrates God's view of the sanctity of blood and should still be observed by Christians who respect God's feelings.

10. Harm the Temple of God

While harming the temple of God isn't explicitly listed as a sexual prohibition, the principle of caring for our bodies is a biblical one. The following scripture, which admonishes us to honor our bodies, is in the context of sexual activity: "Do you not know that your body is a temple of the Holy Spirit, who is in you, whom you have received from God? You are not your own; you were bought at a price. Therefore honor God with your body."[31] Our bodies belong to God as well as our spirits. We are not to do anything that desecrates our bodies, for our bodies are the temple of God. Sexual activity that harms the body should not occur.

BASIC PRINCIPLES OF PROHIBITION

As I finish describing these ten areas to people in our seminars, I ask, "What did you expect to be listed as a prohibition that isn't?"

Sometimes they answer with things that the ten prohibitions clearly imply as being sinful but didn't state explicitly. For example, someone may say, "I don't see sexually abusing a child on that list."

I explain that sexual abuse of a child is there; it's just not stated in those exact words. The ban on homosexuality makes it a sin to have sex with anyone of the same gender, even a child. The condemnation of incest covers almost every other situation we encounter in child sexual abuse. Finally, the prohibition against rape concludes the issue. No child could be a willing participant since neither God nor we view them as capable of making those kinds of mature decisions. Also, because we don't live under the Old Testament acceptance of polygamy, sex isn't allowed with *anyone* other than one's mate. So all child abuse is condemned under one or more of the prohibited categories.

Others in the seminar sometimes say that they expected to see prohibitions of oral sex, various sexual positions, or sex "play" between married partners. Based on the background they come from, various people feel that these and other matters are sinful, even though the scriptures don't condemn them. I reply by pointing out that everything God condemns about sex (with the possible exception of sex during the menstrual period) can be summarized as follows:

1. Sex cannot take place outside the confines of marriage.
2. Sex may never involve:
   - another person besides your mate
   - an animal
   - anything that causes harm to either person's body

And that's it. That's all that God says cannot happen in a sexual relationship in marriage. We don't have to look for things He "specifically authorized" for a couple to do, building great theological arguments, because He left it to the husband and wife to decide what best fulfills each of them. God just gave the parameters discussed above and allows us to choose what we like and don't like within those parameters.

While cultures within families, communities, or churches may add to this "prohibition list" their own preferences of likes or dislikes, they cannot make those preferences the will of God. Only God can do that, and He's already spoken. Unless you can find a specific scripture to the contrary, anything that a husband and wife mutually agree to that fits within the framework above is okay with God.

You may have reacted emotionally as you read the above paragraph. For some, the reaction may have been unadulterated joy; for others, dread.

Dread?

Yes. If either you or your spouse has been selfish or demanding in your sex life, opening the barriers to wider experiences and practices will likely be viewed with apprehension. The "put-upon" spouse may anticipate even more demands and even greater selfishness.

It's a reasonable fear. No one wants to be an object or prop for the other's selfish satisfaction. If one has to endure a partner's insensitivity, at least there could be comfort in having a limited scope. But there is good news. As we tear away man-made barriers and remove limiting inhibitions in this chapter, in the next chapter we will study one of the greatest lovers in history and learn from his interactions with his beloved wife. Our intent is not to remove the binders while leaving on the blinders! No indeed. We remove the misconceptions that bind so we can unhesitatingly learn the methodology of true lovemaking. Intimacy in every dimension.

Personal Application

Make a quiet time to visit together without disturbance or distraction. Make sure you have plenty of time and that each of you feels good physically, emotionally, and spiritually. Then do the following three exercises.

1. Share openly. Discuss slowly and in detail what brings each of you to the greatest levels of arousal and desire. Take turns. Listen carefully. Try to learn more about your spouse.

2. Share a guided tour. Each of you give the other a detailed exploration of his or her body. For example, the wife may slowly guide her husband's hand to help him understand why and when and where swelling takes place in her breast and genitals. She does the same to explain lubrication. He does the same with his body.

3. Discuss inhibitions or guilt feelings that have prevented you from being completely open sexually with your spouse. Take turns. Be understanding and avoid all criticism or contempt. Discuss how what you've learned in this chapter can help you get past these.

If you want uninhibited, passionate, sensual, sexual exhilaration, seek it from the Scripture. God made us; He surely knows what it takes for you and your spouse to be great lovers. (page 155)

If you're a husband who wants to be a consummate lover to your wife, learn from Solomon. Once you start understanding the idioms of Solomon's day, you'll see that he knew exactly how to bring his wife to peaks of sexual ecstasy. Do what he did, and you're wife will respond as passionately as his. (page 158)

If you're a wife who wants to be a consummate lover to your husband, learn from Solomon's wife. She understood the characteristics common to most males and took complete advantage of her feminine charms to erotically charge her lover. Do as she did, and you're on your way to helping your husband become the careful, considerate, complete lover that Solomon was. (page 164)

If you're in conflict over sexual desires—one wants to do something the other doesn't—there is a logical and spiritual way to satisfy you both. (page 168)

Chapter 7

Developing Sexual Intimacy, Part 2

Becoming Consummate Lovers

I stared at the question for several seconds before lifting my head to scan the audience. The *Love, Sex & Marriage* seminar had drawn around four hundred people, and there was no way to know which person in the group had submitted the anonymous question. Nearly a hundred slips of paper had drifted into the question box during our fifteen minute break, and I had been busily sorting them into categories as rapidly as I could so we could start back on time. My dilemma was twofold: No category existed among my neat piles for this question, and how was I to understand the mind-set of the person who would ask this kind of question at a church seminar?

> My spouse and I want to know what you think about our inviting another woman into our bed. We believe it would make our sex life much more exciting and fulfilling. What do you think?

Naturally I looked again at the handwriting. My prejudices made me think it would be a masculine scrawl. Instead it appeared to be the delicate touch of a feminine hand. That didn't prove anything since I'm no expert on handwriting, but it made me contemplate the question longer.

I decided to answer it.

Starting with the more pressing questions—at least my experience with the seminar told me they were the most commonly urgent questions—I worked my way from pile to pile. Occasionally some brave soul spoke up from the audience, but most just sat there grinning at me as I talked about things not normally discussed in church. I could tell I was getting through and that good was being done.

Finally I came to the "third party" question.

As I read it into the microphone, the room froze into complete, soundless stillness. I think everyone was afraid that if they were to breathe the folks around them might take it as a sign that they were the one who had contributed the query. Now that I think about it, I believe there wasn't even a blink of an eye from the time I read the question until I slowly began to answer it several seconds later.

I began by quoting Hebrews 13:4 that says the marriage bed shouldn't be defiled. I went on with a few other pertinent passages. Somber eyes and nodding heads signaled the agreement of the audience. Then, after making sure my objection to the practice questioned was clear and unmistakable, I continued, "But I can understand why you would ask."

Silence.

Deep silence.

That "let's run this pervert out of town," grim, and determined kind of silence.

"Let me explain," I continued. "Sex can become boring when a couple has been married for a while. I surely don't know who wrote this and, therefore, haven't a clue as to whether you've been married twenty days or twenty years. But I do know that many, many Christian couples are bored silly with their sex lives.

"Some folks can live with that. They never longed for fireworks to begin with, and the warmth and closeness they experience in making love is all that they want or need.

"Others are quite different. They crave the warmth and closeness. But they also want something more. They want to be lifted to the heights of sexual ecstasy and have lovemaking experiences that are true mountaintop experiences. I guess that probably is what prompted this question. Either the husband or wife or both feel something is missing and they want it. The trouble is that where they're thinking about looking for it isn't going to give them what they want. Oh, it might carry a temporary thrill. But within that will be the seed of destruction. They'll destroy the unique sanctity of their ONEness and lose the very thing they seek.

"It's okay to want sexual exhilaration. But if you seek it, seek it from the Scripture. Yeah, that's right. Scripture. Believe it or not, the Bible tells us how to be great lovers."

Missed that in your last week's Bible class, did you?

Well, it is there. Right in Solomon's Song of Songs.

REFERENCES TO PASSIONATE SEX IN THE BIBLE

God shows us in the Bible that sex can and should be a passionate, fulfilling relationship between two people that leads them to ecstasy and rapture. Solomon's Song of Songs stands as a classic love story about Solomon and his dark-skinned wife, and anyone who reads it knows that these two people were sexually thrilled with each other. The book is explicitly sexual in several passages, but those references may sometimes slip past modern readers because many of the idioms used in that day don't communicate well to twenty-first century people.

For example, we know that in our culture the phrase "he slept with her" means "he had sex with her." That idiom might not mean the same to someone of another time or culture. Perhaps an even greater example of idiom and culture could be demonstrated by the various nicknames currently used by Americans to refer to various anatomical parts. For example, how many idioms or "nicknames" can you think of that people use to refer to a woman's breasts? In your own marriage, what does the husband call them? The wife? Imagine how someone two thousand years from now reading a love story from today would struggle with our idiomatic phrases about body parts or sexual encounters. While the reader may figure out some of the unusual words we use to refer to breasts, genitalia, lovemaking, etc., some would undoubtedly be lost on him or her.

That same principle holds true in the song of Solomon. We may read the Jewish idioms that held strong sexual meaning for those of Solomon's day and see no sexual innuendo at all. Nevertheless, they exist, and the original audience understood them. Song of Songs is a highly sexual book.

Clear References to Sexual Matters

Of course, some of the statements are very easy to understand. I list some of the clear references to sexual matters here.

- Kissing[1]
- Lying together entwined in an embrace[2]
- Lingering lovemaking that lasts all night[3]
- Admiration of his wife's breasts[4]
- "French" kissing (pardon the use of one of our idioms!)[5]
- Admiration of her husband's body[6]
- Admiration of his wife's body[7]
- A statement of passion[8]

- Wife's statement of the contentment her breasts bring her husband[9]

Idiomatic References to Passionate Sex

The explicit references above don't sound too intensely passionate, do they? A person could read them and think that Solomon and his bride didn't express much variety or intensity in their lovemaking. But the idioms used throughout the book reveal a whole new dimension to their sexual relationship. The workbook that accompanies this book takes a detailed look at several of those idioms and helps you interpret their meanings. Here, we'll look at just one. Keep in mind that Solomon is speaking to his wife in this verse. Also, refer to the hints below. Now see if you can guess what his idiomatic language might mean:

> Until the day breaks and the shadows flee, I will go to the mountain of myrrh and to the hill of incense.[10]

As you try to interpret its meaning, remember that as Solomon speaks to the longevity of his lovemaking, he tells his wife where he will concentrate.

- First hint: Notice that his use of the words "mountain" and "hill" are singular, not plural.

- Second hint: Myrrh and incense are unique and special aromas or fragrances.

- Third hint: It doesn't appear that the mountain of myrrh and the hill of incense are different places but two ways to refer to the same place.

Now, read the verse again and answer this question in your mind: What do you believe he is telling her that he is going to do?

We understand Solomon's reference to the mountain of myrrh and the hill of incense as a reference to his attention to his wife's genitalia during their lovemaking. The fragrances he cites refer to the unique fragrance of the aroused female. His reference to the mountain or the hill is similar to the name we use today: *mons veneris*. He knew that while all the other parts of her body need kissing and caressing, her orgasms emanate from her clitoris. In this section of Scripture, he began with her eyes (v. 1) and moved down her body to her hair (v. 1), her teeth (v. 2), her lips and mouth (v. 3), her neck (v. 4), her breasts (v. 5), and then the area in question in verse 6. In verse 7, he says, "All beautiful are you, my darling; there is no flaw in you." It seems pretty clear to us that as he "worked his way" down her body, verse 6 clearly refers to the genitals. Thus, he makes the "all" of you statement when discussing her beauty.

That verse is just one example of the sexual content of Solomon's Song of Songs. The fact that God included this book in His Book testifies to the pleasure He intends husbands and wives to find in marriage.

SOLOMON SHOWS MEN HOW TO BE GREAT LOVERS

We wanted you to think through Solomon's statement so that you wouldn't think us salacious or provocative in what we write. It's obvious from that passage, and several others discussed in the accompanying workbook, that both Solomon and his wife enjoyed every part of each other's body and that their sexual unions were exquisite times of slow and attentive love. In my *Love, Sex & Marriage* seminar, I read several passages from the Song of Songs and use them to teach men how to be good lovers. There's a lot to be learned from Solomon; Solomon knew how to fulfill his wife through all phases of the sexual experience—from beginning to end.

Start Slow

When I talk to the men in my seminars, I share one of the secrets of lovemaking: "Husbands, I'll teach you a secret you can apply right away: You can become a 50 percent better lover immediately. How? Take your time like Solomon did." Solomon obviously understood that women approach sex differently than men, so he didn't rush his wife. Instead, he made love to her all night long—"until the day breaks and the shadows flee"—when he had opportunity. He also knew that women build to a sexual crescendo slowly, so he took his time to execute what we today call "foreplay."

The most common question we get about sex in our seminars is how to slow down a husband who thinks good sex is trying to make each partner reach orgasm as quickly as possible. We're not sex therapists, and we don't speak to specific people about their sexual dilemmas, but we are educators who speak to these issues in general.

Gentlemen, if you learn to love your wife like Solomon loved his, you will have the same kind of response from her that he received from his wife. We men are much too quick to blame our wives for our lack of sexual fulfillment when the problem is often the masculine approach to sex. We think too much about the immediate and the intense feelings of climax. Women don't. God made their bodies different from ours (aren't you glad!), and their approach to sexual fulfillment is different from ours. They must be loved slowly. It takes time for their bodies to prepare for intercourse. For most women, neither intercourse nor orgasm is the be-all-end-all of sex. They tend to long for and enjoy things like kissing, caressing, and talking.

For men, sex tends to be a series of pleasurable, physical sensations that culminates in an intense, nearly uncontrollable spasm of pleasure called orgasm. For women, sex tends to be a broader experience. Not only are there pleasurable and exhilarating physical sensations, there are also pleasurable and deeply fulfilling emotional sensations. A man may feel satisfied with little to no emotional involvement. That is seldom true of a woman. One reason for foreplay—in addition to giving the woman's body time to prepare itself—is that it allows her to emotionally become more aroused. Therefore, foreplay should slowly and deliberately concentrate on acts that arouse emotions. Things like kissing, touching, romantic words, and the like.

CHAPTER 7

Maintain Her Pleasure

Look at Solomon. He didn't only love his wife *slowly;* he maintained her level of pleasure through the entire experience. One thing he did was *talk* to her—telling her what he was doing or going to do. He understood her love of poetic language. Talk to your wife as you begin making love to her; caress her with words throughout the entire lovemaking experience. Of course, you shouldn't say things that will turn her off; rather, use the poetic language that will "light her fire"— whatever that means for her. Some women like it more primal and some more aesthetic. Solomon also understood her desire to share not only her body but her emotions. He made love to her with every part of his body, including his vocal cords.

Solomon maintained his wife's pleasure by continuing to take his time and give her his full attention. Chapter 7, verse 8 says that he "will climb the palm" rather than taking it abruptly. The image he paints makes one think that he started by kissing her feet—maybe even her toes or the erogenous zone of the soles of her feet—and worked his way up. Since he repeatedly said throughout the book that he wasn't concerned with time, we picture him kissing and caressing any part of her body as long as she continued to find it pleasurable. He wasn't in a hurry to get anywhere or complete anything. He obviously kissed her calves, the backs of her knees, her thighs. (Don't panic; we won't get too graphic here.) And the picture we get from his description is that he constantly spoke to her between kisses. Maybe he softly laughed with her as he kissed her feet. The laughter probably evolved into more softly passionate noises as he moved up her legs. He likely made his words and sounds more urgent as her reactions became more intense. This man was a consummate lover.

You can't read the song of Solomon and picture this woman as disinterested; she was just as excited and passionate as he. But it appears that their wonderful lovemaking ability started with him and then transferred to her. She became a great lover because she wanted to please her husband who was making wonderful love to her.

In my seminars, I use Solomon to teach men that women can continue at a plateau of sexual pleasure for almost indefinite periods of time and can have intense orgasms. Some women can even have multiple orgasms in the same lovemaking session. I've actually had reports from exuberant couples that because the husband listened well in the seminar, the wife for the first time discovered that she could have multiple orgasms. One lady I ran into a few weeks after the seminar said to me in a church foyer, husband right beside her, "I didn't know that was even possible!" I just cleared my throat and glanced away, blushing. She'd heard me discuss sex openly in the seminar, so I assume she (and he) viewed me something like a sexual educator or therapist and had no hesitation discussing their sex life with me.

In public.

While that particular episode embarrassed me a little at the time, I'm very happy for the couple who learned a whole new dimension to their lovemaking.

Their comments told me one thing about them that is decidedly good. The husband had learned a new level of concentrating on the needs of his wife. What makes me think that? Giving one's wife multiple orgasms usually means that a husband has learned how to create orgasms for her without penile penetration. That means he's learned how to concentrate more on her pleasure than his.

One study indicates that the average time of intercourse before male ejaculation is approximately three minutes. (How they learn those numbers, I don't know and don't want to know.) If that is the case—and it seems to be true based on almost universal agreement from audiences when I quote that fact—then the average husband has only about three minutes to give his wife an orgasm if he intends to accomplish that during normal intercourse. Some women could orgasm in that time frame if properly prepared by foreplay and if maintained at a pleasurable plateau for a satisfactory (to her) period. Other women need longer. And some women are incapable of orgasm through penile stimulation altogether. That means that a husband must concentrate on his wife to give her multiple orgasms—or maybe even to give her an orgasm at all! Most often, if a husband wants to create multiple orgasms for his wife, he will do that by bringing her to orgasm as many times as she wishes before he engages in the intercourse that will bring about his own orgasm.

When a husband concentrates on his wife, he has several options for giving her orgasm or multiple orgasms. All female orgasms—whether as a direct result of penile penetration or from other stimulation—emanate from her clitoris. If the woman's genitalia and the husband's penis are harmoniously shaped and sized, and if she is properly prepared through foreplay and plateau so that her genitals have swelled and lubricated properly, she may have an orgasm from intercourse. If there is any discrepancy in any of those areas, other clitoral stimulation will be required.

Sometimes we get questions from husbands in our seminars that indicate they feel something is wrong with their wives or their relationship because the wife cannot orgasm from normal intercourse. Without fail I point out in reply that the husband's question says more about his self-concerns than about concerns for his wife's pleasure. Here's a simple fact: It doesn't say anything about the lack of lovemaking ability on the husband's part if he has to digitally stimulate the wife's clitoris (or, of course, stimulate it in some other way) to give her an orgasm. Actually his adjusting to other methods of bringing her to orgasm says good things about his skill as a lover. It says he understands his wife's needs and will do what it takes to bring her through plateau to orgasm. It says that he understands that the way she's shaped, or he's shaped, or the way they fit together doesn't give her enough physical stimulation to the clitoris.

It says that he's being a knowledgeable and thoughtful lover.

If a wife can have satisfying orgasms from penile penetration, her husband may be able to give her multiple orgasms through that method. Some husbands practice a form of intercourse interruption to give their wives multiple orgasms. That's accomplished by continuing in intercourse until she orgasms—assuming she orgasms before he does—and then interrupting the intercourse for other pleasurable activities until he recedes from the edge of orgasm. When he has sufficiently calmed to resume intercourse without the threat of rapid orgasm on his part, he repeats the process. Some sexual therapists call this a form of multiple orgasm for men if the man can get to the edge of orgasm and then stop just before it occurs—repeating the process again and again until he is ready to have his "final" orgasm. Notice we say this method *may* work. You may be able to make it a part of your marriage, but you may have to practice it a few times before you find the ability to know when to stop and start again. Don't be disappointed by "failures" in the learning process.

I tell the men, "You can be a 'consummate lover' like Solomon if you will slow down, talk, and kiss and caress everything. Learn from Solomon what good loving is. Your wives will *definitely* reward you for it."

Remain Attentive through the Afterglow

Just as a husband should slowly build his wife to her plateau, keep her there as long as she desires, and give her as many orgasms as she wants, he should also continue the lovemaking with his wife during that slow *afterglow*.

For men, lovemaking tends to be over with orgasm. We prepare quickly, have short-lived plateaus (if we aren't concentrating on our spouses), and find ourselves disinterested in sex after orgasm almost as quickly as we were ready for sex in the first place. Our sexual cycle is much faster than our wives'. For women, lovemaking isn't over with their orgasm; it's only over when they've completed afterglow. Remember, for a woman, sex is as much emotional as sensual.

Don't forget what we learned back in chapter 1: Women tend to see intimacy as a *feeling* while men tend to see it as an *action*. Who's right? Both. Intimacy does require action, but those actions must produce the right feelings. Any man who wants his wife to experience feelings of intimacy will help create them by his actions in the foreplay, during the sexual union, and during the afterglow. He, by being attentive in every part of their lovemaking, is building intimacy. Holding, talking, and caressing in a nonsexual way as their wives "relax" during the afterglow are tremendous lovemaking techniques for men to learn. He is helping her relax from her plateau just as gently and expertly as he helped her achieve it. It makes a definite difference in the way the wife responds to him the next time he makes love to her.

Every man should learn to fulfill his wife through her entire sexual cycle. He should start slow, maintain her pleasure, and remain attentive through the afterglow.

SOLOMON'S WIFE SHOWS WOMEN HOW TO BE GREAT LOVERS

Solomon's wife apparently knew how to be a good lover too. She obviously understood that men tend to approach sexual fulfillment both *sensually* and *mentally*. That awareness made her as wonderful a lover for Solomon as he was for her.

Sensual Stimulation

Erotic Appearance

Solomon's wife understood the excitement most men get from sensual stimulation—especially sight, smell, and sound. She made herself beautiful for her husband, creating arousal and longing in him through the appearance of her eyes,[11] hair,[12] teeth,[13] lips,[14] face,[15] neck,[16] and breasts.[17] The descriptions Solomon gives of these aspects of his wife's body make it clear that she knew how to apply cosmetics and how to call attention to her most alluring features. She also used perfumes to stimulate him.[18]

Solomon's wife knew what stimulated her man, and she used every tool at her disposal. Wives of our era should learn from her. There is no shame or embarrassment in making oneself as sexually attractive as possible for one's mate. Wearing stimulating attire (luxurious lingerie, "naughty nighties," or anything that calls attention to a woman's best features) is a wonderful way to broadcast to a husband, "I'm here to give you pleasure." Many husbands today would be just as stimulated and honored by that as was Solomon in his day.

Occasionally a wife in one of our *His Needs, Her Needs* seminars will object to our stating that a man is stimulated by his wife's appearance. Usually the comment is something like, "If my husband really loves me, he won't care what I look like or what I wear. He'll love me in any shape, fashion, or form."

When we hear that, we try to explain that we aren't talking about what a man *should* do or what he *should* be. We're talking about the way men are wired, the way they think and react. We'd all be upset with a husband who left his wife because she wasn't as radiant or alluring at forty as she had been at twenty. No Christian could justify that kind of behavior. But that isn't what we're trying to communicate here. We're not trying to convince a woman that she must be as beautiful as the ex-beauty queen down the street or that it is essential that at her twenty-fifth wedding anniversary she must be able to slip easily into her wedding gown. Society has done enough to make all of us—not just women—feel inadequate because we aren't "Madison-Avenue" beautiful. We won't add to that dilemma. Nor will we ever indicate that our worth or value is tied to physical beauty or charm.

Our point, simply put, is that it surely appears that God made men to be visually stimulated. Men notice the shape of a woman's body, the shine in her hair, and the sparkle in her eye; and they react to those stimuli in positive ways. (Actually, we have pretty good evidence that the fairer sex responds positively to these kinds of things in men as well.) A wise wife knows her husband's visual propensities and caters to it rather than ignoring it.

It wouldn't be right for a husband to say, "I know that you react well to hearing 'I love you,' but that makes me feel hypocritical or unreal to have to say it just because you like to hear it." A comment like that from him would show a complete lack of respect for his wife's feelings. If hearing "I love you" is important to her, he should learn how to say it and to mean it when he does.

In like manner, if a husband is "turned on" by his wife in a low-cut negligée festooned with delicate lace designed to provide provocative glimpses of her thigh, why shouldn't she shop for, purchase, and occasionally wear things like that for him? And if wearing makeup you wouldn't be caught dead in on the street piques his interest, what valid reason would you have for never adorning yourself with it? You can have your own sexy hairstyle just for him, a special perfume that you wear only on sexually provocative occasions (use it only then, and you'll develop a pattern where his heart jumps just at a whiff of the fragrance), and a new alluring outfit to surprise him with. Solomon's wife understood how her doing all that helped make him a better lover.

Provoking sexual desire within your husband isn't lasciviousness. It's love.

What husband wouldn't find himself sexually excited to know that his wife made special effort in dress, makeup, hair style, or perfume to make herself especially attractive to him?

Initiative in Lovemaking

Most men are stimulated when their wives initiate lovemaking. When a man feels that his wife is as interested—sometimes even more interested—in lovemaking as he, he usually responds with great affection for her. She may initiate lovemaking through erotic words, erotic actions, or just by making the environment unusually sexually charged.

Of course, in lovemaking, there is the dimension of giving to the husband what the husband gives to the wife—slow, gentle, all-over lovemaking that pays particular attention to each part of the husband's body. If Solomon made love to his wife "until the shadows flee and the day breaks," it certainly seems valid to assume that she was just as active for just as long in her lovemaking to him.

Mental Stimulation

Appeal to His Need for Praise and Admiration

Solomon's wife also had knowledge of the masculine need for praise and admiration. She told Solomon that he was handsome and charming.[19] She praised the parts of his body she found attractive,[20] telling him that he was "outstanding among ten thousand."[21]

Sexually Charged Language

With her sexually charged words, Solomon's wife inflamed Solomon's desires and enticed him to linger in his lovemaking.[22] (Some of her words were very graphic.[23]) She made it clear that she wanted him, not always waiting for him to initiate sex but making the opening advances herself.[24] She spoke of using aphrodisiacs (people of that era viewed mandrake as an aphrodisiac) and let him know that she had stored them up for his use.[25] She talked sexily and made it clear that she wanted to make love to him.

A wife who understands these concepts stimulates her husband *sensually* by her erotic appearance and by initiating lovemaking, and she stimulates him *mentally* by responding to his need for praise and admiration and by her sexually charged language.

The Basics

Based on all we've studied in this chapter and the one before, the following statements sum up God's view of sex:

- God intends for sex to be *enjoyed* by people married to each other. (Sex isn't just for procreation as with the other animals.)
- God endorses our enjoyment of *every* part of our spouse's body.
- God wants each person in the marriage to *conscientiously fulfill* his or her mate's sexual needs and desires.

Compromise—Overcoming Barriers to Fulfillment

Inevitably when we get to this point in a seminar, someone asks, "What if my spouse wants to do something I don't? Are you saying that I'm wrong not to do it?"

Not necessarily. We believe that the sexual union is spiritual and emotional, as well as physical. When one person carries an inhibition about something, being forced to participate in that activity would inhibit the growth of overall intimacy in the marriage.

For example, what if a woman had been treated terribly by a former husband who continually hurt her physically during sex and damaged her emotionally by constant humiliation? If he finally left her for someone else and she eventually married a wonderful Christian man, she would carry "scars" into the new relationship. Many things that were perfectly permissible for her and her new husband in their sexual union would be difficult for her—not because they were wrong, but because of the negative emotions she would associate with those acts. What's the solution? Does the new husband forever have to forgo certain pleasures because of the sin of the first husband? That isn't fair, is it? Does she have to do whatever the new husband asks, no matter what it does to her emotions and spirit? That isn't fair either, is it?

If we were dealing with that couple (again, not as therapists but as educators), we would strongly recommend they both read the appendix in this book to find biblical principles to help them get beyond past experiences. Then we would recommend that they consider whether they need a marital or sexual therapist. (There are good Christian sex therapists around the nation.) Finally, we would recommend that they adopt a strategy of *compromise*.

Compromise takes place when both mates try to find grounds for agreement as they approach any matter from differing viewpoints. This is especially true about sex. The disagreement could be something as simple as: "Hey, honey, I want to do _____" and the spouse replies, "Not in this lifetime!" Or it could be as complex as the illustration we used just above. Whatever the issue and whatever the level of complexity, the solution may be the same.

Understanding and Acceptance

First, both mates should understand and accept either the desire or hesitation of the other. Sometimes matters can be solved by simply accepting *why* your spouse feels as he or she does, by accepting the other person's "truth."

The hesitant mate needs to accept the truth that the other wants to do something and needs to accept his or her reason. "I've always wanted to" or "I just want to see what it feels like" are valid reasons and should never be discarded as irrelevant or unimportant.

In turn, the requesting mate must also accept the fact that your spouse doesn't want to do a particular thing and must accept his or her reason. "I think that's yucky" or "I don't think I'd like that" are valid reasons and should never be rejected as too selfish or uncaring.

Remember: "When I accept myself as I am, I change. When I accept others as they are, they change." We'll never convince our spouses to abandon their viewpoints or change their actions if we demand that they defend their views or actions. People in defensive postures don't want to change, and if they do, they do it grudgingly.

People who feel accepted can more honestly examine the question at hand and are much more likely to want to please the other.

Prayer

Second, pray for God to solve the problem. Ask Him to give each of you a clear understanding of the other. Ask Him to get each of you past whatever memories, misconceptions, misunderstandings, or hang-ups are causing problems. Ask Him to give you a wonderful, totally uninhibited sex life within the parameters of His boundaries. Ask Him, believing that He will answer.[26]

Fulfill Each Other through Compromise

Make it your unalterable goal to fulfill each other. If your mate wants something that you find uncomfortable, displeasing, or otherwise unpleasant, you should ask yourself if what he or she wants is within the parameters of God. If your spouse desires it and God didn't condemn it, the only barrier to your spouse's fulfillment is you. If you physically cannot do it—if it is impossible—then you won't be able to oblige until you find an available physical remedy. If that remedy is available, you should seek it. For example, if a man is impotent and his wife desires sexual intercourse with him, he cannot deny her based on his impotence. He must seek a cure for his impotency, even if it requires a special apparatus supplied by a physician. His duty is to fulfill his wife, and he cannot deny her that fulfillment without violating biblical commands.

If you can physically comply with your mate's request but are dealing with an emotional barrier, you should seek the remedy to that as well. If a person just finds something distasteful or if he or she carries scars from previous encounters, there is help available. If a counselor, therapist, psychologist, or psychiatrist is needed, the person should seek that help so that any barrier between husband and wife can be removed, removing at the same time any susceptibility to sexual temptation that may come to either spouse from the lack of sexual fulfillment.

A Plan for Compromise

If no professional help is needed, the process becomes one of fulfillment by compromise. Working together, you can make a plan to gradually achieve the requested action—taking as many days, weeks, or months as necessary. Make your plan by delineating specific steps to move you toward the fulfillment of the request. Both of you must agree ahead of time on how often the activity will be participated in after the hesitant person finally can complete that act. It may be that it occurs only once a week or once a month or once a quarter or once a year. The timing must be mutually agreed to.

An Example of Compromise

To illustrate this concept, let's return to the example we used earlier of a wife who had been treated terribly by her first husband. Suppose the second husband requests that she occasionally buy and wear erotic lingerie as part of their lovemaking. She responds that she can't do that because her first husband made her dress and act in ways that made her feel like she was a slut. Just the effort of trying to dress sexily for her new husband would incur those old feelings and destroy her ability to experience true intimacy with him.

Understanding and Acceptance

If her husband pushes the matter—whining or pouting or demeaning her—he will cause her to retreat even further from fulfilling his request. If instead he understands her anguish and accepts it, then she will be more likely to in turn understand his explanation of why it is so important to him, "Honey, I'm a visual person. I get very stimulated by what I see, and I like it when you don't hide your body from me. If I were to see you in a sexy negligée, I would not only be excited by the sight, I would be touched by knowing that you were able to actually do something sexually oriented without feeling shame or degradation. I wish you could do this for me, and I look forward to the day when it can happen."

Their solution would be to find a compromise they would both enjoy.

How?

Prayer

Once they've heard each other out, they should pray. In our example, the husband prays for his wife's healing from her past as she prays for the same. He prays that he will never hurt her as she has been hurt and that God will use him as part of her healing from those emotional scars. He asks for patience that he will not push her too fast or make her retreat from him.

She prays that God will not only remove the scars she carries but that He will make her all that she can be for her loving husband. She prays that God will give her the ability not only to dress sexily for her husband but to enjoy the experience and to feel intimacy with him as she does so. Then they together pray for a plan to make all this happen as God gives them His healing power.

A Plan for Compromise

The next step after prayer would be for the husband to wait until his wife could talk more about the subject, not pushing her but being patient until she could come to that point. She would be putting the pressure on herself to please him rather than reacting to pressure he brought to bear. When ready, she would visit with him about the "stages" for fulfilling his request. Maybe stage one would be that they "window shop" together in lingerie stores for a few weeks as he pointed out what he likes and why he likes it. The next step might be that she actually would buy one of those outfits and wear it some while he's not present, getting used to it and how she looks in it. The final step might be that she would present herself in her new negligée one night. He would know that when she reached that point, he would be very gentle and slow in their lovemaking that night so that she would know that he loves her for herself and that she is pure and holy and beautiful. Once she accomplished that step, she might wear a beautiful negligée at least once a month as she promised back when they worked out their compromise.

If they worked out a compromise like the one we described above rather than drifting apart because of their differing desires or hesitations, they could together fall on their knees and thank God for giving them this unity of heart and bodies.

See how it works?

That simple procedure can and will work for the two of you, no matter what it is that you disagree over in your sex life.

THREE PRIORITIES

As we conclude our brief study of becoming ONE sexually, we point out three priorities that should exist in your sex life together.

#1—Pay Attention to Your Sex Life

Make every effort to keep your sex life healthy. Never forget God's warning in 1 Corinthians 7 about Satan's attack. Sexually unfulfilled people can be tempted through their lack of self-control. Remove that avenue of attack from Satan's forces by keeping your mate thoroughly sexually satisfied!

That means that if you and your mate are on different body clocks—one is a morning person while the other is a night person— you must plan your sex life. It also means that if you and your mate have schedules that don't allow plenty of time together, you must plan your sex life. Don't think that planning makes your sexual encounter less special; it makes it more special!

For example, if a husband came home from work one evening to find that his wife had dispatched the children to other places, filled the house with scented candles, and was leaning against a doorframe in an exotic, sexy outfit while staring at him with unbridled passion, do you think he'd say, "Nope. This is planned. Don't like it that way. Just want spontaneous sex."

When I've used that illustration in seminars and asked how many husbands would enjoy that "planned" scenario, nearly every hand goes up. Enthusiastically.

Planned sex can be wonderful sex. Sex that is just scheduled on a calendar as the next thing on the agenda typically isn't. Planned sex is more than "we'll do that at this time." It's "we'll make this special at this time." So make sex a priority; pay attention to your sex life.

#2—Keep the Bedroom Special

Never argue in the bedroom. Never discipline the children there. Never, ever, pay bills in that room. The bedroom should be for sleeping and lovemaking. Nothing else! Don't let that room be associated with any negative thing in your mind or emotions. If you want sexual intimacy to include emotional intimacy, make your bedroom the most special room in your house.

Teach your children to respect the privacy of that room. Train them from infancy that when that door is shut, parents are spending special time with each other that is not to be violated. If you fear that they may figure out what you're doing in there as they get older, *what better way to teach them healthy attitudes about sex?* They learn to associate sex (although, of course, they shouldn't see or hear anything inappropriate) with love and marriage.

#3—*Make It Your Goal to Be the Best Possible Lover*

Christian bookstores carry books that will teach you more about sex. No matter what your age or level of experience, you can continually learn to be a better lover throughout your lifetime.

Personal Application

1. *Use your intimacy triangle.* As you feel that you experience sexual intimacy to a satisfactory level, use your three dimensional triangle to communicate your satisfaction—or lack of satisfaction—with your mate. Fold the sexual intimacy leg of your model up when you feel sexually satisfied and fold it back down when you don't. Watch to see when your mate's triangle is folded up or down. When you find that your mate's triangle has a side folded down, talk. Find out what's missing, what part of intimacy is going unfulfilled. Then fill it as best you can.

2. *Pray.* Pray for a closer relationship in your spiritual life. Pray for a closer relationship in your emotional life. Pray for the closest relationship any two can have as lovers in your sexual life. God honors those prayers if you honor His commands.

Intimacy is what it's all about—first and last. Intimacy in your marriage in every way for every day of all your lives together.

May God bless you to find it in all its dimensions—spiritually, emotionally, and sexually.

When you and your spouse share deep levels of spiritual intimacy, you've transcended even most good marriages. You've gone beyond. You've reached a level of ONEness few experience but that we were all made to enjoy. (page 180)

◦

Are you afraid of spiritual intimacy because it means there will be nothing within you now that your spouse doesn't see? No part of you he or she doesn't have access to? Everything known? That isn't something to fear but to crave. You will truly become ONE in every sense of the word. (page 192)

◦

If you need to forgive your spouse and feel you can't, hear what we've learned from thousands of couples: You can. Forgiveness isn't an emotion. It's a choice. A series of choices. And if you decide to make those choices, your world—and your marriage—will change forever. (page 198)

◦

When you're ready to remove every inhibition from your marriage—emotional, sexual, or anything else—learn to pray together. (page 203)

Chapter
8

Developing Spiritual Intimacy —As a Couple

Removing Barriers to the Deepest Level of Intimacy

If it weren't happening to me, I think I would have found it comical. Several ladies circled me like rented Indians in an old Hollywood movie, each in turn firing a flurry of verbal darts at me—and I didn't have a single wagon wheel behind which to hide. I didn't even have a quick-witted rejoinder to defend myself with or, at the very least, to use to clear a path for escape. As it was, all I could do was spin from one to the other, mumbling things like, "Yeah, you're right" and "Uh-huh, I see what you mean." Unfortunately, those were *not* the words they wanted to hear. What they wanted were answers, and they wanted them *now*.

I hate getting flayed in the church foyer, don't you?

These agitated sisters had just left a ladies' class where the teacher had rightly insisted that every Christian home should have regular devotionals involving the whole family. Driving her point home, the teacher dramatically ended her class by leaning over the lectern and lashing out at their husbands, regardless of the fact that none of them were there to hear her rebuke. "If your husband won't lead that devotional, guiding you and your children in spiritual matters, he is *failing* in his duty before God and *failing* you and your children in the most important matter of your lives! Go to him immediately and *demand* that he stand up as the spiritual leader of your home and *demand* that he start tonight!"

The class rallied to the call and adamantly agreed that this sinful behavior of their negligent husbands had to stop immediately! Fired up, these sisters solemnly spilled through the classroom door intently engaged in determined discussion as to how to bring their husbands into line. Unfortunately for me, they didn't go to their husbands as directed. Instead, they waylaid me in the foyer.

From the cacophony of voices assaulting me, I deciphered the general meaning of their concern. *"You're* supposed to make marriages better. What are *you* going to do to motivate our husbands to fulfill their God-given responsibilities to us and our children? We've talked about this among ourselves. We're tired of asking them to pray with us, lead us in home Bible studies, and teach our children the ways of God. They have a million and one excuses, and we're not asking anymore. So *you* have to do it. You have to get them to do what God told them to do.

"What are you going to do to get our husbands involved in the spiritual lives of our families?"

At that point in my own study of intimacy, I wasn't at all sure that their request fit within Family Dynamics's mission, although I could understand their dilemma. I reassured them as much as I could, clucked my tongue and wagged my head in dismay over the spiritually insensitive men to whom they were married, and escaped with my scalp generally intact. I was happy to get away. I'm not sure they would've let me go unscathed if they'd thought to ask me how often I prayed with my wife and taught my children in the ways of God. I kept up a good front but felt a twinge of guilt for my own marriage as I listened to their laments.

As much as I taught people around the world about Jesus, I'd fairly well left it to Alice to teach our children, and I couldn't remember the last time she and I had prayed together, except at the beginning of a meal. Part of me wanted to pass off the insistence I heard from these ladies as teacher-generated fervor that would fade in a week or two. But I couldn't. How could anyone deny the intensity on their faces and the pleading of their hearts? They really *wanted* to be married to men who are spiritual leaders in their homes.

As they left me and went to collect their children from classes before the worship service began, I wondered if Alice felt the same about me as these sisters did about their husbands—if she thought that I was failing in my duty as a spiritual leader in my home. I wondered, but I hadn't the courage to ask her. Deep within myself I knew the answer, and I didn't want the hurt of hearing her say it.

Gradually, as I continued to learn about intimacy and all its components, I came to realize that what these ladies requested is vitally needed within marriages and, therefore, a valid goal for Family Dynamics. I'm ashamed to admit that when we interacted in the foyer, I didn't give their concerns much credence. I knew my wife and children were doing very well spiritually and couldn't see what the big deal was about a special time for my input in shared devotionals, Bible study, and prayer. My children were learning the wonderful truths of God in Bible classes taught by capable teachers. We all went to church together, worked on church projects together, and went out of our way to do good deeds for people. I thought this was enough. I didn't understand my wife's or daughters' needs for bondedness, closeness, and warmth with me in spiritual matters. I was yet to learn that warmth and closeness in its ultimate sense could come only when we shared our thoughts and feelings together in a more intimate setting—through shared Bible study, prayer, and discussion of spiritual matters. Developing spiritual intimacy means talking, listening, and understanding. Without that, neither my wife nor my daughters could ever feel the level of spiritual intimacy with me they wanted.

As I admitted earlier in this book, Alice and I had a decent marriage and were being used by God as effective servants in the kingdom, but I was coming to understand that neither Alice nor I would ever overcome our periodic struggles until we developed complete intimacy. *Real* emotional intimacy, *real* sexual intimacy, and *real* spiritual intimacy. Those ladies helped set me on the path to learning that spiritual intimacy is crucial to ONEness. And that awareness slowly started revolutionizing our marriage.

I pray that it revolutionizes yours as well. It will, if you truly grasp the significance of spiritual intimacy and are willing to take steps to attain it.

Complete ONEness must include seeking God *together*. That may sound simplistic to you, but it was a major awakening for me when the concept morphed from a "stained-glass statement" to a crucial, foundational truth. When we at Family Dynamics tried to incorporate this idea into our marriage seminars, we quickly discovered that understanding the significance of spiritual intimacy and knowing how to grow it in a marriage are *not* the same thing. In order to teach couples how to become ONE spiritually, we had to discover why so many spouses fail in this particular area of marital life.

As we analyzed marriage situations we've worked with, we noted that more often it is the wife who feels the need for spiritual union and the husband who is disinterested in the spiritual dimension of their relationship. Of course there are exceptions: Sometimes the husband craves spiritual intimacy with his wife while the wife refuses to invest in spiritual ONEness. But the vast majority of situations we encounter involve a godly woman married to a man—often a godly man—who won't pray with her, study the Bible with her, or teach their children the ways of God. Whether the problem lies with the husband, the wife, or both, the path to spiritual ONEness is the same: (1) the couple must analyze why spiritual intimacy between them doesn't exist, (2) they must remove spiritual barriers, and (3) they must make a plan to bring both of them to spiritual intimacy.

WHY SPIRITUAL INTIMACY DOESN'T EXIST

To help you understand why spiritual intimacy doesn't exist in many marriages, we'll share with you three of the things we've encountered in couples that lack spiritual intimacy: *spiritual lethargy, misplaced priorities*, and *fear of openness*.

Spiritual Lethargy

When spiritual lethargy occurs, it isn't because one or both spouses believe they don't need spiritual intimacy. Usually both partners say they see the value of developing spiritual intimacy, but one (sometimes both) just doesn't seem to be able to pull together the energy to make it happen.

Cecil tried to explain, "Look, Joe, I agree that it would be a wonderful thing to sit down with my kids and teach 'em about the Bible, or just to have quality prayer time with my wife. But when I get home, I'm dead tired. I get up early—five in the morning—and I go wide open from can to can't. I work like a proverbial Trojan all day long. When I get home, it's all I can do to make it to the sofa. I crash there while Margaret finishes supper, and when she calls me I drag myself to the washroom to clean up a little and then drag myself to the table. Now, don't think that makes me totally selfish. I want to know all about the kids' lives, so we spend dinnertime askin' 'em what happened at school, how their little buddies are, and things like that.

"After supper I help Margaret clear the table and get things into the dishwasher. Then it's a little TV just to rest the bones and soothe the brain. After that, we get the kids to bed. And after they're asleep, maybe—if we're not too tired—a chance to make love to each other every once in a while. Now, just tell me when, with all that going on, do I have time for a family devotional?

"Teach my kids? Pray with my wife? I'm lucky if I even get through my own prayer before I fall asleep. I gotta go to bed early, you know. Five A.M., and I start all over again."

Cecil makes it sound as if asking him to pray with his wife or teach his children a Bible story is totally beyond the boundaries of possibility, doesn't he? Before you agree with him, listen to Margaret's side of the story.

"I know Cecil works hard, and I appreciate that with all my heart. But I work hard too: keeping up the house, taking care of two kids in grammar school, being involved with PTA, and then there's hauling them to ballet and soccer. On top of all that, all day long I follow behind my youngest, who can run around enough to get into everything but isn't yet old enough to be potty-trained. When I get supper on the table, I'm about as bushed as Cecil.

"But after supper, he just sits in front of the TV. He gets home at six, we eat at six-thirty, and he's in front of the screen wearing out the remote control from about seven till he comes up for the kids' last good-night kiss a little before nine. Then he's in bed watching TV till he falls asleep sometime around ten.

"Unless, of course, he's feeling a little frisky. Then he might make it to ten-thirty.

"The kids have all their homework done by the time Cecil gets home. He has at least two hours in the evening where he could teach them a Bible story or pray with us or something. It wouldn't have to be every day. Even once a week would be a wonderful change! And I know he could pray with me after the kids are asleep instead of watching that last program from our bed. I just don't think he cares enough about it to do it. He claims he's tired...I think he's just spiritually lazy."

Which would it be in Cecil's case? Fatigue or failure? Is he spiritually lethargic?

Responsibilities of Fathers and Mothers

If a man has a responsibility to be the spiritual leader of his home, then the answer has to be that indeed Cecil *is* spiritually lethargic and, therefore, failing his wife and children. Even if Cecil takes his family to church and teaches his children by example to serve God by serving others, he fails to fulfill what God requires. God commands *both* father and mother to spiritually develop their children, and that means more than church: It means giving true spiritual guidance.

Consider just a few scriptures to see how intent God is about the responsibilities of a father and mother to create a spiritual home.

- A father encourages, comforts, and urges his children to live godly lives: "For you know that we dealt with each of you as a father deals with his own children, encouraging, comforting and urging you to live lives worthy of God, who calls you into his kingdom and glory."[1]

- A father brings up his children in the nurture and admonition of the Lord: "Fathers, do not exasperate your children; instead, bring them up in the training and instruction of the Lord."[2]

- A father commands and a mother teaches: "My son, keep your father's commands and do not forsake your mother's teaching."[3]

- A father also instructs as the mother teaches: "Listen, my son, to your father's instruction and do not forsake your mother's teaching."[4]

- A father directs his children and his *household* (that includes his wife—his children's mother) to keep the way of the Lord:

"For I have chosen him, so that he will direct his children and his household after him to keep the way of the LORD by doing what is right and just, so that the LORD will bring about for Abraham what he has promised him."[5]

The kinds of things God teaches us to do in the above scriptures require the three elements of intimacy that we discussed in chapter 3: *communication* (sharing, telling), *time* (quantitative and qualitative), and *action*. When parents practice these elements with their children, they transfer the love of God from their hearts to the hearts of their children. God said it even more clearly in other passages: "Only be careful, and watch yourselves closely so that you do not forget the things your eyes have seen or let them slip from your heart as long as you live. Teach them to your children and to their children after them."[6] And He said, "These commandments that I give you today are to be upon your hearts. Impress them on your children. Talk about them when you sit at home and when you walk along the road, when you lie down and when you get up."[7]

While God made it clear that the primary responsibility for building faith in children fell to the father, clearly mothers played a crucial role. "I have been reminded of your sincere faith, which first lived in your grandmother Lois and in your mother Eunice and, I am persuaded, now lives in you also."[8]

After examining the overwhelming preponderance of scripture requiring a man to help his wife and children develop spiritually, we must conclude that Cecil—or any other husband who lets that task fall primarily to his wife, his kids' Sunday school teachers, or anyone else—is abdicating his God-given responsibility. He can claim fatigue all he wishes, but lying motionless (except for the thumb on the remote) before a TV is nothing less than spiritual lethargy. If he had a major project due at work, he wouldn't be in front of the TV but slaving on his home computer or working overtime down at the factory. If he can find time to work more, he most certainly can find time to be the spiritual leader of his home.

Responsibilities of Childless Couples

If you read the above and thought, "Whew, you really stuck it to fathers and mothers! I'm glad we don't have children so you can't use those scriptures on us!" think again. While God addressed Himself directly to homes where children lived, He holds similar expectations for childless homes. Just as the father has the final responsibility for ministering spiritually to his children, so a husband has responsibility for ministering spiritually to his wife. Paul wrote that Jesus died for His church—His bride—so that He could make her holy, clean, radiant, blameless, and without stain or wrinkle. As he described the love Jesus holds for His bride, spiritually leading her to God, he said that husbands should love their wives in just the same way.[9] It makes no difference if children live in the home or not, God gave husbands the responsibility to spiritually develop their families—wife as well as children.

Does that mean, then, that husbands must overcome spiritual lethargy but wives mustn't? No. Peter spoke to wives just as strongly as Paul spoke to husbands. Peter told wives that they should spiritually impact their husbands by their godly behavior, purity, reverence, and the "unfading beauty of a gentle and quiet spirit."[10] He said that wives who live in this spiritual fashion may "win over" their husbands to Jesus. They have a responsibility to their husbands just as their husbands do to them.

No Excuse

For husband or wife, father or mother, there simply is no excuse. If you can make time in your life for other matters you feel important—a soccer match, a round of golf, watching TV—you can and must make time to spiritually develop your home. Not only does your spiritual lethargy potentially put members of your family at risk—particularly your children—it also keeps you and your mate from achieving the most wonderful kind of intimacy—spiritual intimacy.

Misplaced Priorities

As some read the above section they thought, "Yeah. I see what you mean, but what you're writing doesn't apply to us. We don't watch TV. I haven't played golf in three years. We're not spiritually lethargic people, we really do have time problems! Don't you know that in homes where both husband and wife work there just isn't time to sit and talk, much less time to study our Bibles together and pray? Haven't you heard of business trips, deadlines, and shift work? Get real; not everyone who doesn't grow together spiritually is spiritually lethargic. Some of us really can't make the time to do what you say we should do."

If the above sentiment characterizes you, welcome to the world of the twenty-first century. Remember how in the sixties experts predicted that with the exponential growth of computers and an increasingly mechanized world, we'd soon have too much leisure time and would need sociological studies to figure how to use it to our best advantage? Really. Newsmagazine articles fretted over how all that extra time and lack of activity would affect our psyches, health, morals, and family units.

What happened?

We could cite all sorts of theories, studies, postulations, and the like, but maybe we'd do just as well to get right to the point: The problem is *misplaced priorities*. If you say that your work and life allow no time for a spiritual life with your spouse or children, we respond by asking what your priorities are.

In our current world the paradigm is clear: Most anyone can find "success" if he or she is willing to drop everything at a moment's notice for the sake of work. Overtime? We're there because we like that money or because we want to prove we're a team player who should be moved steadily up the ladder of success. Travel? Where do you want us to go, and when do you want us there? Long hours? Put us on salaries, and we'll be here from early till late. Family time? Well, maybe this weekend if the company doesn't need us.

Face it. We can choose our families, or we can choose our companies. Only one can have top priority—even if we own our own company or work for some nonprofit organization that serves mankind, like a church. If we want spiritual union with God, we must place Him first in our lives. If we want spiritual union with our spouses and children, they must come next—not our work, no matter how important it is, and certainly not the almighty dollar.

Misplaced priorities come in many forms—two of them being *greed* and *self-gratification*.

Greed

Free enterprise and the American way are wonderful. Money and success are pleasing rewards for good work. But what we're discussing goes beyond that. It's greed for more and more and more. More money, a higher position, more fame, greater recognition. Never enough. Always something beyond. This isn't the American dream; it's pure, unadulterated, sinful greed—a greed that places God and family second to the ambitions of the seeker.

I actually heard a man who purported to be a Christian address a sales force with these words, "Greed is good! You have to want money, and you have to go after it with all your might. To do that you have to fake it until you make it! When I first started in sales, my kids had to wear hand-me-downs because we used our money to buy me expensive suits. We lived in a small house located in an undesirable neighborhood because I needed to use our money to drive an expensive car. My family ate hamburger while I took my clients out for steak. But that's what it takes in this world. You gotta dress the part, act the part, and do what it takes to impress. Now we're rich, and my kids have everything they want! Well, actually, my kids are all grown now, but they know I've got the money to help them when they need help! I'm telling all of you to do the same thing. Go home and tell your spouses and kids that they'll just have to tough it out for a while and that they shouldn't complain or think it unfair that you get the best of everything. Someday they'll thank you for it!"

It so happened that I was the number one salesperson for the company he addressed. Sitting next to me in the meeting was the number two salesperson, Lance Cooper, a dear friend who is also a brother in Christ. We looked at each other, got up without a word, went to our hotel rooms, and changed to blue jeans and loafers. We returned to the room full of suits, shiny shoes, and expensive jewelry and retook our seats. We wanted everyone to know that our wives and our children would never come after our desire to become rich. We, as Christians, wouldn't "fake" anything but would live in total honesty and sincerity. We made sure that everyone, including the head of our organization, understood just what our priorities were.

Far too many Christians with glazed eyes and stressed nerves fall prey to the same spiritual corruption to which King Solomon succumbed. They get caught up in the race—the drive to succeed, win, or maintain—and they sacrifice everything for it. Time and again I've tried to comfort deluded believers when they reach the point in their lives when they realize that in the pursuit they lost everything of value to them—their children, their spouses, a lifetime of missed events and neglected opportunities that can never, ever be reclaimed.

When will we learn the truth that eluded Solomon most of his life, leading him to misery and frustration?

> When I surveyed all that my hands had done and what I had toiled to achieve, everything was meaningless, a chasing after the wind; nothing was gained under the sun.[11]

So I hated life, because the work that is done under the sun was grievous to me. All of it is meaningless, a chasing after the wind. I hated all the things I had toiled for under the sun, because I must leave them to the one who comes after me.[12]

And I saw that all labor and all achievement spring from man's envy of his neighbor. This too is meaningless, a chasing after the wind. The fool folds his hands and ruins himself. Better one handful with tranquillity than two handfuls with toil and chasing after the wind.

Again I saw something meaningless under the sun: There was a man all alone; he had neither son nor brother. There was no end to his toil, yet his eyes were not content with his wealth. "For whom am I toiling," he asked, "and why am I depriving myself of enjoyment?" This too is meaningless—a miserable business![13]

When I read those verses, my heart breaks because many people we work with through Family Dynamics have become just like Solomon in his early life; they are striving for the golden ring and haven't yet become aware of the cost of the ride.

"Yeah," you say, "it's easy to disparage the pursuit of success when you have money and a place to live. What happens when you lose all that? Can you really be happy without money?"

Absolutely.

When Alice and I divorced, I tried a business in Birmingham, Alabama, that I knew nothing about. Foolishly I invested everything into my effort to become rich. Without boring you with all the details, I'll tell you that I lost every cent I had and found myself hundreds of thousands of dollars in debt. I had no place to live, nothing to eat, and nowhere to go. My life spiraled into the pits of evil degradation in every way—financially, morally, spiritually, and emotionally. When I was at the very bottom with no place to turn and nothing to comfort me except a bottle of liquor and a handful of pills, I finally looked up and saw, as it were, God watching. Like Solomon, I finally understood, "Meaningless! Meaningless!...Everything is meaningless!... here is the conclusion of the matter: Fear God and keep his commandments, for this is the whole duty of man."[14]

I, and thousands like me, can tell you with all assurance that in the overall scheme of life, money *is* meaningless. If you have enough to stay warm and dry, to feed your stomach, and to care for your family, you have enough. Boats, cars, mansions, and other material manifestations are fine, and it's wonderful to have them. If God blesses you with money and success, buy all you want as long as you do it as a good steward. But don't sacrifice your life—and especially don't sacrifice your family—to get more money! You sin if you love money, your business, your notoriety, or your ministry more than you love your God and your family.

Success? Meaningless. It won't hug you close at night when you dread being alone or hold your hand lovingly and kiss your brow gently as you die. Prestige? Meaningless. Only a handful of people makes it into the history books, and they usually don't even live to know about it! Power? Meaningless. What good is it to be able to direct thousands of people and be waited on hand and foot when you aren't sure whether people love you for yourself or for what you can do for them?

Alice and I have more money, a nicer house, better cars, and more influence now than at any point in our lives. But we don't care; those things are not important to us, and we won't sacrifice our lives with each other or our children to maintain what we have. We've been poor, we've been hungry, and we've been castaways. We know the reality of life: Once you've lost everything, you discover that it's all meaningless. You just don't need it for wholeness or happiness. You learn that all that matters is God above, the person who can and should be your soul mate through life, and the children you cherish.

When desire for success, prestige, preserving your business, building your church, material goods, or just plain riches interferes with your spiritual growth and the spiritual obligation you have to your family's growth, you've gone too far. Watch out, because that misguided focus will take you from all that you hold dear.[15] "Keep your lives free from the love of money and be content with what you have, because God has said, 'Never will I leave you; never will I forsake you.'"[16]

Self-Gratification

"But, wait," you may cry, "what if it isn't money or greed that drives me but the importance of what I do? I work for an organization that serves people, and it doesn't pay much; so don't accuse me of sacrificing my family for money!"

Okay. We won't. But may we ask if you would sacrifice your own spouse or children for your sense of fulfillment in helping others? We've met far too many church officers, counselors, medical doctors, and the like who were driven by their need to help, to heal, and to nourish the needs of humankind but who didn't feel the same call to minister to their own families. We've talked with embittered adults who still carry great hurt and anger over a minister father who was always someplace else serving some other person and never had enough time for his own children. We've seen wives who left philanthropic husbands whose charity didn't begin or end at home. We've seen husbands emotionally distance themselves from social-minded wives whose focus was on every worthwhile project in their community except for the most worthwhile of all: loving their husbands at home.[17]

May we be as brutally honest with you as we are with those who were driven by greed for money or fame or power? If you neglect your family for some good work—even a godly work—you, too, seek the wrong goal. You cannot honestly justify your neglect of your own family by claiming that God called you to minister to others. He never told anyone to abandon the greatest responsibility of all—the one to our own spouses and children—to do good for someone else. You minister first to your own, then to others.[18] Therefore, if you claim your neglect to spiritually and emotionally fulfill your spouse or children is because of your godliness, we reply that it is much more likely to be your own need for self-gratification. Somehow, something within you is nurtured by your service, and that's what really drives you. If you were truly selfless you'd serve your husband or wife or children— people who typically can't offer you fame, accolades, or paragraphs in the annals of history.

You can make time for your spouse, to talk *and* to study and pray, if you wish. It just takes deciding what is most important in your life.

I know.

I had to face this sin in myself and beg my wife and my children to forgive me for neglecting them too many times because some other priority took precedence. From this point on, they will be the most important part of my life, just behind God. I would have never neglected them for money, but I did for ministry. The sin is the same, no matter what the motive.

What choice do you make about your family?

Fear of Openness

Perhaps the greatest reason that one person won't study or pray with another is because he or she fears being open and vulnerable in the presence of the other. When we bow or kneel before God to pray, really pray, we remove every barrier behind which we hide. Sure, it's true that a person could offer a ritualistic prayer that required no openness at all, like "Now I lay me down to sleep...." We've heard those kinds of prayers in church and before meals all our lives. The head bows, the mouth opens, the recital rolls through the room, and the prayer is done. Any two people could pray like that with each other and have no fear of anything.

But when prayer is a pouring out of our lives and hearts to God, we sometimes have to speak of things that we don't want others to hear. We confess to God the failings and faults with which we struggle. We beg Him for things we can't accomplish ourselves. We tell Him not only what we've done but how we feel about what we've done. Sometimes we even tell Him what we *want* to do, begging Him to prevent us from doing it.

No spouse could pray like that before the other if he or she isn't already living an honest life. The fear of openness is accentuated by at least two things—*shame* and *sin*.

The Effects of Shame

I remember when I first wanted to pray openly with Alice. I had to struggle with the paradox of wanting to grow spiritually with her while at the same time knowing that if anyone on earth knows everything that is bad about me or weak within me, it is Alice. As I struggled through the process of finding the courage to ask her to pray with me, I was hesitant because I knew she'd seen me do so many sinful things. She's seen me shout with anger, act like a selfish buffoon, and lapse occasionally into a hundred other things that a Christian ought not do. It is difficult enough for me when she's in the congregation hearing me preach, because she knows where I fail in my service to God; but praying with her—praising, asking, and confessing—was just too much. I felt this overwhelming dread that surely she'd sit with head bowed and think what a hypocrite I am, wondering what God must think when He hears the prayers of someone as flawed as me.

For me, and perhaps for you, the primary barrier that prevented me from developing spiritual intimacy with my wife wasn't spiritual lethargy or even my occasional misappropriation of priorities. It was shame: fear that she would laugh derisively at me, reject me, or ridicule me.

Don't misunderstand; Alice isn't that kind of person. I hope I'm making it clear that the problem didn't lie with her; it was altogether mine. I wanted the admiration and respect of my wife, but I inwardly feared that because she knows all about me, there must be some secret place within her where she couldn't respect me at all. Trying to lead her spiritually could only reinforce her disgust with me. Praying openly about things I occasionally struggle with might even lead her to finally wash her hands of me.

The only reason I share my struggle so openly with you is that my experience with people, particularly men, confirms that the same dread and fear lives in many of them. Their wives can ask forever about praying together and reading and meditating on the Word together, and these guys will always have an excuse: "Too tired." "Got to go." "Not right now." The list is endless. No matter how frustrated she becomes or how much she cajoles, he refuses to participate. Though she doesn't realize it, the more she pushes, the harder he resists, feeling pressured to be more godly than he believes himself to be. "If I already feel like a hypocrite, a spiritual failure, what am I gonna feel like when she finds out I don't know how to pray or don't know how to understand Scripture? I know she wants this, but I just can't do it."

Again, remember: This isn't only a "man thing." Some women feel it too.

The Effects of Sin

Sin is another factor that causes fear of openness. If a spouse is sinning with or against his or her spouse, the problem magnifies exponentially. A man who convinces his wife to watch pornographic movies with him won't feel right about praying with her either before or after. A woman who continually rips into her husband's self-esteem with jibes, insults, or curses won't end a vicious tirade with "And now, let us pray," unless she's being cruelly sarcastic. A couple who knowingly steals money on their tax returns isn't likely to bow together in prayer the night after they file their taxes and piously ask God to keep them from temptation. A husband or wife who has just lied about something important in their relationship can't take the hand of the other and pray openly to the God who just witnessed that lie.

A Call to Acceptance and Honesty before God

Praying with or studying the Bible with one's spouse calls for complete acceptance of each other so that shame is not a factor, and it calls for two hearts that are honestly seeking to please God and leave sin behind. If either lacks or *thinks* he or she lacks these attributes, that spouse won't work to develop a spiritual life with the other. Most people just can't live with that kind of hypocrisy.

REMOVING BARRIERS TO SPIRITUAL INTIMACY

What, then, can a couple do to start developing a spiritual life together?

If spiritual lethargy, misplaced priorities, or fear of openness prevents their spiritual union, the first step is to deal with those barriers.

Removing Spiritual Lethargy

If you are spiritually lethargic, the solution is simple. Make a schedule of when and how you will work on your spiritual life together and then get a couple of good books for family devotionals. Your church likely has some. If they don't, your local Christian bookstore most certainly will. Tell the clerk what level of study you want to do (children present, just adults, the level of Bible knowledge of those adults), and ask what he or she can recommend. Start with once a week: Turn the TV off, make sure all homework is done, remove the phone from the hook, and put a note on the door telling potential visitors you're not to be disturbed. For the next hour or so, you'll have a wonderful time of study and prayer. Then, reserve another time, at least twice a week, when just you and your spouse pray together without your children present. We'll tell you more in a few pages about how to do that.

Rearranging Misplaced Priorities

If you have trouble finding time for Bible study and prayer with your family, it's time to rearrange your priorities. That might take awhile, but it can be done. Set a goal date for yourself, and by that date, set aside a regular night of the week when your *whole* family will be home to study and pray together. You may have to rearrange your work—you may even have to find another job!—but it will be worth it. The closeness you will gain with your spouse and children—the spiritual intimacy—will bless you for the rest of your life and change all of you for eternity. Once you've made the schedule, follow the suggestions of the previous paragraph about how to begin.

Dispelling the Fear of Openness

If you fear being viewed as a hypocrite because shame or sin stands as a barrier between you and your spouse, you must start at a different place. If you'll faithfully work through the following six steps, you will find that spiritual intimacy can be yours.

Step 1. We recommend that you buy and read together *Forgiven Forever.*[19] This book will show you how to remove guilt that God doesn't want you to feel. Before you read it, buy two colored markers, a blue one for the husband and a pink one for the wife. Whenever the husband reads the book, he highlights in blue those things he feels important, things that speak to him. When the wife reads, she does the same thing in pink. That way each can later look back at the chapter and discover what is important to the other. If both of you think something important, the blue and pink will combine to make a light purple color. After reading each chapter, discuss it. Talk honestly about the biblical truths it teaches. Talk even more honestly about how it applies to you personally.

As you talk, strive to do these two things:

1. *Honestly share with your spouse* any guilt, hypocrisy, or fear of rejection that you feel. Tell him or her any hesitation you have about sharing yourself honestly and why you have that hesitation. Share as honestly and openly as you can.

2. *Reassure your spouse*—if you can do so honestly—of your acceptance of him or her. When appropriate, tell of your forgiveness. Share what you feel about his or her spirituality. You've already had practice with that from earlier chapters in this book. Now is your chance to help your spouse *believe* you accept and understand him or her. If you want spiritual closeness, this is the place to start.

If you can't or don't want to purchase *Forgiven Forever*, try the same exercise just by sharing what's on your heart about your fears.

Step 2. If there is any sin in your life—angry outbursts, pornography, mistreatment of your spouse, lying, stealing, an unconfessed affair, or whatever—now is the time to confess it to your spouse if you haven't done so already. For example, if you have pornography in the house—even porn you may have watched or read together—tell your spouse that you sinned by bringing it in and you want her or him to forgive you. If you've been difficult to live with, confess your haughty or angry or bitter spirit. Whatever the sin, confess it.

Step 3. If there is any physical dimension to your sin, destroy it or return it. For example, if you have pornography in the house, burn it, cut it to pieces, or in some way render it unusable, and then throw it away. Don't return that kind of stuff; make it so that no one can be influenced by it again ever. On the other hand, if you've stolen money from someone, give it back. We are saying that you must *do* whatever needs to be done to complete the confession. Talk is often cheap. Actions prove the validity of your words.

Step 4. If your spouse confesses sin to you, *forgive.* You may hear something you don't want to forgive, but by the grace and mercy of God, try to forgive anyway. For example, a confession like the following will be very hard to take: "Honey, I need to tell you something that I can't hide anymore. It's eating me alive, and I need to get it clear between us. You know when you suspected I was getting too close to _____? Well, you were right, I, ah, I, well, I didn't want for it to happen but...we slept together." If you were to hear something like that, you would undoubtedly reel under the shock of the confession, even if you suspected the sin. While you would have the option to kick your spouse out, divorce him or her, and start looking for someone else, we beg you not to do that but instead to forgive.

In chapter 5 we pointed out that forgiveness has two essential steps and one optional step. We remind you of those steps here and ask you to do all three.

- *Assign your mate value again.* Decide not to view him or her as evil or corrupt or any such thing. View him or her as a flawed human who did a wrong thing—a flawed human who is still important, loveable, and valuable, a person you can live with and build a better future with.

- *Decide not to take vengeance.* Don't even *think* about what you can do to hurt in return, much less *do* anything like that. Decide that what's done is done and that you won't harm yourself emotionally or spiritually by trying to repay your spouse for what he or she has done.

- *Decide to develop your relationship.* This is the optional step that isn't required to fulfill biblical forgiveness but is required if you want to make your marriage what it can be. Once you choose to assign value to your spouse, even though he or she has hurt you, and to forgo any vengeance, you *can* work together to develop wonderful intimacy. We've witnessed hundreds of couples who have done this after unbelievably harmful things happened to their marriage.

Whatever the sin your spouse confesses, we beg you to forgive for several reasons.

1. *Reacting with forgiveness to confessed sin sets the stage for true intimacy like few other things can.* If your spouse confesses a sin to you, there can only be two motives. Either he or she is trying to hurt you, or he or she is trying to remove a barrier between you. We've seen people maliciously throw an affair or some other awful sin into the face of their spouses just to rip into them emotionally. That's evil, and the results are devastating. But let's assume that your spouse isn't doing that (you'll know if he or she has that as a motive by the way they do it) and genuinely wants to restore intimacy with you, removing the barrier of his or her guilt and unconfessed sin. If ever in your life you've had a clear shot at the path to complete intimacy, it is now. Your mate has laid him- or herself bare before you, giving you complete control of his or her future. If you choose to forgive, you and your spouse can step into a new level of intimacy. Sin is heinous, but the opportunity presented by confessed sin is tremendous.

2. *God desires that Christians forgive*, even when the sin committed against us hurts terribly. Jesus forgave those who crucified Him.[20] He told us that God won't forgive us if we don't forgive others.[21] He said that we will be judged in the same way that we judge others.[22] And He demanded of us a level of forgiveness that can come only as He gives us the grace to do it. He said, "If your brother sins, rebuke him, and if he repents, forgive him. If he sins against you seven times in a day, and seven

times comes back to you and says, 'I repent,' forgive him. The apostles said to the Lord, 'Increase our faith!' "[23]

3. *Jesus can and will give you the faith to forgive*—just as the apostles begged in the previous verse. We've witnessed people forgiving mates of anything and everything you can imagine. Affairs? Yes. Drunkenness? Yes. Child abuse? Even that. I specifically remember one man whose wife and daughters forgave him of that sin. He'd come to his senses and told his wife *and* the authorities what he'd done. They placed him in prison for a period of time, but they also got him the help he needed to overcome the sin. I asked his wife if she forgave him, and she, with tear-filled eyes, said yes. I then asked the daughters if they forgave him, and they replied that they did too. Naturally they all had to practice certain precautions to ensure that recurring temptation could never place the daughters in jeopardy of any kind, but the marriage and family survived. Personally I can think of no greater sin than child abuse—not even murder—yet I saw Christianity practiced on superhuman levels by that wife and those daughters. Only God can make that happen, and because they were willing to forgive, God rescued them all, bringing them back into holy intimacy.

Step 5. If you are the confessing spouse, be prepared to answer all questions honestly, without hesitation or complaint. When any partner has been sinned against, it takes time for trust and respect to rebuild. I learned that principle when Alice and I remarried. To rebuild her trust, I told her I would honestly answer any question she asked—no matter what—but I also told her, "Make sure you want to know what you ask, because I cannot 'untell' you." You can imagine how hard it was for me and for her as she asked specific questions about those three years we were apart, wanting to know names and places and details. After asking numerous questions that brought great pain to each of us, she finally knew that I'd hide nothing from her. Then, and only then, could she begin to trust me again. As soon as she knew that any information was hers for the asking, she stopped asking altogether. She didn't really want to know all I'd done; she just wanted to know that I wouldn't lie to her ever again about anything—no matter how much it would hurt me to tell her. So, if you are the confessing spouse, tell the truth. All the truth. Don't volunteer any details your spouse doesn't ask for—don't bring unnecessary pain—but hide nothing.

Step 6. Each of you should vow to each other that from this point on you will do your best to live the Christian life. We know that temptations come and that you will never reach sinless perfection, but your pledge to each other is to try. In order to follow through with this step, it is *essential* that each willingly submits to accountability to the other, reacting neither with aggravation nor self-pity when asked about holiness.

Several years ago a preacher came to me and confessed his struggle with going to pornographic peep shows. He nervously pulled at his tie and mopped continually at a cascade of sweat pouring from his forehead. Trying to look me in the eye but having too much shame to hold back his scalding tears, he told me how he'd stop into some "adult store" and feed quarter after quarter into machines that played hardcore porn. Telling me was the toughest thing he'd ever done in his life, but he needed help and didn't know what else to do. When he finished his confession, he asked, "What do I do? How do I stop?"

"Go home and tell your wife," I replied.

I'm sure he had to throw his tie away after our visit; he continued using it to mop the flood from his forehead. "What? Are you crazy?! If I tell her, she'll kill me!"

"Well, that'll stop you," I dryly replied.

For a moment, he didn't know if I was serious or not. During his confused pause, I continued, "Tell her. She won't kill you, and she won't leave you. I know her, and I know she's gonna be hurt. She'll cry and talk about how ugly she is and how if she were prettier or sexier or younger or whatever you wouldn't do this. Of course, when she goes through all that self-recrimination, you have to reassure her that it's not her fault at all but a spiritual flaw in you. When she gets over the hurt, she'll forgive you. She's not going to destroy you or your home. But I'll guarantee you there's some things she will do: She'll want to know where you're going every time you go anywhere for the next year or so. She'll ask time, places, people you saw, and everything else. She'll start counting your money to see if you're spending any in unusual ways. She'll ask you directly if you're looking at that stuff again. And *every* time she does any of that, you'll hug her and reassure her and thank her. You will *never,* no matter how long it takes, show any aggravation or self-pity. Never. You understand?"

He numbly nodded his head in the affirmative, so I sent the shell-shocked sinner on his way. "Call me after you tell her so I can know how things are going. Okay?"

He nodded again and shuffled to his car. I've never seen a man walking death row to his execution, but I think his facial expression and body language must be similar to what this guy's were as he headed to his car. He was too overwhelmed and too disgusted with himself to do anything but what I told him, but he was sure I was wrong about her not leaving him.

That was five years ago, and they're doing great today. Every once in a while, she still asks him where he's been or pulls out his wallet and thumbs through his cash. He grins at her when she does.

She grins right back.

They both know she's just working on their intimacy.

Personal Application

Once you remove the barriers to spiritual intimacy, it's time to turn what you've learned into a proactive plan. Remember that devel-

oping spiritual intimacy between two people requires three things—
communication, time, and *action.*

1. Communicate with God together. You and your spouse communicate with God through prayer; God communicates to you and your spouse as you study and meditate on His Word. We encourage you to continue your own personal time of prayer, Bible study, and meditation for continual development of your own spiritual intimacy with God, but if you want to grow spiritually together, you must also study and pray together.

In the accompanying workbook, *Becoming ONE: Exercises in Intimacy,* you will find exercises to help you and your mate develop a prayer life together. In this book, we can give two quick suggestions to get you started, in case you don't know how to pray or aren't comfortable praying together.

First, pray together using the ACTS method. The word becomes an acrostic for your prayer outline.

- A—*Adoration.* Spend time just praising God for who He is. For great examples of this, read the Psalms.

- C—*Confession.* Tell God what you've done wrong and ask Him to forgive you.

- T—*Thanksgiving.* Thank God for all He has done, is doing, and will do for you.

- S—*Solicitation.* Tell God what you ask of Him for yourself, your family, your church, and others.

As you pray together, first take turns adoring God with your own words or by praying to God words of adoration you find in the Bible. Then take turns confessing your sins to God. Be specific. After that, take turns thanking God. It's okay to make a list beforehand so you can remember to tell Him just how much you appreciate all He does for you. Finally, take turns asking Him for everything that is important to you. You can ask Him to make your child well from a cold or to begin preparing the person your child will marry so that he or she will have a wonderful, spiritual Christian mate. You can ask for God to bless your sex life, your financial life, and your attentiveness to each other. Ask Him for anything, because He answers all sincere, unselfish prayers.[24]

Second, if you want to be a bit more studious in learning how to pray, read together Matthew 6:9–13, the passage where Jesus taught His apostles to pray. Carefully inspect the verses and outline the model prayer that Jesus gave the apostles. Once you develop that outline, use it as an outline for your own prayer life.

Some couples pray one at a time, each taking several minutes to pray as the other sits quietly. Other couples prefer paragraph prayers where each speaks about a paragraph of thought in prayer to God and then pauses for the other to pray his or her "paragraph," alternating until they finish their time of prayer. It may take you a few sessions to find the method you like best, so be sure to get started right away.

Today.

Pray.

2. Spend time with God—both quality and quantity. The two of you must share quality time with God in great enough quantities to develop spiritual intimacy. You can't rush the development of spiritual intimacy. Two-minute prayers and fifteen-minute studies won't develop the level of intimacy you need. Make sure you have adequate time to read a passage—either directly from the Bible or from some Bible resource—and time to discuss it, learning all you can from it. Make sure that your prayer time isn't sandwiched between pressing matters like the kids' bath time and bedtime. It might even be good if you don't make your spiritual time together the last thing you do before sleep. If you do, you'll be tempted to cut it short on nights you find yourselves exhausted...or on the nights you find yourselves wanting sexual intimacy. Time with God should be special, with no interruptions and no matters hastening it or stealing time from it.

3. Put what you learn into action. Whatever you learn in your study of God's Word, you must put it into action. Don't be just *hearers* of the Word; be *doers* of the Word. It's not enough to learn or understand; you must act! Put it into practice.[25] If you really want to develop spiritual intimacy between the two of you, find a ministry that you can do together. It may be working with your church's children's ministry or volunteering downtown at the homeless shelter. If you're growing together through this study, you may want to develop a ministry to other couples. We at Family Dynamics Institute can help you build a dynamic and effective ministry together.[26]

Whatever it is, find something to do for God in service to Him. Show Him you love Him!

4. Use your intimacy triangle. When you feel that you and your spouse have attained enough spiritual intimacy that you are happy with the progress, fold the spiritual intimacy side up so that it stands. Attach it to any other legs that are standing by using a paper clip or scotch tape. The folded side will stand after a fashion—though not straight—even if it's not connected to another leg. Your spouse can see it and know that you're happy with the progress you two are making in achieving spiritual ONEness. If your 3-D triangle doesn't have that leg standing, your spouse will know that you aren't happy or pleased with the progress you two are making in developing spiritual intimacy.

*L*earning emotional intimacy with your spouse means learning to share the facts and feelings of your life with him or her. Especially the private or potentially threatening ones. The same is true with God. Regularly tell Him the facts and feelings of your life, and you'll fall in love with Him. (page 216)

*A*s you grow closer to God, you *will* draw closer to each other. (page 225)

*M*any view Solomon's song of passion with his wife as a metaphor of our relationship with God. Passionate. Emotional. Spiritual. Similar to a husband and wife unabashedly united with each other, total union with God involves every part of us. (page 222)

Chapter 9

Developing Intimacy
with God—Personally

Becoming His in Mind, Body, and Spirit

My secretary was temporarily away from her desk, but Lark didn't let that small inconvenience deter him. He crossed her office, knocked tentatively on my office door, smiled nervously when I opened it, and asked politely, "You got a minute? Shelly and I would like to talk with you."

I swung the door open and gestured toward the sitting area, happy to see them. They'd only been coming to our church for a few weeks, and I hadn't yet been able to have any interaction with them other than shaking their hands as they exited the foyer. I was a minister, in those days, of a fairly large church and didn't always get to know all the folks who worshiped with us. Because ministry teams followed through on our visitors, I knew they hadn't been neglected, but I was happy for a chance to become friends with them myself.

"Glad you two dropped by. I just happen to have about fifteen minutes before my next appointment and was just sitting here deciding which of a hundred things I should use that time for. You saved me the weight of that decision." I laughed as I said it, because I didn't want to make them feel bad; I just wanted to gently nudge them directly into whatever they'd come to talk about—because I really did have a busy day.

After stumbling through a few niceties about my preaching and how much they liked our church, Lark finally fell to the purpose of his visit. "Well, Shelly and I have been talking. We've listened to your sermons, been in the young marrieds' class for Sunday school, and been invited into some of the class members' homes. Through you and the teacher and those couples, we've heard the call of God. I'm a Christian, but I haven't been active in church in years. Shelly isn't a Christian. We know that God wants us both to be Christians and wants us both to serve Him in this church. We were hoping you'd have time to tell us what to do."

I leaned over the desk and clicked the intercom to see if my secretary had returned. Happy to find that she had, I asked, "Have we heard from the Jernigans yet?"

"Yes, they just called and said they can't make it and hope you understand."

Understand? Oh, I understood all right. I grinned at Lark and Shelly and said, "Not only does God want you to be His, He's not waiting a minute longer. Let's find you a couple of Bibles, and we'll get started."

That day Shelly became a Christian. That day Lark recommitted himself totally and completely to God. Over the next two years that I remained with that church, I watched them grow dramatically in their relationships with Him and with each other. God became first in their lives in every way. They worked tirelessly in our evangelism ministry. In his second year with our church, Lark received a bonus at work and gave every cent of it to a missions program. No minister could ever hope to find a better couple to help build the kingdom of God.

One day as Lark and I went to visit a brother who needed rescuing, Lark confided a bit of information about him and Shelly I'd never known. "When we first came to church here, Joe, it was a 'last gasp' kind of thing. Shelly and I couldn't agree on anything. We fought over money, fought over how to raise the kids, and fought over sex. We discovered within months of marrying each other that we had nothing in common, but we both believed that we were supposed to stick it out. Our seventh anniversary was coming, and we finally agreed that if we couldn't work it out by then, we'd call it quits before we hit that 'official' seven-year mark. I asked her what we could do different than we'd done before, and she snapped back, 'Well, if *you* would *change*, maybe everything would be just fine!'

"That hit me hard. I'm sure she'd said it a hundred—maybe even a thousand—times before, but somehow I heard it this time. I don't know why, but I thought, 'She's right. I need to change. I used to be a pretty good guy, but I'm not so good anymore. I need to be what I was, not what I've become.'

"So I said, 'Okay, I'll change, but I only know one way to do it. I gotta get back in church. I need help to live like I know I'm supposed to live. But here's the deal; you have to go with me.'

"She snorted with contempt and said something about what a hypocrite I was, but she finally agreed. 'Fine,' she said. 'If you think that will change *you*, then *I'm* all for it.'

"And that's how we came to your church. We got up one Sunday, dressed, and started driving. When we saw a church that looked okay, we pulled in. We liked your sermon and decided that next week we'd go a step further and come early for Bible class. Well, as they say, 'The rest is history!'"

I laughed lustily along with him as he shared how God got to him and Shelly. Then it hit me to ask, "How are you guys doing now? How's the marriage?" I had assumed it to be good because of how much they smiled at each other and the gentle caresses they seemed to constantly be giving, but I thought I'd make sure.

"That's the best thing about our finding God. Not only did finding Him save our souls, it saved our marriage. We couldn't be closer. We pray together, read the Bible together, and teach the kids Bible stories. It's great! We share everything in our lives now, where we shared nothing before. And it all hinges on our relationships with God."

Amazing, isn't it? No one in our congregation ever did the first marital intervention or therapy with them, but their marriage went from awful to awesome anyway. They found intimacy with each other by finding a true relationship with God.

That shouldn't surprise us. It always works.

Perhaps you're already experiencing it in your own marriage. In the last chapter we urged you to start studying and praying together. Your participation in those activities should be changing your relationship for the better. In that chapter we emphasized the activities you do together as a couple, seeking a spiritual union with each other as you seek spiritual union with God. As we end this book, we want this last chapter to guide you in your personal relationship with God. Don't quit your *together* spiritual activities, but realize that much of the depth of the intimacy you develop with God will be in one-on-one encounters with Him.

You may be a Christian who already has intimacy with God. Wonderful. Or you may be a Christian who wants intimacy with God but you can't honestly say that you have it. It may be that you aren't a Christian at all. Whatever your situation, we can show you how to initiate, develop, or rekindle intimacy with God—through your *emotions*, your *body*, and your *spirit*.

EMOTIONAL INTIMACY WITH GOD

We said in chapter 3 that humans have a triune nature: We are mind, we are body, we are spirit. We focused there on the emotional aspect of out minds; here we will look at both the intellectual and emotional aspects of this dimension of intimacy with God. The following passage of Scripture will serve as our model for emotional/intellectual intimacy with God. Read carefully the words of the dying David to his son Solomon; then we'll look at the phrases one by one. "And you, my son Solomon, acknowledge the God of your father, and serve him with wholehearted devotion and with a willing mind, for the LORD searches every heart and understands every motive behind the thoughts. If you seek him, he will be found by you; but if you forsake him, he will reject you forever."[1]

Now let's look at key phrases in this passage and see how they apply to you.

"Acknowledge the God of your father." Intimacy with God begins with mentally acknowledging that He is the one and only true God. It means believing that He is there and that He always does what He says He will do. The writer of Hebrews said much the same thing: "And without faith it is impossible to please God, because anyone who comes to him must believe that he exists and that he rewards those who earnestly seek him."[2] Doubters, scoffers, and skeptics never find intimacy with God because they can't trust Him enough to develop it. If you doubt Him—either because you've never known God or because He disappointed you by not giving you a specific request at some point in your life—you cannot have intimacy with Him until you allow Him to replace your doubt or disappointment with faith.

"Serve Him with wholehearted devotion." Jesus said it this way: "No one can serve two masters. Either he will hate the one and love the other, or he will be devoted to the one and despise the other."[3] If we want intimacy with God, we must focus our hearts on God above all else. When work, hobbies, worries, or concentration on unfulfilled needs takes center stage in our lives, our relationship with God immediately begins to wither. Any person, thing, or emotional need that

takes precedence over Him becomes a diversion keeping us from developing intimacy in our hearts for Him. If we want to be close to God, we must hold Him close to us.

"Serve Him with a willing mind." A person performing an act of obedience to God grows closer to God by that obedience...*if the act is done willingly.*[4] "Have to" service usually doesn't breed intimacy; it more often breeds discontent and dissent. Service from a willing mind brings joy, and as a direct result, intimacy. That's why Paul explained to the Corinthians, "Each man should give what he has decided in his heart to give, not reluctantly or under compulsion, for God loves a cheerful giver."[5] And it is the cheerful giver—not the pressured giver—who in turn learns to love God.

The next three key phrases tell us *why* the above things are so important:

"The Lord searches every heart." God knows how we think, and He knows how we feel. Nothing within us is hidden from Him nor ever can be. He wants to be close to us, but unlike all others in our lives, He cannot be fooled into thinking we have a relationship if one doesn't really exist. If you love Him, He knows. If you never think about Him unless you're in church—or in trouble—He knows that too. If you want Him to be close to you, you must do as David said and *acknowledge* God, serve Him with *wholehearted* devotion and a *willing* mind. If you lack any of those, the Searcher of the Heart knows.

"The Lord understands every motive behind the thoughts." If we pray in order to receive the accolades of men rather than to draw closer to Him, He knows.[6] If we fast in order to appear more spiritual to others instead of to grow more dependent on Him, He knows.[7] If we give to the needy in order to have people think us generous rather than to please our Lord and Friend, He knows.[8] And if we find ourselves drifting into sin, all the time justifying our actions with one rationalizing thought after another, He knows the motives behind those thoughts as well. We may fool everyone with clever words and devi-

ous explanations—sometimes even ourselves—but we never fool Him. He always knows why we think as we do, why we feel as we do, and why we do as we do.

"If you seek Him, He will be found by you." Interesting how that's phrased, isn't it? Almost sounds as if you aren't the one doing the finding, He is. It sounds as if He allows Himself to be found by those who seek Him. Since He searches the heart and understands the motive behind every thought, it makes sense, doesn't it? He knows who wants intimacy with Him and who seeks Him for other purposes. When He knows a person's heart is good and his or her motives are good, He *allows* Himself to be found by that person. Intimately. Perhaps the opposite is also true: When he knows a heart is bad and a motive corrupt, he *doesn't* allow Himself to be found.

If we want true intimacy with God—not just a contractual relationship where we do "this" and He does "that"—we must seek Him with our whole hearts. And as we do this, we'll find that we're falling in love with our God and Savior.

Falling in Love with God through Bible Study

Remember what it was like when you first fell in love? You hung on to every loving gesture, every romantic word—especially the words that were written down. There's nothing like the special communication of the written word. Whether it comes in the form of a beautiful card with a handwritten message or a lengthy love letter, words penned especially for you by your loved one are treasured and guarded and kept close to your heart. In a letter, the love-struck couple shares devotion, information, humor, concerns, and anything else that's important to them. No conversation—by phone or in person—could ever replace the words we fold into special places and read over and again for the rest of our lives, dwelling on certain passages that touch us deeply.

Do you think that's how lawyers feel as they dig through law books and case histories? Do you think they're filled with anticipation for the next line? Can you imagine them longing at night to switch on the light and read through a favorite paragraph once more? Who can picture them watching impatiently out the window for the mailman, hardly getting any work done, when a new volume of a legal quarterly is due?

Maybe there's a lawyer like that, but I'm having trouble picturing it. Reading and understanding law is *work*—valuable *work*—but work just the same. There may be passion in it, but it isn't the passion of romance. Reading a letter from someone you're falling in love with is altogether different from ingesting the intricacies of the law.

When God wrote His Bible for us, He didn't give us a law book in the technical sense of the word. Instead, He gave us love letters so that we could know how much He loves us and so that we may fall in love with Him.

That's right, fall in love with Him.

My friend Ken Young of Midland, Texas, is one of the most gifted worship leaders I've ever had the privilege to work with. He gets so caught up in worshiping God that the congregation can't help but do the same. He told me that the first time he led a church in a beautiful song titled, "When I Fell in Love with You," some of the congregants approached him afterward to tell him how uncomfortable the song made them.

"Why?" Ken, flabbergasted, wanted to know.

"Because it feels too personal, too much like a love song that one lover would sing to another," they replied.

Ah. That's it, isn't it? Too many Christians have been taught that the Bible is a law book, not a book of letters from God to the people He loves, and they view God as the judge, not as the friend Jesus specifically said He wants to be.[9]

Friendship. Love. Intimacy. God loves us, and He wants us to love Him in return. He wants us to feel friendship (intimacy) with

Him, His Son, and His Spirit. To develop that intimacy, we must spend time with Him in deep levels of communication. We can never reach this level of communication if we only read our Bibles to prove some doctrinal point or pray just to make sure we've fulfilled our duty.

If you want to develop deeper intimacy with God, get a good Bible reading plan—quite a few are available at your Christian bookstore, and some may be available through your church—and begin to read the Bible as a book of letters from God on high. On this journey through the Word, don't read for the law; don't look just for the rules or even the loopholes! Read the love of God demonstrated from the time He made this world right through the lives of the apostles and New Testament writers. Read to learn of Him and what He wants you to know of His nature, His love, and His heart. Read His love letter to you and make note of all the ways He tells you He loves you.

If you say that you have emotional intimacy with God but don't have a regular time of reading and meditation on what you've read from Him, you're fooling only yourself. You don't fool God. He searches your heart and knows what is there. And you won't even fool *yourself* when you finally find yourself in some situation that a follower of God should never be in. You'll know then that the intimacy you claimed wasn't anything more than a casual acquaintance or a legal contract.

You can't love God if you don't know Him, and you can't know Him if you don't let Him communicate from the depths of His heart to yours. He already did His part, He wrote you those love letters we call the Bible. To learn to love Him, you have to do your part of reading, meditating on, and cherishing those letters. You must spend time with Him in that way, listening to His communication to you.

When finally you learn to let God communicate to the deep levels of your soul, you must communicate with Him in the same way.

Sharing Your Heart in Prayer

When Hannah suffered the agony of childlessness, she spread her pain before the Lord, seeking Him above all else. She prayed in bitterness of soul, weeping, and pouring out her soul to the Lord.[10] God searched her heart, saw her motives, and He *was found by Hannah*.

When David brought the ark of the covenant back to the city of Jerusalem, he celebrated by leaping and dancing before the Lord with all his might.[11] God searched his heart, saw his motives, and He *was found by David*.

Hannah and David experienced two very different emotions—she felt agony, and he felt celebration. And they responded in two very different ways—she with a tearful prayer and he with dancing before the Lord. But they had one thing in common: They both took their thoughts and feelings before the throne of God. By doing that, each did exactly what God wanted them to do: "Is any one of you in trouble? He should pray. Is anyone happy? Let him sing songs of praise."[12]

The surest sign of emotional intimacy between two people is how much of themselves they share with each other. As they share the facts of what they've done, who they are, and what they're doing now, they come closer to each other. As they move on to share their innermost feelings, pains, disappointments, joys, and desires, they come closer still. It works that way in marriage, and it works that way in one's relationship with God. No one can honestly claim intimacy with God who doesn't pray and worship in total openness before Him.

What should we pray about?

Everything.

What should we leave out of our prayer lives?

Nothing.

We should tell God the facts about what we've done—good or bad. We should tell Him we're sorry when we've done wrong and how thankful we are when He blesses us for doing right. We should talk to Him about our pasts, our presents, and our futures. As we grow in our relationship with Him, we should move from facts to feelings, discussing with God our pain, like Hannah, or shouting to Him with glee about our happiness, like David.

If you lack intimacy with God even though you pray, perhaps you pray without truly sharing yourself. Maybe you thank God and even ask things of Him, but do you share your heart with Him? He never hesitated to share His heart with you in His book of letters to us. He spoke freely of His anger, His joys, His disappointments, His love, His frustrations, and His desires. No one can read the account of His thundering from Mount Sinai and conclude that God hides His emotions.[13] No one could read Luke's description of Jesus crying in brow-bleeding anguish for deliverance from His impending crucifixion and say that God doesn't share openly with us what He feels.[14]

When we pray we should do the same with Him.

If you ever find yourself asking for the life of your dying child, tell Him how you hurt, how scared you are, and why you so desperately need your child to live. If you find yourself overwhelmed in your business and don't know what to do next, let yourself cry before Him, releasing all your anguish and frustration as you seek His guidance and sustenance. He wants you to "cast all your anxiety on him because he cares for you."[15] When you seek Him without hiding any of yourself—not even your doubts, fears, or hurts—you come closer to Him, learning intimacy in its most intense form.

I know.

In 1970 I begged God for the life of my daughter, Angela. Although not nearly as important, in more recent years I wept bitterly before Him because I didn't know where the money would come from for payroll for a company I headed. I discovered, as have so many other Christians, that when I open my heart completely to Him, I grow closer to Him. And that's not just when I share fretful emotions with Him, but it's also when I share my excitement or happiness.

We feel closer to God when we trust Him enough to share all that we feel. Our feelings should show not only when we pray but when we sing, when we connect with God during communion, or when we cheerfully throw money into the collection to help some distressed family.

Emotional intimacy is based on feelings. So, let go! Let God know what you feel about *everything!* Give Him your praise, tell Him your life, present to Him your requests, and share with Him your heart. All of it. Don't be uncomfortable with the idea of falling in love with God, seek it!

As long as your motives are good and your heart is devoted to Him and not something else, *He will be found by you.* It will happen when you read and meditate and pray and worship with total openness before God.

What about it? Are you communicating with God? Have you given Him your whole heart or just certain portions of it? If you're still holding back, ask His help in letting go. He'll meet you right where you are.

PHYSICAL INTIMACY WITH GOD— GIVING YOUR BODY AS A LIVING SACRIFICE

When we speak of our bodies being intimate with God, we refer to yielding our bodies to Him completely. We've already mentioned passages in 1 Corinthians that refer to our bodies as "temples" of the Holy Spirit, which definitely is part of our physical intimacy with God. But right now let's concentrate on another passage:

> Therefore, I urge you, brothers, in view of God's mercy, to offer your bodies as living sacrifices, holy and pleasing to God— this is your spiritual act of worship. Do not conform any longer to the pattern of this world, but be transformed by the renewing of your mind. Then you will be able to test and approve what God's will is—his good, pleasing and perfect will.[16]

The truth of this passage may fly past a modern-day American or European. We think of a sacrifice as going without lunch or having to miss our favorite team playing on television. That *isn't* the type of sacrifice Paul is writing about here. For people in the first century who routinely witnessed animal sacrifice, the meaning of sacrifice conjured up a more intense image. Though I didn't like it at the time, I learned about that as a child when I saw an animal slaughtered and butchered. While it wasn't a sacrifice per se, it mimicked the process.

When I was only ten or so, my grandparents lived on a simple farm in lower Alabama and tenaciously clung to a rapidly passing way of life. My grandfather never plowed with a tractor but with a plow, sending more than one overtaxed mule to a premature grave. By the time tractors became the norm for farming, he was too old to bother with them. A hard-working man, he and my grandmother farmed several hundred acres, raising nearly everything they needed and selling enough crops to make a comfortable living. I guess by the standards of their world, they were wealthy people; I know they were highly respected in their community as leading citizens—though probably not by their hogs.

Because meat spoiled in warm weather before it could be smoked, country hogs were butchered only when it was cold. One year, we were visiting them in the late fall when the temperature had dropped enough to butcher the hogs. My frugal grandfather didn't believe in wasting shells, so he took a blunt end of an axe and dispatched the two porkers.

My job was to keep the fire burning under large, black cauldrons full of boiling water. That water was crucial to the butchering process, but I'll spare you city folks the description. Let's just say that in the space of a few hours, I observed how to remove all the blood from an animal, how to remove the parts that you didn't want, how to make sausage from parts I didn't understand why you would want, and how to cut that animal into predetermined pieces for the smokehouse.

Needless to say, it was *awhile* before I ate sausage again. And I'll never, ever, eat chitlins. Years later when I proposed to Alice, I asked her if she'd ever eaten chitlins. She replied in the negative and inquired as to why I'd asked. I told her solemnly, "Because lips that have touched chitlins will never touch mine."

I learned more about slaughtering than I wanted to know. Of course, you may be shaking your head right this moment thinking the same thing. So why lead you through all that information about hog slaughtering? Because that's what many first-century people thought of when they were told to present their bodies as living sacrifices. They'd seen animal sacrifices and could easily picture some animal being ritualistically killed, bled, and cut into pieces. When they read Paul's admonition to be a living sacrifice, they had an instant conflicting mental picture of a person totally annihilated and dissected but somehow put back together and alive again.

And that's just what Paul wanted them to think.

We've heard stories about people in certain parts of the world having alleged voodoo powers to raise dead people and make those resurrected zombies their slaves, doing anything the master commands. While I don't believe in the power of voodoo, I do see a similar image in what God wants of us. We place ourselves on a sacrificial altar, willingly, in devotion to Him. We die there, all the life drained from us. Then a miracle happens, and God puts us together again, making a new person from the old, a person living only by His power. When we rise from that altar, we leave our old lives on it, gone forever, and take within us the new life that will sustain us forevermore. The One who gives us life is the One to whom we give ourselves as completely dedicated servants, doing whatever He wishes. We are living sacrifices.

When we give God that kind of power over our bodies, we can say with Paul: "I have been crucified with Christ and I no longer live, but Christ lives in me. The life I live in the body, I live by faith in the Son of God, who loved me and gave himself for me."[17] When we read those words, we get the impression that Paul felt physical intimacy with God. Not only did he feel close to God in his emotions and intellect, he obviously felt God's very presence within him. He knew he wasn't alone; he knew that God's Spirit was with him all the time. I believe Paul felt that strongly and that he wanted all Christians to feel that way.

Why?

Because it's hard to join ourselves to a sin, any sin, when we view our bodies as totally sacrificed to God and filled with His presence. For example, who could join his body to a prostitute if he viewed his body as alive only by the power of God? Or who could abuse her body through drunkenness if she understood that her body was God's building?

When we give our bodies totally to God, we have no excuse for drunkenness, drug abuse, gluttony, homosexuality, or any other sin against our God-owned, God-powered body. If we would take wonderful and precise care of someone's precious and expensive car that we have temporary custody of, we certainly ought to take even more care of the body that now belongs to God and is precious to Him. It's His, and He wants it treated right!

Examine your life. Is your body truly the property of God? You can read your Bible and pray for hours a day, sharing every part of yourself with God in prayer as He reveals Himself to you, but if you aren't *acting* in accordance with that *communication*, you don't have intimacy with Him. You may express your emotions to Him and tell Him all day long how much you love Him and how close you feel to Him, but His perception of your love and intimacy isn't based on what you say; it's based on what you *do*. Playing on the words of James 2:18, we might well say, "You say you have love for God, but it doesn't translate into action. Show me how much you 'love' Him by doing nothing, and I'll show you real love for Him by what I do."

Are you yielding your body to God? Are you taking your body into any situation or relationship where He doesn't want it to go? Do you consciously think of how you treat your body and consciously avoid sinful situations because you know He wants you to take good care of His temple? Are you drinking too much? Eating too much? Letting your body deteriorate through laziness?

Remember, when you have physical intimacy with God, your body belongs to Him. Live according to the truth that He is the power giving you life. Consciously serve Him by doing what He asks. Consciously serve Him by avoiding what He condemns. Go nowhere, say nothing, and do nothing that in any way demonstrates a lack of living sacrifice. For it is when you *live* as a Christian, doing what Christians do and avoiding what Christians avoid, that you ultimately find the fruition of your study, meditation, and prayer.

Emotions/intellect and body. Two crucial parts of us that we consciously join to our God so that we can achieve intimacy. That leaves one part of us: the most important part.

SPIRITUAL INTIMACY WITH GOD— JOINING YOUR SPIRIT TO HIS

The ultimate goal of serving God with a willing mind and presenting our bodies as living sacrifices is to attain true spiritual union with God Almighty. We become His in actuality, married to Him as it were, when we join not only our minds and bodies with Him, but also the essence of our being—our spirits.

Quite simply that means that a person cannot be spiritually intimate with God if that person hasn't been born again.

If you're reading this as a non-Christian, no one can tell you how to have God in you—having spiritual intimacy with Him—until you have been *transformed* by Him. You may have noticed in the Romans 12 passage, which we discussed in the last section, that those who give their bodies as living sacrifices are to also be "transformed" by the "renewing" of their minds. Spiritual transformation, becoming ONE with God, takes place as a person's mind becomes new. Without that change of mind, transformation doesn't take place. But note carefully the language; they didn't transform themselves by their own renewing of their minds—they were transformed when their minds were renewed by another power outside themselves. Confusing? Let Jesus explain it.

> Jesus answered, "I tell you the truth, no one can enter the kingdom of God unless he is born of water and the Spirit. Flesh gives birth to flesh, but the Spirit gives birth to spirit. You should not be surprised at my saying, 'You must be born again.' The wind blows wherever it pleases. You hear its sound, but you cannot tell where it comes from or where it is going. So it is with everyone born of the Spirit."[18]

You Must Be Born Again

When you came into this world, your mother's body gave birth to your body—flesh gave birth to flesh. That's simple enough to understand; it occurs thousands of times a day all over the world. But to be changed by *God*, something has to happen beyond the human, or fleshly, realm. The Spirit of God must act on your spirit like your mother's body acted on your body. Her body took the seed planted by your father and produced a human being—slowly, carefully, wondrously.[19] After you left her womb, your mother continued to shape you (if she was the person who raised you), but now she shaped not only your body but your mind, heart, and character. The flesh that gave birth to flesh now gave guidance.

Spiritual birth is similar to human birth, but instead of a woman's womb, it requires a different kind of miracle altogether. Spiritual birth takes place when God's Spirit gives life to your spirit, forming it, changing it, and taking it from an "embryo" to a fully mature spiritual being. At the point of spiritual birth, the Spirit who gave you birth doesn't abandon you but instead continues to guide you—influencing your mind, heart, and character. That same Spirit who gives you life continues to live in you. I love the poetic way the King James Version translates that truth in this next verse: "But ye are not in the flesh, but in the Spirit, if so be that the Spirit of God dwell in you. Now if any man have not the Spirit of Christ, he is none of his."[20]

That indwelling, guiding Spirit brings us into total union with God Almighty. The Spirit attests to our relationship with God.[21] He helps our weaknesses and intercedes for us in prayer.[22] As we yield to His direction, He produces in us love, joy, peace, patience, kindness, goodness, faithfulness, gentleness, and self-control.[23]

But don't forget that the Spirit won't live in you, giving you complete intimacy with God, until you are a born-again believer in Jesus. So before we can go further, we must pause to ask: What about you? Have you experienced that new birth, that transforming by the renewing of your mind? If you aren't a born-again Christian, you *don't* have intimacy with God, no matter how much you like Him, how much you pray to Him, or how much of His Word you know by heart. Knowing about God and knowing God aren't the same. You may go to church, participate in Bible class, and even write wonderful essays on foundational Christian doctrines, but none of those things are enough. Spiritual union with God comes only when we seek God in our intellects and emotions, yield our bodies to Him, and become His through the "wedding ceremony" of new-birth conversion.

Shelly, whom you met at the beginning of this chapter, was transformed the day she became a Christian. She "married" God that day. Lark allowed his mind to be transformed again, like it once had been when he first became a child of God, as he recommitted himself to God. Both were transformed, but the transformation wasn't accomplished by their pulling themselves up by their own bootstraps or because they finally discovered the right course of discipline. God changed them. Both of them. And by transforming and renewing them, He at the same time transformed and renewed their relationship with each other.

As they grew closer to God, they grew closer to each other.

If you aren't a Christian, are you ready to be transformed and renewed? If you say yes, we say "Praise the Lord!" Study your way to Jesus.[24] Usually, the best way to do that is to talk to a real human being who can answer your questions and guide you through verses of Scripture that tell you how to be God's. If your spouse is a Christian, ask him or her to tell you how to be born again. It may well be the best conversation of your entire marriage. If your spouse isn't a Christian or isn't sure how to guide you, ask if he or she will go with you to visit a minister in your church. If it is more comfortable, contact the couple facilitating your *Becoming ONE* course so that you together can ask them about how to be born again. They will be able to tell you, or they can guide you to the people who can. If you aren't enrolled in our course and don't know where to turn, call us at Family Dynamics Institute, and we'll send you a wonderful little book called *ABCs of the Christian Faith*[25] that will clearly and simply guide you to God.

Live by the Spirit

The next step after being born of the Spirit is to live by the Spirit. "So I say, live by the Spirit, and you will not gratify the desires of the sinful nature. For the sinful nature desires what is contrary to the Spirit, and the Spirit what is contrary to the sinful nature. They are in conflict with each other, so that you do not do what you want."[26] How does one "live by the Spirit"? Just as in every other relationship, intimacy with God through His Spirit requires focusing the "river" in your heart on Him every day.

THREE WAYS TO DEVELOP INTIMACY WITH GOD

You develop intimacy with God the same way you develop intimacy with your spouse: through *communication, time,* and *action.*

- *Communicate with God.* Speak to God through prayer as He speaks to you through His divine Word.

- *Spend time with Him.* Spend both quality and quantity time in prayer, meditation, and service.

- *Act.* Serve God by doing what He requires and avoiding what He condemns.

Remember, becoming ONE with God is the final step to a great marriage, not to mention the only step to eternal life. If you want the best relationship you can possibly have with your spouse, seek God right now.

Intimately.

A QUICK PERSONAL EVALUATION

Remember how in chapter 3 you made a quick evaluation of the kind of intimacy you felt for your mate by using our model that showed the seven kinds of ONEness? Before we finish this chapter on intimacy with God, will you place yourself on a similar chart in terms of your relationship with Him? And would you be willing to share your analysis with your spouse?

You've read in this chapter our descriptions of intimacy with God in emotions/intellect, body, and spirit. Take a moment now to see the seven kinds of intimacy that can exist in a person's relationship with God. (Of course, if a person hasn't yielded his or her body to God, has no emotional or intellectual intimacy with Him, and hasn't been born again, there is an eighth category—nonintimacy.)

Types of Intimacy with God

Unemotional
Spirit + Body

New Birth
Spirit Only

ONEness
Spirit + Emotions/Intellect + Body

Sacrificial
Body Only

Nonsacrificial
Spirit + Emotions/Intellect

Searching
Emotions/Intellect Only

Nonspiritual
Emotions/Intellect + Body

Before we ask you to decide which of these kinds of intimacy you have with God, we give very brief descriptions of each kind.

1. Emotions/Intellect Only: Searching Intimacy

People in this category haven't become Christians yet—they have not experienced the spiritual rebirth—but they are seeking God with intellect and emotion. Their lifestyles haven't changed—they have not yielded their bodies to God—but they are honestly searching for God. They sometimes pray and will participate when surrounded with worshiping Christians, but their spirits aren't truly intimate with His. They want God, they just aren't yet ready to commit or yield to Him.

2. Emotions/Intellect + Body: Nonspiritual Intimacy

These people have found enough of God in their search that lifestyle changes have taken place. They live good and moral lives because they want God to be happy with them. They seek intimacy with Him and enjoy the level of intimacy they have. But because they haven't been born again, the Spirit of God doesn't live in them yet. They are "not far from the kingdom" but lack the most crucial element of all, spiritual conversion. All their efforts at holiness are self-powered rather than God-powered.

3. Body Only: Sacrificial Intimacy

These people have neither emotional/intellectual intimacy with God nor the spiritual intimacy with God that comes through a conversion experience; but they are good people. They live quite exemplary moral lives and are often pillars in their communities. By living a sacrificial lifestyle, they have a form of intimacy with God, but they aren't His. Any discussion of God beyond the superficial makes them uncomfortable, and church is only a social occasion.

4. Body + Spirit: Unemotional Intimacy

These people have been born again and have totally surrendered their bodies to God. Good Christian people, they are at church often and may even hold leadership positions there. They want to go to heaven, but they aren't too interested in reading about it. They'd rather search the Scriptures to find the law, prove their points, or develop a teaching. They aren't dedicated to personal Bible study and meditation or even to personally fulfilling prayer. The only intellectual intimacy they have with God comes from what they've heard from their preachers or found in their legal research. Emotionally they have little or no tie to God at all. As a matter of fact, they don't understand why anyone else gets emotional about their relationship with God either. They worry that Christians who evidence strong emotions in worship may be "ungrounded" in their faith and certainly are getting too emotional for their own good.

5. *Spirit Only: New-Birth Intimacy*

These are new Christians who haven't had time to get into the Word and become one with God in intellect. The emotional aspect of intimacy with God exists in limited form, but that emotion is young and not yet firmly rooted. Their path to ONEness with God lies in learning to be ONE with Him in mind (emotions/intellect) and body, but they may not get there. If discipled by mature ONEness Christians, they will achieve ONEness also. If mentored by someone in another kind of intimacy with God-like unemotional intimacy— they will likely inherit the intimacy type of their mentors. These are truly "babes in Christ," whose future depends on the nourishment they get.

6. *Spirit + Emotions/Intellect: Nonsacrificial Intimacy*

These born-again Christians love to learn of God and love to come closer to Him through prayer and worship, but somehow their learning and joy doesn't lead to action. Living selfish lives, they haven't committed themselves to becoming living sacrifices. They may even be teachers of the Word, but while what they know of the Word affects their understanding of God and their worship of Him, it doesn't affect how they live. They are hearers of the Word but not doers of the Word.[27] These Christians struggle continually with temptation and sin, losing the battle constantly.

7. *Emotions/Intellect + Body + Spirit: ONEness Intimacy*

This, of course, is the ideal. It is everything that the New Testament teaches us to be: one in emotions and intellect, one in body, and one in spirit with the God of heaven. Though we see so many Christians operating in other types of intimacy, this is the type God considers the norm, where He expects everyone to be.

Personal Application

Do you see yourself there on the ONEness triangle? Which of the seven (eight if you count nonintimacy) best describes the intimacy you have with God?

1. Accept input from your spouse. Before you settle on a category, ask your spouse to tell you where he or she believes you to be in your intimacy with God. Ask why he or she believes you to have that kind of intimacy. Listen carefully without rebuke or retribution. Try to see yourself through your spouse's eyes. His or her view of your intimacy with God is ultimately crucial to your marital intimacy, so learn it now.

2. Ask yourself what needs to happen. Once you think you know where you are, ask yourself quite honestly what it would take to bring you to the middle of that triangle, to having ONEness with God in every part of your being.

3. Ask your mate what needs to happen. When you think you know what you should do, there's one last step. Ask your mate what he or she believes would take you to the middle of that triangle, to ONEness with God. Hear carefully and wisely what you are told. Whether your mate is right or not, you are now hearing exactly what this person wants from you spiritually.

As soon as you close in on complete ONEness with God, you will be that much closer to complete ONEness with your spouse. Start working on it today.

Appendix

Overcoming Negative Sexual History
Getting Past the Bad to Enjoy the Good

We realize that even as we ask you to pray that God will give you a great sex life, some people who read this book have difficulty believing that it can happen for them. They read the story of Ernie and Sal in chapter 6 with either disbelief or dismay, thinking either that there can't be a real couple like Ernie and Sal[1] or that they could never have the kind of relationship that Ernie and Sal have. There are at least four categories of people who have trouble believing God can make their sex lives the wonderful experience we describe in chapter 7.

1. Those who've had bad sexual experiences forced on them

2. Those who've willfully participated in sinful activities

3. Those whose painful pasts have influenced sinful choices

4. Those who believe their spouses could never learn to be good lovers

CATEGORY 1:
THOSE WHO'VE HAD BAD SEXUAL
EXPERIENCES FORCED ON THEM

Some folks read our emphasis in chapter 6 on the truth that sex is good and think, "You think I could see sex as good? You don't know what I've been through!" I recall one woman who sobbed out the awful truth that she couldn't remember a time in her life when she was a virgin. From her very early childhood, both her father and mother sexually molested her. Although she's a Christian and married to a wonderful Christian man, she was trained early that sex is evil and dirty and should be hidden in the darkness. But at the same time she also was taught that sex can be used to get your way, to manipulate people into giving you what you want. As she talked about her marriage she said, "My husband so much deserves a wife who can be a loving companion, but I'm forty years old, and I still use sex only to get what I want. I don't know how to do it any other way; it's the legacy my parents left me. Not only do I suffer from what they did to me; my husband does too. It would be so wonderful if only I could hold him and love him from my heart."

Another man shared nearly unbelievable agony from his early sexual experience: "My father let his homosexual lover molest me for years. I was only about seven when it started. The first time it happened, I went to my father and told him what that man had done to me and begged him not to let him hurt me like that again. His response was to beat me till he broke my arm. Do you hear me? I went to my dad for protection, and he broke my arm! He said that I was to make his friend happy and that if I told anyone else, he'd send me to the hospital again. Now I'm thirty-five years old and been married for thirteen years. Thirteen years, and I've had at least a dozen affairs. Matter of fact, I've been sleeping with anything I could get into bed since I was a teenager. You think what happened to me as a kid has anything to do with my continual adultery? I'm asking 'cause I don't know what to do to stop."

In one seminar a lady practically screamed at me, "How am I supposed to learn to enjoy sex after what my first husband did to me?! He made sex into a sick torture that hurt my body and twisted my emotions. You know what it's like being raped? Humiliated? Treated like filth? That's what I felt every time he did the next perverted thing to me." Then she revealed why she felt so frustrated to hear me say sex is good. "I finally got the nerve to leave him and after a few years met this wonderful Christian man sitting beside me. Marrying him was the best thing that ever happened to me. How do I have a fulfilling sex life with him...how can I be a good lover for him...when I recoil at his very touch? He's never been anything but good to me, but every part of my mind and body hates sex and never wants it again." Then in a soft, plaintive voice she begged, "What do we do?"

I could go on with the stories. I've heard them from so many people in so many places that I could recite them until you screamed, "Enough!" And that's exactly how we feel; it's already been enough. Every person who has been hurt by relatives or a spouse or anyone else has had enough pain. They now need the healing of God.

If you are one of those people (or if you're married to one of those people), we have good news. We'll show you how God will heal this terrible past. Before we do, we need to speak to the second category of people who think sex could never be good for them.

Category 2:
Those Who've Willfully Participated in Sinful Activities

Some people carry bad sexual memories because of their own promiscuous sexual history, and now they believe they can never have the sexual union in marriage described in this book. They carry at least one of three scars in their hearts:

1. Their heart is weighed down with degradation for having been immoral.

2. They fear that because of their exposure to sexual variety, they cannot be satisfied with one sexual partner for the rest of their lives.

3. If their former sex life had homosexual or other divergent dimensions, they fear they won't be able to live within the boundaries of normal heterosexual marriage.

I've met many people with these scars who are Christians and who want to be godly and holy and fulfilled in their relationship with God and a mate. As with every sin, God restored their purity when they yielded to Him, but He didn't destroy their memories of what they'd done. God can and does make us pure again, but He never makes us innocent—at least not in the sense of naiveté that exists within those who've never done a particular thing. Their memories of what has been—similar to the process of those who've been molested or abused—keep them from enjoying what can be.

Some of these people I've worked with strayed into sexual sin because they wanted to explore the unknown or because they desired adventure and excitement, but they didn't have the maturity to see where their ungodly quest would take them. Others were led into sexual sin by skillful and seductive guides. If a person is susceptible to a particular temptation, it seems there is never a lack of Satan-powered humans around to help him or her find the path to perdition. Sometimes the guides are truly evil; other times they are just as manipulated as the one they are used to corrupt.

Several years ago, one teen tried to explain her wanton lifestyle to me by explaining her self-willed exploration into hedonistic pleasure: "We have sex with whomever we want to whenever we want to because it feels good. We don't have to love the person or be married to them or anything like that to have pleasure." Then she went on to use several graphic words that we can't print in this medium to differentiate the various kinds of sex you could have with a partner. Each street word represented a different type of relationship, but the action was always the same—sexual intercourse. Her crude words described relationships that ranged from "recreational" to "being in love," with several kinds in between.

She's married now and is trying to live the Christian life, but she and her husband struggle with her past. He struggles because she doesn't seem to be satisfied with their lovemaking; he thinks she mentally compares him to all her previous lovers and gives him less than a passing grade. She struggles because she can't get past what she's been or done; she can't give herself completely to her husband because she feels she long since gave away the essence of herself to a host of men, some of whom she can't even remember.

In order for them to have what God can give them, she must allow God to heal her of her past.

CATEGORY 3:
THOSE WHOSE PAINFUL PASTS HAVE INFLUENCED SINFUL CHOICES

Sometimes people suffer from a mixture of what they've done and what's been done to them. They've committed sexual sin because of what happened to them earlier in their lives. At Family Dynamics, we've discovered that many who were molested or mistreated "act out" their pain and rage by living at least a portion of their lives in blatant sexual sin, creating even more pain and guilt in their hearts. They usually don't understand why they do it but feel they can't control themselves. They learned early that they could gain acceptance or rewards by being used sexually, so they participate in various kinds of sex with a number of people to gain either acceptance or benefits or both. Though they live sexually active lives, they hate what they do because sex in that context is destructive to their hearts and souls, circumventing any sense of intimacy and destroying every shred of self-worth. Satanic forces use their malformed view of sex as a springboard to tempt them into more degrading acts, leading these poor, manipulated people to heap more disgust on themselves even as they crave healing and wholeness. When finally, by the power of God, they free themselves from the trap and want an intimate relationship with a spouse, all their "training" about sex makes that difficult to attain.

Like the people we described in the paragraphs above, they, too, need the healing power of God.

STEPS TO HEALING

If you carry bad feelings or sexual hang-ups because of what someone did to you either as a child or an adult or because of what you've done on your own or both, we offer you the hope and healing available from God. He can and will take away your hurt, your previous wrongful training of mind and body, and your current struggles with sexual fulfillment. He can, as He promised, make all things new. Even you. Read the encouraging words written by the Holy Spirit through Paul: "Therefore, if anyone is in Christ, he is a new creation; the old has gone, the new has come!"[2]

Do you see the truth of that? God promised to make you a "new creation"[3] and a "new self"[4] so that you can "be made new in the attitude of your minds."[5] Whether your corrupted view of sex was birthed in your being molested, raped, degraded, seduced, or selfishly sinful, God's promise of a new life and a new you will heal your hurts and give you that promised new life—especially a new sex life.

Yes, a new sex life. Brand-new. Different from anything you've ever experienced before.

How?

If God can make a person new spiritually, He certainly can make a person new emotionally and sexually. His power doesn't work on just the spiritual part of us but on all of us.

If you want His power to unchain you from your past—what was done to you or what you've done to yourself—follow these five spiritual steps.

1. Believe what God tells you about you and your past if terrible things have been done to you.

2. Believe what God tells you about you and your past if you willfully sinned sexually.

3. Let go of harmful emotions.

4. Replace harmful thoughts with holy thoughts.

5. Implement His healing power through confession and prayer.

1. Believe What God Tells You about You and Your Past If Terrible Things Have Been Done to You

It appears to be universal. People who were abused in some sexual way—or abused in other ways—tend to think that somehow they caused it. Though the sin was committed by the person who molested them or raped them or degraded them, they still feel that somehow it was their fault.

I remember the first time I encountered it nearly twenty-five years ago. I'd read about it, but I'd never witnessed it until that night. We'd just finished the evening service of a revival I was preaching. God had worked powerfully that night, and several people had given themselves to Jesus. Several more had decided to rededicate themselves into the service of the Lord. One respondent, a teenage girl, continued to cry bitterly afterward, so I approached her to see if I could minister to her. Clutching my lapels with desperate hands, she practically dragged me to a corner of the hall and sobbed her sorrow onto my shoulder. "It's all my fault," she said. "Me. I'm the one who's turned her from God."

It took a few minutes to calm her enough to get the story. I won't shock you with the heartrending details, but I can tell you this much:

This fifteen-year-old Christian was involved in a homosexual affair with a twenty-eight-year-old woman. The teen knew it was wrong, knew it affronted God, and that night had promised Him that it was over, done. But her heart continued to shred before Him because she believed that she was the perpetrator who had seduced the older woman into the sin. She quickly told me how it had first happened and how the older woman would be pure today if she, this disheveled teen in front of me, hadn't lured her into degradation.

"Wait, slow down," I stopped her. "It isn't necessary for me to hear all of this. We'll get you a qualified counselor to help. But I just want to ask you one thing: Do you really believe you have the sophistication to seduce someone nearly twice your age? Someone much more experienced in life than you?"

Yes. She did believe that.

I didn't for a minute.

I knew that she'd been slyly manipulated, but she, at least at that point, wasn't going to believe it.

Since that night, that story in one form or another—changing genders, ages, and the sins forced on them—has been repeated to me more times than I'd like to remember. Just a couple of months ago, I heard another version.

It was a young lady again. This one was about twenty-five years old. She'd been raped by her stepfather when she was about fourteen or so. She absolutely believed him to be a terrible, evil man, but she just as absolutely believed it was her fault that he raped her. "After all," she said, "I knew what he was like but accepted the ride to the beach with him anyway. Sure, it's my fault. I shoulda known how he'd react when he saw me in my bikini. He raped me, but I'm the one who's corrupt. Can't you see that?"

I could see that what she'd done was anything but smart. I could see how a teenage girl who didn't like her stepfather could actually try to demonstrate her contempt for him by dressing seductively. I couldn't approve of it. But I could see it. I could see how her immature mind would justify that kind of sin just to see if it would cause him some kind of mental anguish. But I couldn't see how that made his rape her fault. He was forty. She was fourteen. A child. A misbehaving child, but a child nevertheless.

Now she sat in front of me, her life a mess because she was living up to her self-concept. Corrupt people do corrupt things. But my sermon in the revival at the church she visited cut her to the quick. She wanted to do right, but she had this one major problem: She believed she was incapable of it.

If you've been abused in some way in your life, you may have the same problem. You may find that temptation has inordinate power over you because you believe deep in the core of your being that you're no good. Or it may be that you have trouble being intimate with your spouse because in the secret part of you there resides a small but sure belief that you don't deserve intimacy because of what you "made" someone do to you earlier in your life—maybe even as far back as early childhood.

Would you like to know how God views you—even if some evil thing befell you?

You Were His Precious Little Child

When you were a child, God viewed you as His precious little one whom He cared for in a special way. He saw you as naive—which you were—and in danger of being led astray by older people who knew more of the ways of the world than you. It wasn't to you, as a child, that He gave warning. It was to every adult around you. He said to them,

> Whoever welcomes a little child like this in my name welcomes me. But if anyone causes one of these little ones who

believe in me to sin, it would be better for him to have a large millstone hung around his neck and to be drowned in the depths of the sea.

Woe to the world because of the things that cause people to sin! Such things must come, but woe to the man through whom they come![6]

Notice that He said that "such things must come." In an evil world where Satan has power, where "the whole world is under the control of the evil one,"[7] evil things happen. Don't think it shocking or unusual that Satan's forces want to hurt children. What better way, from their point of view, to injure the kingdom of God than to attack people when they're young and defenseless so that maybe they'll have difficulties when they get older?

But God takes note, and He will act in vengeance.

Jesus made it clear that any adult who lets him- or herself be used as Satan's pawn to hurt the young will hear His shout of justice: "Woe to the man through whom they come!" He warns any person contemplating it, "It would be better for him to have a large millstone hung around his neck and to be drowned in the depths of the sea."

If something happened to you when you were young, take heart from that passage. Jesus clearly placed the blame, the fault, the responsibility on the adult, not the child. And when you think logically, you know that's right. If someone were to hurt your child, you wouldn't blame the child, you'd blame the adult who brought the pain on the child.

Loving parents know the truth of that.

Society makes laws based on that undeniable reality.

God verifies it in His word.

Why don't you believe it in your heart?

If you need therapy to get past it, contact a local church to find a good therapist. But when you were a child, God saw you as naive and innocent, not as a person causing others to sin.

It Was Not Your Fault

You may be thinking, "But what about me? What happened to me didn't happen to a child. I was old enough to be responsible."

Both of the young ladies I just told you about thought themselves to be adults when the sinful things happened to them. One was fifteen. The other fourteen. Old enough to know a thing or two and no longer wanting to be considered a child.

I understand that. Felt the same way myself when I stumbled through the maze called adolescence. If you're past your teen years, maybe you did too. But for the adults reading this who are struggling with something done to you in your teen years, can we just be logical about what we were really like when we were in our early- to mid-teenage years?

We were bright, but we weren't yet that smart. We were still gullible and no real match for the sophistication or experience of most of the adults around us. We may have thought them old fogies or dinosaurs, but the truth of the matter was that our quick brains usually weren't quite the match of their hard-earned knowledge gained from living in the world longer than we had.

I'll put it in perspective for you by getting you to look at teens from our adult perspective. If your fifteen-year-old daughter were involved in a sexual sin with a twenty-eight-year-old, would you for a moment consider that she was skillful enough to have seduced that person into the sin?

No.

You'd immediately determine that the "user" was the twenty-eight-year-old and the "used" was your daughter. Your daughter might believe she's reached full maturity and that she was the equal of her lover, that she matched his or her knowledge, skill, and cunning in every way.

You'd know better.

241

You'd know that a child—even a child almost grown—is still a child.

So why don't you use that same reasoning process about what happened to you in your teen years? Yes, teenagers do carry responsibilities for their actions. Yes, they are old enough to be held accountable for most of their actions. But when they are involved with people older than they, almost without exception the older one is in control and the teen's ability to make logical and sound decisions diminishes. For example, the fourteen-year-old raped by her stepfather wasn't the seducer. Couldn't have been. She did wrong by wearing a bikini as he drove her to the beach, but her error was cloaked in immaturity, not a desire for sexual intercourse with that filthy man.[8]

Even if the fourteen-year-old *had* thought she was willingly participating, most states would have convicted the man of statutory rape anyway. Why? Because society realizes the inability of a girl that young to understand the consequence of a decision that important.

Whatever happened to you, it's very likely that society wouldn't think it's your fault.

If the same thing happened to your teenage son or daughter, you probably wouldn't think it his or her fault either, would you?

And God never charges the sinner's sin to the sinner's victim.

I'll explain that in the next section.

You Are Not Responsible for Another's Sin

Even if the terrible thing that happened to you happened after you reached full maturity (if any of us ever really do), you still cannot take responsibility for the actions of another person. None of us can make anyone do anything. We may help in some cases, but every responsible person who decides to do wrong makes that decision on his or her own.

God explained the principle in Ezekiel. He described it by comparing the actions of two people very close to each other—a father and his son: "For every living soul belongs to me, the father as well as the son—both alike belong to me."[9]

That's the first thing to remember: God is in control. He knows each person, and He makes the decisions about that person's destiny. The person who hurt you belongs to God, not you, and God looks to that person's actions and life just as He looks to yours. "The soul who sins is the one who will die."[10]

As He views all of us—all those who belong to Him—He doesn't hold any of us accountable for the sins of another, not even when our relationship is as close as father and son: "Suppose [a father] has a violent son who sheds blood or does any of these other [sinful] things (though the father has done none of them)....Will such a [son] live? He will not! Because he has done all these detestable things, he will surely be put to death and his blood will be on his own head."[11]

Notice: The guilt is on the head of the son, not the father. The father didn't do the sin, and God doesn't hold him responsible for it. Only the son who actually did the sin is held responsible. Ezekiel continues the thought for the next few verses, carrying the scenario to the son of the wicked son. He says that if the grandson doesn't do wicked things, he doesn't have any punishment coming. The fact that his father sinned doesn't make him a sinner. Then he concludes with his point: "The soul who sins is the one who will die. The son will not share the guilt of the father, nor will the father share the guilt of the son. The righteousness of the righteous man will be credited to him, and the wickedness of the wicked will be charged against him."[12]

Do you see that? Do you grasp its importance?

We are judged by what we do, not by what someone else does. Even if the thing he does, he does to *us!* God doesn't hold you responsible if you've been raped; He directs His vengeance toward the rapist.[13] If you wish in retrospect that you'd had more clothing on, that you'd parked in a different spot, that you hadn't so foolishly trusted a kind word and gentle smile, or any of a thousand other things, don't let your hindsight somehow become "guilt-sight." Every person is responsible for his or her actions, including the person who brought pain or degradation into your life. God doesn't charge you or in any way hold you responsible for his or her sin.

If He doesn't charge you with that, then it follows that He doesn't want you to charge yourself with that!

The only beings who can benefit from that kind of lingering guilt and the painful self-concept it fosters are the forces of Satan. They know that tying you to that ball and chain of false and hopeless misery makes you a poor spouse, a poor parent, and a poor Christian. Yes, they'll plant in your head a hundred ways that you could have prevented it, but the truth of the matter is that it happened.

Accept it.

It happened.

And playing mind games with yourself to find why or how you caused it is a foolish venture in every sense of the word—emotionally, sexually, and spiritually.

Accept what God says about you and that awful thing that happened to you. It isn't your responsibility!

A little later in this appendix, we'll give you spiritual direction as to how to get over the hurt, but the first step begins here: Accept God's view of the matter. It is the person who did the sin that God holds accountable. Not the person the sin was done to.

Even if that person might have avoided it if only…

God sees you as innocent. See yourself that way.

2. Believe What God Tells You about You and Your Past If You Willfully Sinned Sexually

We've already shown you verses in this chapter and elsewhere in this book that should convince you that when God forgives you, He views you as if you'd never sinned before. When He makes you new, everything you've ever done is gone, washed away, stricken from the heavenly record. It makes no difference what you've done—even the most degrading sexual acts are forgiven. Notice some of the sexual sins the Christians at Corinth had committed: "Do you not know that the wicked will not inherit the kingdom of God? Do not be deceived: Neither the *sexually immoral* nor idolaters nor *adulterers* nor *male prostitutes* nor *homosexual offenders* nor thieves nor the greedy nor drunkards nor slanderers nor swindlers will inherit the kingdom of God."[14]

Those Corinthian Christians had done some pretty bad things, including self-degrading sexual sins. But note what God immediately writes to them in the next verse. We've italicized the verbs to make His glorious truth jump from the passage: "And that is what some of you *were*. But you were *washed*, you were *sanctified*, you were *justified* in the name of the Lord Jesus Christ and by the Spirit of our God."[15]

He wants us to know that He cleansed everything we've done from His records when He forgave us—even sexual sins of any kind.

Believe what God says about you!

You Are Dead to Your Past Sin

God tells us that as He changes us spiritually, He makes it possible for us to change the way we feel and act. For example, when in Romans 6 He tells us to "reckon" (KJV) or "count" (NIV) ourselves dead to sin, He is telling us to acknowledge the spiritual change He made in us at our conversion.[16] As we intellectually and emotionally accept that great spiritual truth, He expects that as a direct result we will *think* and *feel* differently. He actually anticipates a different set of behaviors from us as we emotionally accept His spiritual truth that we are no longer what we were but are now a different person in Him.

> In the same way, count yourselves dead to sin but alive to God in Christ Jesus. Therefore do not let sin reign in your mortal body so that you obey its evil desires. Do not offer the parts of your body to sin, as instruments of wickedness, but rather offer yourselves to God, as those who have been brought from death

to life; and offer the parts of your body to him as instruments of righteousness.[17]

Christians who "count" (acknowledge and accept the truth of) themselves as dead to the past and alive in Christ can find within themselves the power of God to refuse to "offer" themselves to sin. When they believe and trust God's truth about their new status, they will be set free[18] from the past, free from its history, free from its guilt, and free from its power.

You Are New

God is the ultimate truth. He is true over all else that appears to be true or that anyone might believe to be true. When He tells you that you are no longer what you were and that the record of your past is expunged in heaven, then the truth is just that. The old has gone and the new has come.[19] When you truly accept the "new" truth with which God replaced the "old" truth, you will let go of what was and grasp firmly to what is.

If you want to have the life you desire—including a sex life free from evil encumbrances—believe Him when He tells you that you're brand-new. When you finally and completely accept that powerful truth, everything in you—intellectually, emotionally, spiritually—will feel and act differently than before. Everything in your life will be different, including your sex life with your spouse.

Your Past No Longer Exists

You must believe what God tells you about you and your past if you want to create the future you deserve in Him. The future He promises lies in believing Him when He tells you that you didn't do it, that you're not guilty. If you're in Him, you've been declared justified (that means not guilty!) by the Judge of all judges, the Chief Justice of every universe and all that is therein.[20]

If God were to speak to you, He would say something like, "In the annals of the history book that will be read throughout eternity, your sin isn't mentioned. It never happened. If it continues to exist, it does so only because some human wants to remember it, not because I do."

That's all I need to hear: What about you? My past partners in sin may remember my actions. My enemies may choose never to forget. But God says it's over and washed away and no record remains. The history books have been rewritten in heaven, and that's where my faith lies.

You don't have to live in the past because the past no longer exists—at least not the way it first happened. God rewrote it, and He has the power and privilege to do that. For me. For you. For us all.

3. Let Go of Harmful Emotions

If you have accepted God's truth about you and your past, you need to move to the next step: You need to let go of any spiritually or emotionally harmful feelings you have for those in your past. You'll never be set free from your past—no matter what God does for you—if you choose either to (1) hold a death grip on the hateful feelings you have for those who hurt you or (2) cherish intoxicating emotions you felt for those with whom you sinned.

God offers a new present as He continually points you to a wonderful future, but all sinful emotions you hold in your heart act like superglue to cement you to the evils of your past—either the evils you've done or the evils that were done to you. For both types of continued harmful emotions—as drastically different as they are—the solution is the same. Whether it's love or hate, passion or bitterness, fondness or revenge, you can only find peace in the present if you let go of the past and look to building an intimate future.

Forgive and "Forget"

You can't let go of harmful emotions if you can't forgive. Earlier in this chapter I told you about a man who confessed having one affair after another throughout his marriage and who told us about being molested as a young boy by his father's homosexual lover. As I worked with him and his wife in an effort to save their marriage, it became quite clear that he possessed an intense furor and hatred toward his father and his father's lover. He couldn't let go of the hate. Both men were dead, depriving him of the opportunity to thrash them in hopes of finding some kind of physical catharsis. Now that he was big enough to fight back, there wasn't anyone to fight.

There was only one solution for him: He had to let go of the pain he felt and all the negative emotions that attended it.

Anyone who holds hatred, rage, bitterness, anger, or desire for revenge must forgive and "forget" if he or she ever wants to be truly free from the past. We put quotation marks around the word *forget* because in the technical sense of the word, forgetting is impossible. Any intense event in our life can be summoned by willing it to memory (unless, of course, it was so distressing that the mind refuses to catalog it in memory in an event-specific amnesia). But God, who is all knowing, says that He "forgets," so there must be some way that a person can do it. He gives us a clue to how it is done as He tells the people in Isaiah's day to forget: "Forget the former things; do not dwell on the past."[21]

Forgetting doesn't mean erasing the memory banks; it means not dwelling on the past, not holding it in active thoughts. Isn't that what God Himself does when He removes our sin from us as far as the east is from the west?[22] Isn't it what He means when He says "I will forgive their wickedness and will remember their sins no more"?[23] Forgetting is not remembering; refusing to bring it up, agreeing not to discuss it, never throwing it back at the forgiven sinner—this is forgetting.

God basically says, "I choose not to think about it again. Once it's forgiven, I have better things to think about than what happened in the past."

Find Freedom in Forgiveness

I told the man who clung to his hatred for his father and his father's lover, "They do more harm to you now than they did then. They tormented you for a few years when you were a child, but your continuing bitterness toward them has allowed them to torment you for nearly thirty years beyond that. Only when you forgive them and refuse to let your mind drift back to those evil acts will you be free of them.

"Don't worry that you'll somehow set them free from the guilt of what they did to you by forgiving them. Your forgiveness doesn't affect their accountability to God. Your forgiveness doesn't free *them*; it frees *you*. It lets you get on with your life without having to be chained to the events of your past. You can never forget those events until you let go of the emotions that accompany them.

"If you want to be free, you must forgive."

In chapters 5 and 8 we share three steps of forgiveness. Review those again, and open your heart to applying them and finding freedom in forgiveness.

Let Go of Evil Emotions Connected to Sexual Sin

Letting go of harmful emotions does not only apply to people who hold on to hatred but also to people who hold on to love or passion for someone other than their spouses. We at Family Dynamics sometimes work with people who have had affairs and have asked for reconciliation with their partners. We rejoice with the angels in heaven when we encounter these penitent sinners,[24] and we gladly affirm the offended mates for their tremendous spiritual maturity, evidenced by their forgiving and accepting back their straying spouses.[25] We remind these couples that they have many things to work out and do our best to give them a good "jump start" on their healing through one of our eight-week marriage courses. Most of the time, we see great spiritual and marital growth as we watch God work in marvelous ways in the renewed relationship.

Unfortunately it doesn't always happen just that way.

Sometimes straying spouses don't let go of the past. They can't live in the present with their marriage or build a great future with their spouses because they can't let go of the emotional involvement they developed with their paramours. Until they let that go, there isn't much any of us can do for them.

I recall a woman who told me in one of our *Love, Sex & Marriage* seminars that she could never again enjoy sex with her husband because every time she closed her eyes as she made love with him, she saw only her past lover. I remember a man in a different seminar asking me if he would ever quit dreaming about his lover. He wondered if perhaps he could learn to love his wife again—if only he could forget the other woman. Occasionally I even hear someone talk about lingering love for high school sweethearts or former boy- or girlfriends.

If you find yourself dreaming, fantasizing, or longing for a lover, you must accept the fact—both intellectually and emotionally—that the relationship was sinful and distasteful to God. He made it abundantly clear what He thinks of sexual sin, sin outside the confines of marriage.

> The acts of the sinful nature are obvious: *sexual immorality, impurity* and *debauchery*; idolatry and witchcraft; hatred, discord, jealousy, fits of rage, selfish ambition, dissensions, factions and envy; drunkenness, *orgies,* and the like. I warn you, as I did before, that those who live like this will not inherit the kingdom of God.[26]

If you continue to romanticize any sinful relationship you've had—either before or during your marriage—you give the memories of that relationship the power they need to keep you from growing in love and intimacy with your spouse. If you want to make your marriage all that it should be, you must recast your thinking about any adulteries, homosexual encounters, sex before marriage, or any other sexual activity which does not meet the strict standard of God: "Marriage should be honored by all, and the marriage bed kept pure, for God will judge the adulterer and all the sexually immoral."[27]

Whenever you find yourself thinking about a former lover, remind yourself that the relationship was sinful. If you can't find penitent remorse for that sin, we suggest you read *Seeing the Unseen*[28] to see just how satanic forces lured you into your misconception or *Forgiven Forever*[29] to make the consequences clearer. Only when you admit to yourself intellectually and emotionally the enormity of the sin will you find the whole power of God to overcome it.

Once you know how sinful you've been, you can let go of the sin by accepting God's total forgiveness. Grace has little meaning to those who think they've done no harm, but it has life-changing qualities to those who face head-on their sin and guilt.

4. Replace Harmful Thoughts with Holy Thoughts

Once we've let go of harmful emotions—either our hatred of someone who hurt us or our romantic view of sexual sin—the next step is to gain control over our thoughts by replacing wrong thoughts with holy thoughts. When we learn to do this, the peace of God will guard our hearts and keep them free of all the junk. How do we get that peace? Paul explains: "The peace of God, which transcends all understanding, will guard your hearts and your minds in Christ Jesus. Finally, brothers, whatever is true, whatever is noble, whatever is right, whatever is pure, whatever is lovely, whatever is admirable—if anything is excellent or praiseworthy—think about such things."[30]

For those who are haunted by memories of abuse and pain, God's peace comes to His children as they replace bad thoughts with thoughts that are noble, right, pure, lovely, admirable, excellent, and praiseworthy. When the bad memories come, make a conscious effort to think about Jesus and something He did that was noble or good.

Live out that story in your imagination. Or think about a time when someone you care about did a praiseworthy thing. Watch it again in the theater of your mind. You can't live two memories at the same time. What you want to do is replace the bad one with a good one—one that is strong enough to force the bad one out.

Paul's spiritual counsel was given by direction of the Holy Spirit, and it works.

As I explained all this to the man who was sexually abused as a child, I told him: "Give it a try. You'll be able to replace your painful memories with good ones as soon as you forgive those guys who did that terrible stuff to you. Until you forgive them, your hatred will give your memories too much power and your mind will not be able to force them out. You must remove the sin of hatred before you can replace your painful memories with the holy thoughts of God."

There it is. A truth so simple we may disregard it, but it stands the test of time just the same. Remove the sin by the power of God, and remove the memory by consciously remembering events that are good. It worked in the first century, and it works now.

For those who are plagued by memories of their own past sexual sin, the solution is the same: Replace evil thoughts with holy ones. If the memory of an encounter or a fantasy about a lover intrudes (especially during sexual times with your spouse), remind yourself that what you did together was sinful and then remind yourself that God has forgiven you of that sin. Revel in that sense of forgiveness. Rejoice that you are now clean and forgiven. That forgiveness will give you the ability to concentrate on loving your spouse. Concentrate not on what he or she is doing for or to you, but on what you can do to enhance the sexual pleasure for him or her. If you are concentrating on your spouse's pleasure, you will *not* be thinking about someone else.

If fantasies or memories of a former lover come at times other than when you're making love with your spouse, replace those thoughts by planning scenarios of fulfilling lovemaking with your spouse. To replace the wrong thoughts with the right thoughts, actually think of what you will do, where you will be, what time of day, and plan every aspect—even the most minute—of that future lovemaking session.

You ask, "Hey, is that kind of thinking really noble and pure and all that stuff?"

Absolutely. There is nothing nobler in marriage than fulfilling your mate. Nothing at all.

When you've accepted God's truth about you and your past, let go of harmful emotions, and then replaced bad thoughts with holy thoughts, you're ready for the last step.

5. Implement God's Healing through Confession and Prayer

In dealing with the man who was molested by his father's homosexual lover, I explained to him that without knowing it, we sometimes provide Satan with a comfortable place within ourselves from which to tempt us. Let me explain. In a section of Scripture where Paul wrote about lying and stealing and the like, he placed this statement: "'In your anger do not sin': Do not let the sun go down while you are still angry, and do not give the devil a foothold."[31]

The word *foothold* there is *topos* (top'-os), which refers to a place or location like a room or a home. Paul tells us that if we cling to negative things (the general context includes lying and stealing; the specific context points to holding on to anger), we give the devil a room, a place to live within us. Paul doesn't seem to be discussing demon possession, a state where the evil being takes complete control of the host body, but a lesser situation where the evil being has a protected place from which to operate. Some folks today call this "demonization" (as opposed to demon possession). *Demonization* has come to be the current in-vogue word in many religious circles to describe a host of things. For the sake of convenience, we'll use that word here to mean "allowing satanic forces a place in one's life"—a place where they can live and operate as they attempt to tempt or torment their host.

I told this tormented young man what he already knew, that his continual adulterous affairs were rooted in his susceptibility to sexual temptation. I agreed with him that his "wiring was crossed" when he learned the wrong view of sex at the hands of his father's homosexual lover and that at least a part of his healing lay in therapy, which would in essence "rewire" his evil education with the correct education. But then I pointed out that until the anger was let go, not only would he be tormented by memories of the past, he would also leave a "foothold" within himself that satanic forces would use to best effect. They would have their place, their room, from which to operate to lure him into the right places at the right times to do the wrong things.

His ultimate cure from his sinfulness would result from the saving grace of Jesus. To remove any future edge or advantage the devil might have in tempting him, we needed him to close off that room which satanic forces took advantage of. He could do that by forgiving his father and his father's lover.

One result of his decision to forgive would be his eventual ability to let go of the anger he felt for them.

To get him started on his road to healing, I asked him to confess his sin of anger and bitterness so we could pray for his healing from his heartache and his susceptibility to temptation. When he asked why, I quoted, "Therefore confess your sins to each other and pray for each other so that you may be healed."[32] I let him know that as soon as he confessed, we would ask God to heal his heartache and deliver him from his susceptibility to temptation. But he still didn't understand why he should confess when it was they who did the sin. I pointed out to him that while what they had done *was* a grievous sin, he had sin in his own life to deal with. No, he in no way caused what was done to him or carried any blame for it. His sin was allowing his hurt and anger to fester inside of him until it became a root of bitterness. And now he had to deal with his sin, not theirs. His healing wouldn't come from continuing to confess *their* sins against him. It would come when he confessed the sin *he* unwittingly let find a home in his own heart. The scripture spoke to him, "Therefore confess your sins to each other and pray for each other so that you may be healed." I let him know that as soon as he confessed we would ask God to remove any satanic presences in his life and to protect him from all the flaming arrows of the evil one.[33] As in the model prayer, we would pray that he be led "not into temptation" but delivered "from the evil one."[34]

If you need to be healed of your past, we encourage you to do the same thing. It does you no spiritual good to confess the sins of those who hurt you. It only helps you spiritually—and, consequently, emotionally—when you in faith confess your own sins, whatever they may be. Therefore, we gently urge you to pray in faith and courage about your own sins. Satan's forces won't like it when you do that because you will be closing off their "room." But don't let them scare you. God prevails.

Remember that forgiving, letting go, and thinking about holy things are part of the process for being healed from all that's bad in one's past—even sexual sins—but beyond the obedience required of us there is something we require of God. His power. His power to heal and His power to deliver.

Remember the lady we told you about earlier who said that she couldn't remember being a virgin, that her mother and father had sexually molested her from the beginning of her memory? We followed the same process with her as we did with the man who was sexually molested. We taught her the truth of how God sees her and her past because she is a Christian. We encouraged her to let go of her past by forgiving and to replace horrible memories or thoughts with noble and pure ones. Then we prayed for her, asking God to seal the foothold in her life and to deliver her from the evil one just as Jesus taught us to pray.

We saw God work mightily in the lives of this tormented man and woman—two people in two different parts of the country who don't even know each other. But they know God. We've seen Him do the same thing all over America and other parts of the world. He'll do it for you too, if you ask Him. You may want your minister or some godly Christian friends to help you pray for God's powerful deliverance. But there is absolutely no reason to let yourself carry sexual hang-ups or inhibitions because of anything in your past. God wants you to have complete intimacy with your spouse. Complete. Every part. Spiritual. Emotional. Sexual. He can give it to you.

God can heal and deliver you of all that's been done to you and all that you've done. He can make you whole and in your right mind.[35] He can make you into a good husband or wife, no matter what you've been. He can make you a great, caring, gentle, fulfilling lover, no matter what experiences you've had.

The power is His, and it's available for all His children who by faith seek it.

CATEGORY 4:
THOSE WHO BELIEVE THEIR SPOUSES COULD NEVER LEARN TO BE GOOD LOVERS

The first portion of this chapter spoke to those who are haunted by bad sexual pasts—whether it was forced on them or they chose to participate in sinful sexual behavior. Now we'll speak to those who believe that sex with their spouse can never be good because their spouses are incapable of being good lovers. They usually think their spouses are too selfish or too inhibited or too shy. Or perhaps they think their spouses are disinterested in sex and could never be sexy in dress or physical appearance or lovemaking activities. They just can't imagine that their sex lives could ever become all they are meant to be, and they blame all that on the person they married.

But for most couples, there is hope, and you may be the one who can open the door to the sexual intimacy God intended for you and your spouse to share.

Helping Your Spouse Overcome a Painful or Sinful Past

If your spouse suffers from the consequences of a painful or sinful past, the preceding section of this chapter may have given you new insight into him or her. What you've been interpreting as inhibition or lack of interest may actually be emotional scars from molestation or rape or guilt from previous partners and lifestyles.

If your spouse hasn't told you the truth about why he or she feels negatively about sex, perhaps it's because he or she fears your rejection. This fear of rejection could stem from your spouse's poor self-perception or it could stem from past experiences with the way you've reacted to other facts or feelings honestly shared with you. If you create a home where honesty is honored rather than rejected, you can help your spouse through the healing processes we described earlier in this chapter. You will not only free your mate from a tortured past but will provide for your marriage a fulfilling sex life for you both.

If your spouse has told you the truth about his or her past and you reacted in shock or horror or with rejection, it's time to revisit that discussion. If your spouse shared that information with you hoping to find healing and acceptance, it's not too late to give it. Sit down with him or her and tell how sorry you are that you didn't understand his or her pain or shame. With tenderness and gentleness, make it explicitly clear that you will never hold that shameful event against him or her. Firmly, though gently, state your unequivocal love and commitment. Ask if he or she would like to talk about it, and state that you're willing to listen and comfort. Rather than your spouse's past being a barrier to your intimacy, your loving understanding can transform that event into the door that leads to the deepest levels of intimacy for the two of you.

Enhancing Your Spouse's Self-Perception

Your mate's lack of interest or desire may not stem from a painful or sinful past but from poor self-esteem. He or she may think, "I'm not pretty," "I'm too fat," "I'm not smart," etc. If so, you must help him or her work through chapter 4 again, learning to love him- or herself as God wants us to. Your mate will never learn to overcome inhibitions that prevent him or her from loving you as you want if you don't help him or her first learn to love self as God requires.

If you read that and thought, "But my mate *is* too heavy for my tastes" or "My mate *isn't* physically attractive," then hear us well as we say that your mate will *never* change until he or she first learns to accept him- or herself and until you learn to love your spouse as he or she is—right now. Making people feel that love is tied to their appearance does *not* motivate them to change. Only those who feel loved and accepted as they are can find the motivation change. The most powerful motivation for losing weight or enhancing one's appearance comes from the desire to please the one who loves you—unconditionally, right now, just as you are.

When mates feel loved, they are much more likely to respond positively to encouragement to become more attractive in dress, appearance, and every other way. They even hear suggestions for improved lovemaking in a different light: They will be less likely to resist suggestions or feel rejection and more willing to please the mate who already loves them. Only those who truly love their mates as they now are can ask the favor of lost pounds or enhanced technique and expect concurrence.

And when your mate responds by making changes—no matter how small—you can encourage him or her to continue to grow and change by your expressed admiration and appreciation. Don't wait until the entire goal has been reached before complimenting and showing appreciation. If you want someone to do something for you, reward every step, every increment, every effort with lavish praise.

Several years ago Charlie Shedd wrote *Letters to Philip* to his son and *Letters to Karen* to his daughter. Each chapter was a letter about life and love and marriage. I remember reading as a young man a story in *Letters to Philip* about a man who married a woman who, to be quite honest, was rather homely. Shedd wrote that the husband continually told her how beautiful she was, how desirable and voluptuous. Years passed before Shedd saw them again, and when he chanced to encounter them, he noted with surprise and delight that the formerly homely wife had evolved into a graciously attractive woman. She'd learned how to fix her hair and apply makeup to her best advantage, and she'd learned how to dress with confidence and flair to accentuate all her best features. She would never have done those things to please a husband who continually told her how ugly she was. (If she had, she probably would have left him after learning how to attract male attention.) But she did learn to do it for a husband who loved her just as she was and complimented every effort on her part to become more attractive for him.

LEARNING TO LOVE

In the atmosphere of acceptance and warmth, anyone can learn quickly to become a wonderful lover. In chapter 7 we showed you biblical examples of what it means to be a good lover and explained them simply and in a straightforward manner. Both you and your spouse can be good lovers; it really is a learned process. As you've seen from this chapter, sometimes it means "unlearning" some things that never should have been learned in the first place.

Your mate can learn to be a good lover.

But first, *you* must learn to be a good lover. Never expect your mate to fulfill your desires until you first learn how to fulfill his or hers. Start the process and watch what God can and will do for your marriage. To paraphrase teachings of Jesus, "Give wonderful lovemaking and you'll get wonderful lovemaking in return" (see Luke 6:38), and "Seek great lovemaking skills first in yourself and you'll find great lovemaking skills in your mate" (see Matthew 7:7). Do we blaspheme by adapting those verses that way? No. While these are paraphrases and not direct quotes from Scripture, they are based on scriptural principles. If you prefer a direct, unaltered verse, try this one: "So in everything, do to others what you would have them do to you, for this sums up the Law and the Prophets."[36]

If you want your spouse to be a good lover, you must become a good lover first. Love your mate enough to help him or her spiritually and emotionally conquer his or her past. Love your spouse enough to be the best lover he or she can possibly have.

The quality of your sex life starts with you.

Notes

Preface

1. Willard Harley, *His Needs, Her Needs* (Grand Rapids, Mich.: Fleming Revell, 1988). Dr. Harley has shared tremendous insights into marriage relationships in several books including *Give and Take*, *Surviving an Affair*, and *Love Busters*. For more information about his books or tapes, contact Family Dynamics Institute at 706-667-6674 or visit his Web site (www.marriagebuilders.com).

2. For more detail on my sin that led to our breakup, all that we suffered because of it, and the amazing grace of God that put us together again, read the introduction to Joe Beam, *Forgiven Forever* (West Monroe, La.: Howard Publishing, 1998).

Introduction: Intentional Intimacy

1. The *Becoming ONE* interactive course meets for a two-and-a-half-hour session once a week for eight weeks. For more information on how to

have this course in your church, call 1-800-650-9995 or read more detailed endnotes in subsequent chapters.

Chapter 1: The Craving for Intimacy

1. I tell more about my story in *Forgiven Forever*.

2. I've made no secret of the struggles of my life and have recorded some of them openly in the book *Forgiven Forever*. I wrote that book to help all of us who have been burdened with guilt to find the power of God that heals that guilt. Yet some continue to ask why I'm so open. My answer is threefold.

(1) I'm convinced that we are supposed to comfort others with the comfort with which we have been comforted. "Praise be to the God and Father of our Lord Jesus Christ, the Father of compassion and the God of all comfort, who comforts us in all our troubles, so that we can comfort those in any trouble with the comfort we ourselves have received from God" (2 Corinthians 1:3–4). The things God allows me to learn about temptation, sin, deliverance, and forgiveness must be shared with others who need the same comfort.

(2) Openness is one of the most powerful tools I have to keep me from continuing to sin. Though still tempted, as I imagine you are, I find that my times of greatest spiritual strength are when my life is laid open. Satan's forces work so much better in the dark (hiding, secrecy) than they can in the light (openness, honesty).

(3) I've not yet arrived at the level of spiritual strength and healing that I want. If anyone were to ask me about my errors, I could only respond, "I justify nothing I've done in my life through the last breath I drew just a moment ago. I'm a sinner saved by grace, and I would never try to make you think anything else of me. That's why I talk so openly about my sin and my struggles. To this day I am far from perfect, and to this day I'm susceptible to sin, as is everyone [1 Corinthians 10:12]. I envy those people who haven't done what I've done and who haven't been tempted by the things that tempt me. Though still an imperfect, forgiven sinner, I don't dwell on my sin, even as I openly admit it. I'm not anchored to my past but to my future. 'Brothers,

I do not consider myself yet to have taken hold of it. But one thing I do: Forgetting what is behind and straining toward what is ahead, I press on toward the goal to win the prize for which God has called me heavenward in Christ Jesus' [Philippians 3:13–14]. Openly admitting my sinfulness helps me leave it behind, in the hands of the God who forgave me."

3. From what I wrote in the preface, you know that my wife, Alice, and I are married to each other for the second time. When we first remarried in 1987, we struggled terribly. We had foolishly ignored analyzing what had gone wrong in our first marriage and getting the right kind of help to repair those structural flaws before reuniting.

I've read that most divorces take place before the third anniversary, and I remember thinking how ironic it would be if we divorced before the third anniversary of our second marriage with each other. In those first few years, there were things that nearly ended our relationship forever, but by the grace of God we survived and started finding ways to make our marriage work.

After several years of toughing it out through rocky times—mostly my fault—we actually made our own marriage good enough that we felt we ought to share what we'd learned with others. Never claiming to have all the answers or to have the best relationship anyone could have, we knew we'd outdistanced so many marriages that we started the nonprofit corporation Family Dynamics Institute in 1994, offering the first seminars in 1995. We found it wonderful to teach others what we'd learned and to see God work in them as He worked in us.

But Alice knew what I still hadn't learned: We hadn't reached the level of relationship we needed. She tried to tell me, but I could never get clear on what she meant. "Look how well we're doing," I'd say, "and how God is using us to touch marriages around the world." Like too many men I thought in terms of action, and like so many women she thought in terms of feelings.

When I finally experienced the epiphany I describe in the text, I also understood. Our marriage was good, but it still had good times and bad. It wasn't yet what it was supposed to be because it wasn't a ONEness marriage.

ONEness marriage is crucial because it is the kind of marriage that God intends and the only kind of marriage that completely satisfies any human in the totality of his or her being.

4. Genesis 2:20–24.

5. Genesis 1:26.

6. Genesis 2:18.

7. Genesis 2:24.

8. Paul wrote in 1 Corinthians 7 that the ability to live without a mate required a special spiritual gift from God (v. 7). If you are a single person who takes offense at the bold statements about humankind only being complete when married, please note verses 7 and 8 carefully. If you, like Paul, have the gift of singleness, you don't need a mate. If you don't have this gift, then you probably are very much aware of this need for a mate. God intended humankind to be completed by intimacy with a spouse; only He can change that for any human so that the person can find fulfillment alone.

He also encouraged the Christians suffering persecution in the city of Corinth to remain single, forgoing marriage during their time of persecution (v. 26). Why? Because when one must witness the persecution of the special person who completes him or her, the suffering is more than doubled. What hurts one hurts the other because they are one.

But even as Paul recommended the strategy of singleness in times of persecution, he knew that those without the spiritual gift of being single wouldn't be able to endure long without their special companions who completed them. He tells them that God would not consider it a sin that they marry, even during that crisis (v. 28).

9. Psalm 63:1, 3–4, 6, 8.

10. For a more detailed discussion of this, see *Forgiven Forever*, chapter 3.

11. If you purchased the accompanying workbook, *Becoming ONE: Exercises in Intimacy*, you can find out if you fit this one-in-four category by answering the questions and charting your answers. If you also are enrolled in our *Becoming ONE* interactive class through your church, the facilitator couple from your church will lead you through exercises in class that will do more than show you which category you currently fit in. They will start you on a process to ensure the ONEness God intended for your marriage.

If you would like more information about how to have Family Dynamics train facilitator couples in your church, please contact FDI at 1-800-650-9995.

12. For an in-depth study of the spiritual warfare waged on earth today between the forces of evil and the forces of God, read Joe Beam, *Seeing the Unseen* (West Monroe, La.: Howard Publishing, 1994).

13. Only a few of the exercises in *Becoming ONE: Exercises in Intimacy* are specifically mentioned in this book. *Becoming ONE: Exercises in Intimacy* is designed to accompany this text and lead you to discover where you are in your relationship, how you got there, where you want to go, and how to get there. Some of the exercises are biblical studies, some are analyses, and the remainder are practical exercises to lead you into greater levels of intimacy.

14. *Becoming ONE* is an intense eight-week study led by a trained facilitator couple. Twelve couples meet together for two-and-a-half hours each week for eight weeks (for example, every Tuesday evening from 7 to 9:30 P.M.) for a lively and intense interactive session. Each couple also completes "homework" each week before coming to class. The sessions are fun, informative, and life-changing. Multiplied thousands of couples from hundreds of churches around the U.S., Canada, and other parts of the world have grown tremendously in their relationships with each other by enrolling in Family Dynamics Institute's interactive courses. For information on how to have one or more couples from your church trained as facilitators, call 1-800-650-9995.

Chapter 2: The Triune Nature of Intimacy

1. This particular model, "Falling in Love," is used primarily in our *Love, Sex & Marriage* seminars. Our LSM seminar is a Friday night, Saturday lecture-format seminar. Friday evening we spend two-and-a-half hours explaining in detail how to "fall in love" with your spouse forever. Saturday morning we conduct a frank discussion of sex in marriage that is based on several scriptures. Saturday afternoon we explain the differences in individuals and how to communicate with each other with an awareness of those differences.

The seminar is fun, upbeat, and extremely informative. For information on how to have this seminar at your church, call 1-800-650-9995.

2. To learn seven steps to learning how to love, go to our Web site (www.familydynamics.net) or call us at 1-800-650-9995 and ask for our free booklet "Seven Steps to Marital Ecstacy."

3. For a more detailed discussion of the trinary nature of humankind, see *Forgiven Forever*, chapter 3.

4. Psalm 139:13–16.

5. Ecclesiastes 12:7.

6. 1 Corinthians 15:35–54.

7. Genesis 1:28.

8. Genesis 2:24.

9. Genesis 5:2, in the beautiful language of the King James Version: "Male and female created he them; and blessed them, and called their name Adam, in the day when they were created."

10. Genesis 4:1, 17, 25, et. al.

11. W. E. Vine, *An Expository Dictionary of Biblical Words* (Nashville, Tenn.: Thomas Nelson, 1985).

12. Hebrews 13:4.

13. The following quote and corresponding endnote from *Forgiven Forever* (pp. 66 and 235) explain the three parts of the mind:

> The intellect thinks logically. It processes information and compares it to previous experiences and core values.
>
> The emotions feel a spectrum of sensations both through mental and physical stimulation. The heart is where the intellect and emotion come together to form the center of a person's reasoning, the point where decisions are made and actions are taken.

From this quote, I place the following endnote:

> Those in the first century saw the heart as the place where the emotions and intellect came together into a center of reasoning. Many passages use heart to mean the combination of intellect and emotion (e.g. Matthew 5:8; 6:21; Luke 6:45; Acts 2:37; Colossians 3:23; Hebrews 4:12). Occasionally Bible writers separated the heart from the mind when they wanted to make a point about involving

every nuance of our being (e.g. Luke 10:27; Acts 4:32). But most of the time they used heart to refer to the combination of intellect and emotions. For example, in Matthew 13:15, Jesus said, "They…see with their eyes, hear with their ears, understand with their hearts, and turn." In this verse, heart includes understanding and emotion. In Romans 10:10 it's even clearer: "For it is with your heart that you believe and are justified." Here, heart obviously includes more than just emotion and more than just intellect. Faith is trust placed in Jesus, and it is with the heart that we place our trusting faith in Him. Unless you think of faith as a dry, intellectual acknowledgment, you will agree that heart in this passage means both intellect and emotions.

Therefore, to New Testament writers, "guard your heart" (Philippians 4:7) meant guarding the combined intellect and emotions so that a person reasoned correctly and acted accordingly.

14. I am not a certified therapist or counselor and never want to appear that I am trained to be either. Besides that, I think it is dangerous for non-professionals (and, perhaps, sometimes even for professionals) to discuss too much about sex in a private conversation with a person of the opposite sex. I'm quite convinced that minions of the evil one use every opportunity they can to lead people into temptation. I don't want to be tempted, nor do I want to tempt anyone.

Besides, some things are just proper and others aren't, even at the dawn of the twenty-first century!

15. Zechariah 12:1.

16. Proverbs 20:27; James 2:26; Ecclesiastes 12:7; Isaiah 14:9; 19:3.

17. Genesis 1:26.

18. John 4:24; Philippians 3:3; Romans 8:11; Romans 8:16.

19. 1 Corinthians 6:15–20.

20. 1 Corinthians 7:13–14.

21. You can learn more about Sternberg's models of love in his book *The Psychology of Love*, ed. Robert J. Sternberg and Michael L. Barnes (New

Haven, Conn.: Yale University Press, 1988). We use an exercise from Dr. Sternberg's model of love in chapter 1 of *Becoming ONE: Exercises in Intimacy.*

22. Romans 8:14–15; Ephesians 3:14–15.

23. 2 Corinthians 8:4; Philippians 1:5; 1 John 1:3.

24. 2 Samuel 1:26.

Chapter 3: Repairing Intimacy Diversions and Drains

1. Matthew 19:16–24.

2. William F. Arndt et al., *A Greek-English Lexicon of the New Testament and Other Early Christian Literature* (Chicago: The University of Chicago Press, 1957), 856–57.

3. Ibid., 857.

4. Ibid., 816–17.

5. Matthew 6:1–2, 5, 16; John 12:42–43.

6. Luke 14:26.

7. Matthew 10:37–38.

8. Dr. Willard Harley, *Love Busters* (Grand Rapids, Mich.: Fleming Revell, 1997). We base the course on his book *His Needs, Her Needs.* We reference *Love Busters* in the first session of the eight-week seminar.

9. 1 Peter 3:7.

10. James 5:16. Also see the discussion of confession in *Forgiven Forever.*

Chapter 4: Developing Emotional Intimacy, Part 1

1. Titus 2:3–5.

2. 2 Timothy 3:2.

3. John 13:3–5.

4. Matthew 23:6.

5. Romans 12:3.

6. Matthew 5:33–37.

7. Proverbs 12:22.

8. Psalm 15.

9. John 3:16.

10. 2 Corinthians 3:4–5.

11. Matthew 22:39.

12. Matthew 7:1–5.

13. Proverbs 16:28.

14. Matthew 23:26.

15. Luke 7:47–48.

16. Romans 3:23.

17. Romans 5:12.

18. Romans 5:8.

19. Romans 5:20–21.

20. Romans 8:14–17.

21. Psalms 51:7; 103:12; Hebrews 9:13–14.

22. Beam, *Forgiven Forever*.

23. Isaiah 53:2.

24. 1 Peter 3:4.

25. 1 Corinthians 15:35–58.

26. 1 Corinthians 12:18.

27. 1 Corinthians 12:28–30.

28. Romans 12:4–8.

29. Romans 12:6.

30. Philippians 4:11–12.

31. Philippians 3:12.

Chapter 5: Developing Emotional Intimacy, Part 2

1. James 5:16.

2. Although I've known this principle for years, I reverified it during the writing of this book. I called my very dear friend Julie Lindsey. She serves as program director for the Council against Rape, which is part of the Lighthouse Counseling Center in Montgomery, Alabama. Readers of *Seeing the Unseen* will remember the story of Julie being raped several years ago. During the last fourteen years, she has counseled many rape victims. She says, "While it's not common, occasionally a woman tells me that she orgasmed during her rape. That revelation is always accompanied by extreme guilt. I immediately explain that it was only a physiological response that occurred because of her lack of control during her trauma and that she has no reason to feel guilty."

The following quote from Sedelle Katz and Mary Ann Mazur, *Understanding the Rape Victim: A Synthesis of Research Findings* (n.p.: John Wiley & Sons, Inc., 1979) will provide even more insight. "A few women may have been sexually aroused and even have reached an orgasm during the rape (Medea and Thompson, 1974; Greer, 1975). Medea and Thompson felt that this sexual reaction was not necessarily a pleasurable experience but was more related to the excitement of terror. Like a child who wets his pants when excited, a victim may have had a sexual orgasm as a result of the excitement caused by fear. The authors explained that the body and mind are not completely coordinated, so that terror can trigger a reaction so similar to sexual arousal that one's body cannot distinguish between them. The result is that a woman may have a physical reaction (orgasm) while she is mentally horrified and revolted (ibid.). Greer added that even if a woman did have an orgasm during the rape, 'it need not necessarily lessen the severity of the trauma that she suffers'" (178–179).

3. For more information, contact FDI about the *A New Beginning* seminar.

4. Romans 12:19, 21.

Chapter 6: Developing Sexual Intimacy, Part 1

1. Titus 2:3–5.

2. Our oldest daughter, Angela, is educably mentally retarded and operates on about a seven-year-old level. We've never had this discussion with her and don't anticipate the need ever to occur. We are open with our children, but we only teach them about sexual matters to the level of their intellectual and emotional capacity. Our third daughter, Kimberly, has already had some discussions about sex with us at her young age of nine, but we are reserving the kind of conversation we describe in this chapter until she is older—probably as she enters puberty.

3. John 3:19–20.

4. 1 Corinthians 7:2–5.

5. We agree wholeheartedly that procreation is an essential part of our sex drive, but we contend that our emotional, physiological, and spiritual need for sexual union transcends that basic drive.

6. Leviticus 18:7.

7. Leviticus 18:8—under penalty of death, Leviticus 20:11.

8. Leviticus 18:9, 11—penalized by being cut off from the people, Leviticus 20:17.

9. Leviticus 18:10.

10. Leviticus 18:12–14—penalized by dying childless, Leviticus 20:19.

11. Leviticus 18:15.

12. Leviticus 18:16—with an exception made for a man to marry his brother's wife if his brother died childless so as to raise up an heir to his dead brother, Deuteronomy 25:5–10.

13. Leviticus 18:17—penalized by death, Leviticus 20:14.

14. Leviticus 18:22—penalized by death, Leviticus 20:13.

15. Romans 1:24–28—penalized by spiritual death, Romans 1:27; 6:23.

16. Deuteronomy 22:23–27.

17. Deuteronomy 22:28–29.

18. Exodus 22:16–17.

19. 1 Corinthians 7:2–5.

20. Galatians 5:19–21.

21. Leviticus 20:10; Deuteronomy 22:22.

22. Hebrews 13:4.

23. Exodus 20:17.

24. Matthew 5:27–28.

25. Deuteronomy 23:17–18.

26. 1 Corinthians 6:15.

27. Leviticus 20:15–16.

28. Leviticus 17:11.

29. Acts 15:29.

30. Leviticus 15:24; 18:19; 20:18.

31. 1 Corinthians 6:19–20.

Chapter 7: Developing Sexual Intimacy, Part 2

1. Song of Songs 1:2.

2. Song of Songs 2:6.

3. Song of Songs 2:16–17.

4. Song of Songs 4:5.

5. Song of Songs 4:11.

6. Song of Songs 5:10–16.

7. Song of Songs 7:1–7.

8. Song of Songs 8:6–7.

9. Song of Songs 8:10.

10. Song of Songs 4:6.

11. Song of Songs 4:1.

12. Song of Songs 4:1; 7:5.

13. Song of Songs 4:2.

14. Song of Songs 4:3.

15. Ibid.

16. Song of Songs 4:4.

17. Song of Songs 4:5.

18. Song of Songs 1:12.

19. Song of Songs 1:16.

20. Song of Songs 5:11–16.

21. Song of Songs 5:10.

22. Song of Songs 2:16–17; 4:16.

23. Song of Songs 5:4–5. This verse appears to be her telling him graphically how she responded to his touch, even when she first appeared to be disinterested in sex. To see the full effect of her sentence, remember that in other places in Song of Songs, myrrh referred to the fragrance of her aroused genitalia.

24. Song of Songs 1:4; 3:1–2.

25. Song of Songs 7:13.

26. Matthew 21:22.

Chapter 8: Developing Spiritual Intimacy—As a Couple

1. 1 Thessalonians 2:11–12.

2. Ephesians 6:4.

3. Proverbs 6:20.

4. Proverbs 1:8.

5. Genesis 18:19.

6. Deuteronomy 4:9.

7. Deuteronomy 6:6–7.

8. 2 Timothy 1:5.

9. Ephesians 5:25–28.

10. 1 Peter 3:1–4.

11. Ecclesiastes 2:11.

12. Ecclesiastes 2:17–18.

13. Ecclesiastes 4:4–8.

14. Ecclesiastes 12:8, 13.

15. 1 Timothy 6:10.

16. Hebrews 13:5.

17. Titus 2:4–5.

18. 1 Timothy 5:8.

19. Beam, *Forgiven Forever*.

20. Luke 23:34.

21. Matthew 6:15.

22. Matthew 7:2.

23. Luke 17:3–5.

24. 1 John 5:14–15, but make sure you ask with pure motives, James 4:1–3.

25. Philippians 4:9.

26. Contact Family Dynamics Institute about how to register for either a three-day training seminar that will teach you how to build a ministry to couples or for information on a three-day seminar that will teach you how to develop a ministry to parents and children. We train several hundreds of couples each year to do these kinds of family ministries in their home churches. Call us at 1-800-650-9995 to find out how God can build that kind of co-ministry in your marriage.

Chapter 9: Developing Intimacy with God—Personally

1. 1 Chronicles 28:9.

2. Hebrews 11:6.

3. Matthew 6:24.

4. "Willingly" here means that one makes a conscious choice to obey,

not because he fears God will punish if he doesn't, but because he knows that is what God wants him to do. Sometimes the "willingness" isn't charged with great positive emotion but dread and fear. In that sense obedience may be "have to," but we still consider it to be willing. For example, Jesus begged for a way to avoid the cross (Matthew 26:39) because He didn't "want to" do it. Yet He did it because He "had to" do it for our salvation. We consider that a "willing" act because His obedience wasn't based on fear of punishment but love for those who needed Him to die for them (1 John 3:16).

5. 2 Corinthians 9:7.

6. Matthew 6:5.

7. Matthew 6:16.

8. Matthew 6:2.

9. John 15:15.

10. 1 Samuel 1:10–20.

11. 2 Samuel 6:14–16.

12. James 5:13.

13. Exodus 32.

14. Luke 22:42–44.

15. 1 Peter 5:7.

16. Romans 12:1–2.

17. Galatians 2:20.

18. John 3:5–8.

19. Psalm 139:14.

20. Romans 8:9 (KJV).

21. Romans 8:15–16.

22. Romans 8:26–27.

23. Galatians 5:22–23.

24. Mark 16:16 and Romans 10:10, for starters. We also recommend you read your way through the entire book of Acts, paying close attention to every conversion story and making notes of what God required of each of them. When you finish your study, your course of action will be in the notes before you.

25. Call 1-800-650-9995. An invoice for a modest amount for the book and shipping cost comes with the book. If you cannot afford to pay the

invoice for any reason, instead of sending money, send us a letter telling us if you indeed found a relationship with Jesus.

26. Galatians 5:16–17.

27. James 1:23.

Appendix: Overcoming Negative Sexual History

1. As we mentioned in the introduction, nearly all stories in this book are disguised and some are compilations of several real stories that are merged into a representative story. Ernie and Sal are fictitious only in one sense: Certain facts of their story—including their names—are disguised so that I don't inadvertently cause them any embarrassment. They are a real couple that I love dearly, and my view of their marriage is that it is one of the best I've ever encountered. Ever. Especially in their healthy attitudes toward their sexual union.

2. 2 Corinthians 5:17.

3. Galatians 6:15.

4. Colossians 3:10.

5. Ephesians 4:23.

6. Matthew 18:5–7.

7. 1 John 5:19.

8. His rape was exactly that. Rape. And rape isn't sex; it's domination. He exerted his power over that little girl. If you agree with me that he is responsible, not her, then I beg you to use the same logic on whatever evil thing happened to you when you were a teen.

9. Ezekiel 18:4.

10. Ibid.

11. Ezekiel 18:10, 13.

12. Ezekiel 18:20.

13. Romans 12:19.

14. 1 Corinthians 6:9–10 (italics added for emphasis).

15. 1 Corinthians 6:11 (italics added for emphasis).

16. For a discussion of this, see Beam, *Forgiven Forever*.

17. Romans 6:11–13.

18. John 8:32.

19. 2 Corinthians 5:17.

20. Romans 3:24.

21. Isaiah 43:18.

22. Psalm 103:12.

23. Hebrews 8:12.

24. Luke 15:10–32.

25. Matthew 18:21–35.

26. Galatians 5:19–21. Italicized words come from koine Greek words that include such sins as adultery, consensual sex between non-marrieds, homosexuality, and wanton sexual activity.

27. Hebrews 13:4.

28. Beam, *Seeing the Unseen*.

29. Beam, *Forgiven Forever*. See especially the last chapter.

30. Philippians 4:7–8.

31. Ephesians 4:26–27.

32. James 5:16.

33. Ephesians 6:16.

34. Matthew 6:13.

35. Luke 8:35.

36. Matthew 7:12.